CRITICAL
TERRAINS

CRITICAL TERRAINS

French and British Orientalisms

LISA LOWE

Cornell University Press

Ithaca and London

First published 1991 by Cornell University Press.
First printing, Cornell Paperbacks, 1994.

International Standard Book Number 0-8014-2579-4 (cloth)
International Standard Book Number 0-8014-8195-3 (paper)
Library of Congress Catalog Card Number 91-55058

Printed in the United States of America

*Librarians: Library of Congress cataloging information
appears on the last page of the book.*

∞ The paper in this book meets the minimum requirements of the
American National Standard for Information Sciences—
Permanence of Paper for Printed Library Materials, ANSI Z39.48-1984.

*for Mei Lee Lowe
and Donald M. Lowe*

Contents

Preface

This book treats orientalism as a tradition of representation that is crossed, intersected, and engaged by other representations. The object is not to describe a continuous history of literary orientalism, nor is it to identify a unified and consistent meaning of the notion of the Orient—tasks perhaps more appropriate to a traditional literary history or history of ideas. Rather, I consider here four disparate and nonanalogous orientalist situations and argue the contrary: that orientalism is not a single developmental tradition but is profoundly heterogeneous. French and British figurations of an oriental Other are not unified or necessarily related in meaning; they denote a plurality of referents, do not necessarily have a common style in the production of statements about their Orients, and are engendered differently by social and literary circumstances at particular moments. Although this project has benefited from the critique established in *Orientalism* (1979), by Edward Said, who holds that there is a discernible history of European representation and appropriation of the Orient, and that this history has a relationship to the history of European colonialism, my study ultimately challenges that work to the extent that I query the assumption that orientalism *monolithically* constructs the Orient as the Other of the Occident. In each chapter I consider a specific form of orientalism and contend that each orientalist situation expresses a distinct range of

concerns with *difference:* the conflicts and collaborations among narratives of cultural, class, and sexual differences in eighteenth-century
English and French travel literature; the discourses of orientalism,
romanticism, racialism, and capitalism in the corpus of Gustave Flaubert; the Anglo-American and Indian literary critical debates about
E. M. Forster's novel *A Passage to India*; and finally, the utopian projection of China in French post-structuralism, represented by the work of
Julia Kristeva and Roland Barthes, and in the journal *Tel quel*. The
purpose of distinguishing among four distinct orientalist situations is
to challenge critical perceptions of a consistent, univocal discourse that
dominates, manages, and produces cultural differences, an oversimplification proliferated in certain criticism since the publication of
Said's book. My work ultimately rejects a totalizing framework that
would grant such authority to orientalism, and that would understand
all forms of resistance to be contained by that single determining
tradition. I also argue strongly for the heterogeneity of the orientalist
object, whose contradictions and lack of fixity mark precisely the
moments of instability in the discourse; although orientalism may
represent its objects as fixed or stable, contradictions and noncorrespondences in the discursive situation ultimately divulge the multivalence and indeterminability of those fictions. It is through this attention to the heterogeneity of objects that the interpreted texts of my
study come to represent an incongruous variety of orientalist examples. In discussing these differently unstable moments of French and
British orientalism, I suggest ways in which interventions in managing
or colonizing discourses, such as orientalism, are observable from our
postcolonial position and can indeed be located in the heterogeneity of
different textual, intertextual, and discursive situations. Even so, as I
write this, I am forced by recent events in the Persian Gulf to acknowledge the persistent legacy of orientalism. These events demand that
questions of resistance be more than theoretical, and remind us that
despite practical resistance, newly configured orientalisms will continue to demand our critical attention.

During the years I worked on this project, many people offered me
their interest and attention. I am most grateful to Page duBois—
teacher, mentor, and friend—who helped and inspired me at all
stages. I especially acknowledge Susan Kirkpatrick, whose clarity of

mind and generous comments made it possible for this book to say what it needed to say. Kathryn Shevelow guided me to Lady Mary Wortley Montagu; and Stephanie Jed was a uniquely sympathetic reader. Other colleagues and friends at the University of California, San Diego—Masao Miyoshi, Roddey Reid, Rosaura Sanchez, Don Wayne, and Winnie Woodhull—offered helpful questions, criticism, and encouragement; among them, George Mariscal has been an important interlocutor. I am grateful to former teachers for having opened, each of them, very different intellectual doors: Harry Berger, James Clifford, the late Joel Fineman, Donna Haraway, Fredric Jameson, Kristin Ross, and Hayden White. Equally, I thank Ian Barnard, Luis Madureira, and Margaret Sale, graduate students with whom I have worked at UCSD, for asking me stimulating questions. I am also indebted to a variety of readers, some of whom provided comments at an early stage—Sandra Azeredo, Deborah Gordon, Barbara Gottfried, Christine Grella, Julie Hemker, Marta Morello-Frosch, and Cathy Reback—and others who, at a later stage, offered me enormously instructive conceptual advice—Nancy Armstrong, Cora Kaplan, and David Lloyd. Ultimately I must thank Edward Said, not only for having written *Orientalism* but also for his gracious encouragement.

A fellowship from the American Council of Learned Societies and research and sabbatical leaves from UCSD have permitted me to complete the writing and editing of this book. Chapter 2 includes a revised version of an essay published as "Rereading Orientalism: Oriental Inventions and Inventions of the Orient in Montesquieu's *Lettres persanes*," in *Cultural Critique* 15 (Spring 1990): 115–43; Chapter 3 contains revised portions of two essays, "The Orient as Woman in Flaubert's *Salammbô* and *Voyage en Orient*," *Comparative Literature Studies* 23, no. 1 (Spring 1986): 44–58; and "Nationalism and Exoticism: Nineteenth-Century Others in Flaubert's *Salammbô* and *L'éducation sentimentale*," in *Macropolitics of Nineteenth-Century Literature: Nationalism, Exoticism, Imperialism*, ed. Jonathan Arac and Harriet Ritvo (Philadelphia: University of Pennsylvania Press, 1991). I thank each for permission to republish these materials here. Ideas for a few chapters were presented as papers at meetings of the Modern Language Association and the Philological Association of the Pacific Coast. Many of the literary and theoretical texts I have treated in Chapters 2, 3, and 5 exist only in French; unless I note otherwise, I have translated these texts myself, citing the French when I felt my translation could not capture the ambiguity or nuance of the original.

Above all, there are two to whom I give other than intellectual acknowledgment: Joseph Nebolon, for his equanimity and unwavering support, and Juliet, who delights, and gives me reason.

LISA LOWE

San Diego, California

CRITICAL
TERRAINS

1

Discourse and Heterogeneity: Situating Orientalism

Par la diversité de son humeur, tour à tour mystique ou joyeuse, babillarde, taciturne, emportée, nonchalante, elle allait rappelant en lui mille désirs, évoquant des instincts ou des réminiscences. Elle était l'amoureuse de tous les romans, l'héroïne de tous les drames, le vague *elle* de tous les volumes de vers. Il retrouvait sur ses épaules la couleur ambrée de l'*odalisque au bain*; elle avait le corsage long de châtelaines féodales; elle ressemblait aussi à la *Femme pâle de Barcelone*, mais elle était par-dessus tout Ange!

[According to her changing moods, in turn meditative or gay, talkative, silent, passionate, and nonchalant, she awakened in him a thousand desires, called up instincts or memories. She was the beloved mistress of all the novels, the heroine of all the dramas, the vague "she" of all the volumes of verse. On her shoulders, he rediscovered the amber color of Ingres's *Odalisque au bain*; her waist was long like the feudal chatelaines; she resembled the "Femme Pâle de Barcelone," but above all, she was a complete Angel.]

Flaubert, *Madame Bovary* (1857)

In Flaubert's *Madame Bovary*, a novel reflecting the tedium and homogeneity of French provincial life, Emma's young lover Léon imagines that he finds on her shoulders "the amber color of the *Odalisque au bain*." The workings of masculine desire are illustrated by the young lover's metonymic substitution of Ingres's Turkish bather's shoulders—smooth-skinned and distantly exotic—for the doctor's wife whom he holds in an adulterous embrace. As Léon imagines the shoulders of one of Ingres's oriental women, his conflation enunciates and reiterates an established association of the oriental with the feminine erotic. Throughout Flaubert's writing versions of this theme abound. Masculine romantic desire is often introduced by an oriental motif: an oriental ballad accompanies Frédéric's meeting with Madame Arnoux; Salammbô's golden ankle chain piques Mâtho's desire; the Egyptian courtesan Kuchuk-Hânem uses rosewater to perfume the traveler's hands. Such associations of orientalism with romanticism are not coincidental, for the two situations of desire—the occidental fascination with the Orient and the male lover's passion for his female beloved—are structurally similar. Both depend on a structure that locates an Other—as woman, as oriental scene—as inaccessible, different, beyond. At this moment in *Madame Bovary*, the structural similarities make it possible for romanticism to figure itself in orientalist terms, and likewise for orientalism to figure itself in the romantic tradition.

Léon's conflation of Emma and Ingres's odalisque also reveals that some romantic and orientalist desires function fundamentally as a matter of cultural quotation, or of the repetition of cultural signs. Léon "quotes" Ingres's orientalist painting to signify and to enhance his romantic desire; but, ironically enough, the orientalist painting is itself a "quotation" of other orientalisms. We know that Ingres never traveled to North Africa or the Near East. He derived the colors and textures for his bathers and Islamic interiors from the eighteenth-century illustrations and the descriptions he found in the letters of Lady Mary Wortley Montagu[1] and in Montesquieu's *Lettres persanes*. The Orient of Léon's reference to Ingres is a heterogeneous amalgam: Ingres's paintings of Turkish odalisques bring together iconographies of a multiplicity of Orients—derived at times from painted scenes of Tangiers, Cairo, and Jerusalem, at other times from literary fictions of Persia.[2]

In this particular example from Flaubert, we understand that orien-

---

[1]The editor of Lady Mary Wortley Montagu's *Turkish Embassy Letters* observes that key passages from Montagu's letters enumerating the customs and decor of the Turkish female chambers are found copied into Ingres's notebooks. See particularly "Letter to Lady——,1 April 1717," in *The Complete Letters of Lady Mary Wortley Montagu*, vol. 1 (1708–1720), ed. Robert Halsband (Oxford: Clarendon Press, 1965), pp. 312–15.

[2]See MaryAnne Stevens, ed., *The Orientalists: Delacroix to Matisse: The Allure of North Africa and the Near East* (London: Weidenfeld and Nicolson, 1984), p. 17.

talism—the tradition of occidental literary and scholarly interest in countries and peoples of the East[3]—is hardly a discrete or monochromatic phenomenon. To the contrary, the representation of Léon's quotation from the Ingres painting illustrates how literary figures and narratives express a nexus of various modes of representation; in this case, romantic poetry's representation of women, orientalist literature's representation of the Orient, orientalist paintings of women, and romantic paintings of women are all enunciated in the moment when Léon substitutes the shoulders of the odalisque. As the intertextuality of this scene demonstrates, none of these individual traditions of representation can be discussed as if it were simple or uniform; nor can the social contradictions of which they are crucial representations be equated or analogized. In Flaubert's France, for example, the discursive representations of gender have social determinants—including the organization of the family, the construction of sexuality, medical practices—which are distinctly different from the conditions that produce discourses about cultural and racial differences; yet these diverse means of inscription traverse one another in *Madame Bovary*. The means by which the French culturally dominated and occupied Algeria after 1830, significant determinants of the discursive produc-

[3]Since 1838 the French term *orientalisme* has implied the diverse interests during the romantic period in all varieties of oriental matters, although it also included the more established meaning of oriental studies, the scholarly studies of the languages, cultures, and customs of Asiatic peoples from the Mediterranean to Japan. The term *orientaliste* appears in 1799 in the *Magasine encyclopédique* 25, 122: "Le savant orientaliste le père Paulinus," even though the Académie did not recognize it until 1835. It appears also in the *Journal asiatique* in 1824 in an obituary for Louis Langlès (1763–1824): "Le nom nouveau d'orientaliste sous lequel quelques personnes aiment à confondre ceux qui étudient les langues de l'Asie et ceux qui cherchent à approfondie l'histoire de cette partie du monde, ce nom aurait pu être inventé pour M. Langlès, tant il exprimait bien ses goûts et les habitudes de son esprit." See Daniel Reig, *Homo orientaliste: la langue arabe en France depuis le XIX ᵉ siècle* (Paris: Éditions Maisonneuve et Larose, 1988).

Thus, *orientalism* was already an established term of reference for European literary and scholarly interest in the Orient when Edward Said elaborated his critique of orientalism in his 1979 work, *Orientalism*. Said defines the phenomenon as the body of occidental representations of the oriental world which both constitute the Orient as Other to the Occident and appropriate the domain of the Orient by speaking for it. Orientalism is a discourse, Said argues, which is on the one hand homogenizing—the Orient is leveled into one indistinguishable entity—and on the other hand anatomizing and enumerative—the Orient as an encyclopedia of details divided and particularized into manageable parts. The discourse manages and produces information about an invented Other, which locates and justifies the power of the knowledgeable European self.

tion of cultural and racial difference, are in turn different from the circumstances of emerging industrial labor in France which gave rise to discourses about the working class. But as we will see, these distinctly different concerns overlap in the construction of the warring factions in Flaubert's *Salammbô*. Hence, the means of representation of various discourses are fundamentally heterogeneous and unequal; furthermore, these discursive apparatuses differ over time, and do not necessarily correspond across national and cultural boundaries. Yet, despite their essential nonequivalences, discursive means of representation overlap and are mutually implicated in one another at different moments.

My study treats orientalism as one means whereby French and British cultures exercised colonial domination through constituting sites and objects as "oriental." The discussions that follow are inscribed within an unqualified criticism of the persistent hegemonies that permit western domination of non-Europeans and the Third World. Yet, as much as I wish to underscore the insistence of these power relations, my intervention resists totalizing orientalism as a monolithic, developmental discourse that uniformly constructs the Orient as the Other of the Occident.[4] Therefore I do not construct a

[4]This is one implication of *Orientalism*. Said states: "Orientalism is a style of thought based upon an ontological and epistemological distinction made between 'the Orient' and (most of the time) 'the Occident.' . . . In short, Orientalism is a Western style for dominating, restructuring, and having authority over the Orient." Edward W. Said, *Orientalism* (New York: Random House, 1979), pp. 2–3. It is in this sense that Homi K. Bhabha observes in "The Other Question: The Stereotype and Colonialist Discourse," *Screen* 24, no. 6 (November–December, 1983): "There is always, in Said, the suggestion that colonial power and discourse is possessed entirely by the coloniser, which is a historical and theoretical simplification" (p. 25). Said's tendency to generalize orientalism as a constant and monolithic discourse is also noted by others: see for example, James Clifford, "On *Orientalism*," in *The Predicament of Culture* (Cambridge, Mass.: Harvard University Press, 1988); and B. J. Moore-Gilbert, *Kipling and "Orientalism"* (London: Croom Helm, 1986). Moore-Gilbert, for example, argues for the need to reappraise Said's presentation of orientalism as monolithic by calling attention to the incongruity between the West's relation to Arabs and Islam and Britain's relation to India.

Since *Orientalism*, Said's attention to the question of a Palestinian homeland, as well as to other issues of postcolonial emergence, makes it clear that he is not a proponent of the kind of monolithic rendering that does not account for resistance on the part of the colonized. See his "Identity, Negation, and Violence," *New Left Review* (December 1988): 46–60; *The Question of Palestine* (New York: Times Books, 1979); *After the Last Sky: Palestinian Lives* (New York: Pantheon Books, 1986); and, co-edited by Said and Christopher Hitchens, *Blaming the Victims: Spurious Scholarship and the Palestinian Question* (Lon-

master narrative or a singular history of orientalism, whether of influence or of comparison. Rather, I argue for a conception of orientalism as heterogeneous and contradictory; to this end I observe, on the one hand, that orientalism consist of an uneven matrix of orientalist situations across different cultural and historical sites, and on the other, that each of these orientalisms is internally complex and unstable. My textual readings give particular attention to those junctures at which narratives of gendered, racial, national, and class differences complicate and interrupt the narrative of orientalism, as well as to the points at which orientalism is refunctioned and rearticulated against itself. I suggest that the elucidation of these heterogeneous sites may prove useful, in terms of both method and political strategy, because they mark the places where orientalism is vulnerable to challenge. In focusing my interpretations on these sites, I hope to demonstrate how the logic of a discourse that seeks to stabilize domination is necessarily one that makes possible allegories of counterhegemonies and resistances to that domination; at the same time, these allegories suggest that it may not be possible to essentialize one privileged mode or site of struggle against domination, for each site is already multiply constructed. In this sense this book is a consideration of the unevenness of knowledge formations—the nonequivalence of various orientalisms in French and British culture, and the incommensurability, within specific orientalisms, of different narratives that concurrently challenge or corroborate the power of orientalism—in order to suggest, ultimately, that a critical acknowledgment of noncorrespondence, incommensurability, and multiplicity is necessary in effective contestations of colonial domination.

The Limits of Orientalism

It is necessary to revise and render more complex the thesis that an ontology of Occident and Orient appears in a consistent manner throughout all cultural and historical moments, for the operation that lends uniform coherence and closure to any discourse risks misrepre-

---

don: Verso, 1988). At the same time, Said's work does continue to stress the dominance of an imperialism of a single character, and to deemphasize the heterogeneity of different imperialisms and specific resistances.

senting far more heterogeneous conditions and operations. When Michel Foucault posits the concept of discursive formations—the regularities in groups of statements, institutions, operations, and practices—he is careful to distinguish it as an *irregular* series of regularities that produces objects of knowledge. In other words, a phenomenon such as the notion of the Orient in early-eighteenth-century France may be said provisionally to be constituted by some sort of regularity—that is, the conjunction of statements and institutions (maps, literary narratives, treatises, Jesuit missionary reports, diplomatic policies, and so forth) pertaining to the Orient. But the manner in which these materials conjoin to produce the category "the Orient" is not equal to the conjunction constituting "the Orient" at another historical moment, or in another national culture. With the idea of an irregular series, Foucault emphasizes that neither the conditions of discursive formation nor the objects of knowledge are identical, static, or continuous through time. In this way he seeks to avoid some of the overdetermining idealities of traditional historical study, with its desire for origins, unified developments, and causes and effects.[5]

In a similar manner, my book works against the historical desire to view the occidental conception of the oriental Other as an unchanging topos, the origin of which is European man's curiosity about the non-European world. If we misapprehend that an object is identically constructed through time, we do not adequately appreciate that the

[5]Foucault devises the concept of discursive formation as part of a "historical" project that seeks to avoid some primary idealities—of origin, continuity, and development—that are the instruments of interpretation in traditional historical method. Conceiving of history as an irregular series of discursive formations is an alternative method that takes into account nonlinear events, discontinuity, breaks, and the transformations of both the apparatuses for producing knowledge and that which is conceived of as knowledge itself. After rejecting four hypotheses concerning the unifying principles of a discursive formation—reference to the same object, a common style in the production of statements, constancy of concepts, and reference to a common theme—Foucault characterizes the active principle of discourse as "dispersion": "Whenever one can describe, between a number of statements, such a system of dispersion, whenever, between objects, types of statement, concepts, or thematic choices, one can define a regularity (an order, correlations, positions and functionings, transformations), we will say, for the sake of convenience, that we are dealing with a *discursive formation*. . . . The conditions to which the elements of this division (objects, mode of statements, concepts, thematic choices) are subjected we shall call the *rules of formation*. The rules of formation are conditions of existence (but also of coexistence, maintenance, modification, and disappearance) in a given discursive division." Michel Foucault, *Archaeology of Knowledge*, trans. A. M. Sheridan Smith (New York: Pantheon, 1972), p. 38.

process through which an object of difference—in this case the Orient—is constituted, is made possible, precisely by the nonidentity through time of such notions as Occident and Orient. That is, fundamental impermanence and internal discontinuity undermine the stability of both the relationship between the terms and the terms themselves. When we maintain a static dualism of identity and difference, and uphold the logic of the dualism as the means of explaining how a discourse expresses domination and subordination, we fail to account for the differences inherent in each term. In the case of orientalism, the misapprehension of uniformity prohibits a consideration of the plural and inconstant referents of both terms, Occident and Orient. The binary opposition of Occident and Orient is thus a misleading perception which serves to suppress the specific heterogeneities, inconstancies, and slippages of each individual notion. This heterogeneity is borne out most simply in the different meanings of "the Orient" over time. In many eighteenth-century texts the Orient signifies Turkey, the Levant, and the Arabian peninsula occupied by the Ottoman Empire, now known as the Middle East; in nineteenth-century literature the notion of the Orient additionally refers to North Africa, and in the twentieth century more often to Central and Southeast Asia. Notions such as "French culture," "the British Empire," and "European nations" are likewise replete with ambiguity, conflicts, and nonequivalences. And, as we shall see, nineteenth-century British literature about India is marked by an entirely different set of conventions, narratives, figures, and genres from those in the French literature about Egypt and North Africa for the comparable period. The British and French cultural contexts for producing such literatures at that particular moment are distinct: not only are there many noncorrespondences between the individual national cultures and literatures, but also, in the nineteenth century, the governing methods derived from Britain's century-old colonial involvement in Indian culture, economy, and administration are in contrast to those typifying the French occupation of North Africa, a contrast that exemplifies nonequivalent degrees of rule and relationship.

In addition, the assumption of a unifying principle—even one that must be assumed to be partly true, that the representation of the Orient expresses the colonial relationships between Europe and the non-European world—leaves uninvestigated the necessary possibility

that social events and circumstances other than the relationships between Europe and the non-European world are implicated in the
literature about the Orient, and that the relative importance of these
other conditions differs over time and by culture. To allegorize the
meaning of the representation of the Orient as if it were exclusively
and always an expression of European colonialism is to analyze the
relation between text and context in terms of a homology, a determination of meaning such that every signifier must have one signified and
every narrative one interpretation. Such a totalizing logic represses the
heterologic possibilities that texts are not simple reproductions of
context—indeed, that context is plural, unfixed, unrepresentable—
and that orientalism may well be an apparatus through which a variety of concerns with difference is figured. The Orient as Other is a
literary trope that may reflect a range of national issues: at one time the
race for colonies, at others class conflicts and workers' revolts, changes
in sexual roles during a time of rapid urbanization and industrialization, or postcolonial crises of national identity. Orientalism facilitates
the inscription of many different kinds of differences as oriental otherness, and the use of oriental figures at one moment may be distinct
from their use in another historical period, in another set of texts, or
even at another moment in the same body of work.

There is, of course, a very important political statement contained in
the thesis that orientalism is an expression of European imperialism.
Yet, when one proposes polemically that the discourse of orientalism
is both discrete and monolithic, this polemic falsely isolates the notion
of discourse, simplifies the power of this isolated discourse as belonging exclusively to Europe, and ignores the condition that discursive
formations are never singular. Discourses operate in conflict; they
overlap and collude; they do not produce fixed or unified objects.
Orientalism is bound up with—indeed it reanimates some of the
structuring themes of—other formations that emerge at different historical moments: the medical and anthropological classifications of
race, psychoanalytic versions of sexuality, or capitalist and Marxist
constructions of class. Moreover, the means of representation of any
discursive production are uneven, unequal, and more and less enunciated at different moments. For example, in various texts by a single
writer such as Gustave Flaubert, the representation of the Egyptian
courtesan Kuchuk-Hânem in *Voyage en Orient* (1850) and *Correspond-*

ance (1853) figures her oriental otherness in both racial and sexual terms; whereas in *Salammbô* (1862) the drama of the barbarian oriental tribes builds on a concurrent set of constructions of the French working-class revolts of 1848; and in *L'éducation sentimentale* (1869) the oriental motif is invoked as a figure of sentimental and romantic desire, offering a literary critique of this theme. In this sense this orientalist situation represented in Flaubert's texts is hardly uniform or monolithic; rather, it constitutes a site in which a multiplicity of heterogeneous discourses engage and overlap, not limited to dominant orientalist formations but also including emergent challenges to those formations. The orientalizing figures articulated in *Salammbô* and *Voyage* are imitated and parodied in *L'éducation sentimentale*; the textual instabilities of Flaubert's divided corpus mark those moments in which orientalist domination is simulated and then troubled, counterfeited and then ironically mocked.

An examination of the broader discursive relation between dominant formations and the emergent critiques of those formations provides a further opportunity to appreciate the multivocal character of discursive terrains. In Chapter 4 I pursue this theme of discursive heterogeneity by considering the interventions of Indian scholars into the exclusive tradition of Anglo-American literary criticism of E. M. Forster's *Passage to India*. To the degree that dissenting positions and practices are implicated in the very formations they address and oppose, the articulations of resistance and opposition by emergent or subaltern positions are not in themselves necessarily powerful or transforming. But, as the Forster debates illustrate, every position and practice shifts the conditions and alters the criteria, arguments, and rhetorical terms of enunciation and formation in the discourse. In this sense power is not static, nor does it inhere in an agency or a position or practice in itself; rather, it is found in the spatial and relational nonequivalences of the discursive terrain, in the active shifting and redistribution of the sites of inscription.

As I do not consider orientalism to be a continuous and discrete formation that constitutes a stable, essentialized object, the Orient, in this study I consider four orientalist situations that exemplify a heterogeneous variety of discursive formations of cultural difference. The social and historical context is different in each case, and the variety of literary materials is also heterogeneous, including travel narratives,

letters and correspondence, novels, literary criticism, and literary theories. Rather than suggesting that there is an evolution or development of a uniform notion of the Orient as Other from the eighteenth
through the twentieth centuries, I argue precisely the opposite: although it may be possible to identify a variety of different models in
which otherness is a structuring trope, these differences demonstrate
that to discuss a discourse of otherness is to attempt to isolate and
arrest an operation that is actually diverse, uneven, and complicated.
Even as I bracket the "discourse of otherness" as a heuristic notion, my
ultimate purpose is to present a series of observations that provides
the basis for resisting and challenging the notion of a closed discourse
that manages and colonizes otherness. I should say that one of the
paradoxes built into my discussion is that even as I argue against the
closure or singularity implied by the term *discourse*, I must name it in
order to write about it. Thus I encounter the problem of what to call
this nexus of apparatuses that is not closed but open, not fixed but
mobile, not dominant although it includes dominant formations, and
so forth. Rather than placing *discourse* in quotation marks each time I
want to call its monolithic quality into question, I hope it is understood
that I refer to discourse with the faith that the reader follows my
intention to displace a fixed, discrete, exclusive notion with one that
implies a multivalent, overlapping, dynamic terrain.

Discourse, *Heterotopia*, Hegemony, Subalternity

In the readings that follow, I am interested in tracing the discursive
intersections in particular French and British orientalist situations;
these moments of intersection destabilize the power of orientalism,
and the conflicts and convergences among different productions of
otherness mark places from which resistances to orientalism may be
articulated. It is useful here to define and interpret some of the terms,
and their implied theoretical projects, that form the basis for these
readings. Although the starting point for my critique of orientalism is
Foucault's concept of discourse, his use of the term is both ubiquitous
and inconsistent. In order to redefine *discourse* and to be specific about
my use of the term—as an open, mobile terrain of overlapping formations—I situate Foucault's concepts of discourse and *heterotopia* in

relation to Antonio Gramsci's theories of cultural hegemony and sub-alternity. In bringing together these diverse ideas, I sketch a picture of cultural production in which discourse designates the complex and uneven terrain composed of heterogeneous textual, social, and cultural practices; this is the terrain on which the organization of social life, or cultural hegemony, is achieved, maintained, challenged, and ultimately transformed.

Although I concede an essential incongruity between Marxian and Foucauldian paradigms and methods, I believe that there is an important dialogue to be posited between Foucault's notion of discourse and the Marxist concept of hegemony, and in particular the notion of hegemony elaborated by Gramsci as the entire social process through which a particular group exercises dominance.[6] On the one hand, bringing a Marxist discussion of hegemony to bear on Foucault's notion of discourse can elaborate the persistent, though not exclusive, role of economic forces in the production of cultural practices, supplementing what remains obscure in Foucault's work regarding the role and character of the practices that affect discursive transformation. Furthermore, Gramsci's concept of the "subaltern" classes—the emergent, not yet unified groups who may ally to create a "new historical bloc"—begins to open up, within a Foucauldian idea of discourse, specific and concrete arenas of dissent, resistance, accommodation, and change. On the other hand, the Foucauldian critique of totalizing narratives, unities, and origins can modify the tendency of some Marxist theories to isolate the notions of economic base and ideological

[6]It is apparent from the outset that the purposes and methods of Marx and Foucault are fundamentally incompatible. The Marxian paradigm emphasizes the productive structure of the economic in relation to a cultural superstructure, whereas in Foucault the importance of economic structure is diminished in relation to the greatly emphasized discursive modes of production. To the former, *power* refers to the economic power of one class over others, and history is the history of class struggle, whereas in the theories of the latter, power is at once hypostasized and pervasive, inscribing all areas of human life: social, intellectual, sexual, and so on.

Foucault's project is generally hostile to, and critical of, the most traditional Marxist narratives (a totalized history of class struggle, economic determinism, zero-sum notions of class hegemony) which Foucault's theories would deem too fixed and absolute, themselves parts of a discursive production of false origins, unities, and objects. The most traditional Marxism, by contrast, would view Foucault's theory, which emphasizes the productive power of discourse, as misguided and exemplifying the false consciousness that supports bourgeois class hegemony to the degree that it prevents oppressed classes from recognizing the revolutionary means necessary to throw off their oppression.

superstructure and to understand the former as determining the latter. Foucault's premise—that power is not localized in or limited to a ruling body but saturates the entire discursive field—brings to Marxist discussions of hegemony the possibility of many diverse forms of struggle, including those not easily recognizable as political or economic. This de-essentialized understanding of power is consonant, too, with my discussion of orientalism as a discursive formation not exclusively deployed by European or colonial rule, but articulated alternately and simultaneously by a variety of dominant and emergent positions on the discursive terrain.

In discussing discourse, I am invoking Foucault's notion to refer to networks of texts, documents, practices, disciplines, and institutions, which together function as matrixes in the production of certain objects and forms of knowledge. For Foucault, discourses can both discipline and manage forms of human subjectivity by constituting classifications such as madness, sexual deviance, and racial inferiority; these discourses regulate objects of knowledge through a variety of means, including criteria that exclude, limit, or eliminate. The discursive management of race is among the topics examined in Donna Haraway's work, for example; she writes about instances in the western scientific discourse of primatology in which Africa was conflated with primates and thus African races were discursively excluded from definitions of human species; this exclusion was instrumental in establishing and maintaining the coherence of the European races as well as the legitimacy of racism and colonialism.[7] Foucauldian method is likewise concerned with the productive function of discursive controls and exclusions; paradoxically, discursive means of appropriation and policing are accompanied by articulations of responses to these prohibitions, which are themselves enunciations of categories that are being policed. In this sense we might understand certain forms of African nationalism as responses generated, in part, from positions policed and excluded by racism or colonialism.[8] Because Foucault's

[7]Donna Haraway's far-reaching book, *Primate Visions: Gender, Race, and Nature in the World of Modern Science* (London: Routledge, 1989) can hardly be paraphrased in a brief sentence; I am drawing out only one strand of a complex weave of arguments.

[8]In *Les damnés de la terre* (Paris: F. Maspero, 1961), for example, Frantz Fanon suggests that the bourgeois nationalism practiced by neocolonial governments may be linked to, and implicated in, the structures of the former colonialism. Although Fanon stresses that nationalism and African unity are crucial concepts in the struggles of independence groups against colonialism and cultural obliteration, he also argues that bourgeois nationalism is easily perverted into forms of racism and separatism in which the colonial

books on madness, the prison system, and sexuality imply that resistance to exclusion and prohibition is itself implicated in discursive regulation, his work has often been interpreted by some readers as asserting the omnipotence of discursive apparatuses, the unchanging regulation of the social field, and, equally, the impossibility of resistance or dissent, which is not inevitably incorporated in the dominant terms of the discourse. To the contrary, it seems to me that Foucault refers generally to transformations of the social field, as well as to the disruption and change of discursive apparatuses. Foucault does not describe these changes as being enacted by individual agents necessarily in anticipated forms of resistance; rather, he sees them as originating in other practices and from unexpected sites and functions on the social terrain.[9] Foucault writes:

> The positivities that I have tried to establish must not be understood as a set of determinations imposed from the outside on the thought of indi-

---

power is replaced by an ethnic group while the order of social relations remains the same. Ironically, these tribal separatisms, or "micro-nationalisms," are congruent with the logic of colonialism, and are themselves legacies of the colonial structure.

Fanon's argument—that decolonization may either provide for a new set of relationships or reproduce the old order—illustrates precisely the problem of *transforming* structures of discipline, regulation, and power, a matter that is left inexplicit by Foucault, and one that critics after him have often debated. Fanon's discussion of decolonization suggests that interventions, resistances, and even changes of government or political party do not in themselves guarantee that a changed order or changed social relations will result; of utmost importance are the sites from which interventions originate, as well as the nature of these interventions. In Fanon's account, the old logic and social relations persist, particularly through the ties of the national bourgeoisie to the colonial order, and the racism inherited from the colonial order cannot be expelled in decolonization except through a deep, fundamental transformation of the social and material relations of colonialism. This work of transformation does not come from the national bourgeoisie, he suggests, but is generated "sous la poussée et sous la direction des peuples, c'est-à-dire au mépris des intérêts de la bourgeoisie" (p. 124) (through the upward thrust of the people, and under the leadership of the people, that is to say, in defiance of the interests of the bourgeoisie).

Foucault's theories never achieve the levels of either concreteness or practical engagement that Fanon's work epitomizes; and indeed, although the two men are not historically dissimilar (Foucault, a Frenchman writing after 1968, and Fanon, a Martiniquan who worked as a doctor in Algeria during the Algerian war) they write from very different social positions on the question of race and colonialism. Yet I juxtapose the two in order to suggest that the kinds of interventions described by Fanon are not precluded by Foucault's concept of discourse, and indeed may be the sort of intervention to lend concreteness to Foucauldian discussions.

[9] By "anticipated" and "unexpected" I do not mean to imply that there is somehow a central agency that controls forms of resistance. Rather, I mean to invoke a sense of temporality; the sites, functions, and practices of resistance that succeed in transforming the specific hegemonies in discourse may be identifiable only in hindsight. These forms

viduals, or inhabiting it from the inside, in advance as it were; they constitute rather *the set of conditions in accordance with which a practice is exercised, in accordance with which that practice gives rise to partially or totally new statements, and in accordance with which it can be modified.* These positivities are not so much limitations imposed on the initiative of subjects as *the field in which that initiative is articulated* (without, however, constituting its centre), rules that it puts into operation (without it having invented or formulated them), relations that provide it with a support (without it being either their final result or their point of convergence). It is an attempt to reveal discursive practices in their complexity and density; to show that to speak is to do something . . . to show that a change in the order of discourse does not presuppose "new ideas," a little invention and creativity, a different mentality, *but transformations in a practice, perhaps also in neighboring practices, and in their common articulation.* I have not denied—far from it—the possibility of changing discourse: I have deprived the sovereignty of the subject of the exclusive and instantaneous right to it.[10]

Foucault does not describe the regulating activity of discourse as either a set of fixed laws imposed from the outside or a series of determined utterances recited by individuals. Rather, discourse is a changing set of conditions that regulates the range of possible articulations at any time; yet with each articulation, the set of conditions shifts and adapts. The transformation of the set of conditions includes not only changes in the means of regulation but also modifications of the means and relations of representation as well, changes in the frequency and modes of articulation, fluctuations in locus and register, and ultimately "partially or totally new statements . . . in accordance with which it can be modified." In Chapter 4, for example, I observe that when Indian scholars enter the previously exclusive Anglo-American field of Forster studies, they alter the conditions of the discourse. Their interventions shift the criteria for inclusion and exclusion as well as the permissibility of certain subjects and objects of discourse. A condition

---

of resistance are not "anticipated" in the sense that at the moment of their articulation they may not be understood as transforming, whereas other forms deemed as such may ultimately be appropriated or neutralized.

[10]Foucault, *Archaeology of Knowledge*, p. 209; emphasis added. This is one of the rare texts in which Foucault outlines his method. In citing it I want to be careful not to represent it as the "real Foucault," or the key to understanding Foucault. For amidst Foucault's "histories" in which method is not delineated but is demonstrated—for example, *Madness and Civilization*, *Discipline and Punish*, *The Birth of the Clinic*, and *The History of Sexuality—Archaeology* is an anomaly.

of multiple and interpenetrating positions and practices—what we might call *heterotopicality*—is one way of describing the dynamic through which discursive conditions are transformed.

By heterotopicality I mean several things: first, I am evoking the sense in which discursive terrains are spatial and are composed of a variety of differently inscribed and imagined locations. The first and more general sense of heterotopicality—as a heterogeneous spatial designation—I derive from Foucault's notion of *heterotopia*.[11] Foucault argues that in institutional and social practices, certain spaces are coded as "public" and others as "private," some domains "legal" and others "illegal," some areas are for "work" and others for "play," and so on. He further distinguishes between cultural designations of *utopias*, which are the imaginary inversions of the real spaces of society, and *heterotopias*, which he describes as spaces of otherness: spaces of crisis, illiteracy, deviance, enslavement, or colonialism. Second, I want to render more complex Foucault's sense of oppositional spatial heterogeneity by taking it out of its ultimately binary frame of oppositions to recast spatial difference in terms of *multiple* sites. That is, on discursive terrains, such as the one in which orientalism is one formation, articulations and rearticulations emerge from a variety of positions and sites, as well as from other sets of representational relations, including those that figure class, race, nation, gender, and sexuality. Some of these articulations may intervene in and contest orientalist formations, while others may reiterate them. Each articulation shifts and alters the terms, conditions, and emphasized sites of the terrain. In this sense I employ the term *heterotopicality* to refer to this sense of multiplicity and interpenetration—the continual yet uneven overlappings, intersections, and collusions of discursive articulations.

This expanded notion of multiple spatial differences within discursive fields necessarily leads us to consider the processes through which certain formations maintain dominance over time, and in turn the processes through which resistance to these formations is suppressed or incorporated. In this effort the Marxist notion of hegemony provides a useful model. Although hegemony has been traditionally defined as political rule or economic domination in the relations be-

[11]Foucault's notion of *heterotopia* is elaborated in a posthumously published text "Des espaces autres," translated by Jay Miskowiec in *Diacritics* 16, no. 1 (Spring 1986):22–27, as "Of Other Spaces."

tween social classes, in Gramsci's thought hegemony is elaborated as a much broader notion, one that also includes the complex interconnected relations between social, cultural, and ideological practices through which a ruling group exercises domination. Hegemony is Gramsci's way of describing the entire process of negotiation, dissent, and compromise whereby a particular group or ideological formation gains the consent of the larger body to lead. In this sense hegemony does not refer exclusively to the process by which dominant groups exercise and maintain influence, but it denotes equally the process through which other groups organize, contest, or accommodate any specific domination. It is thus a question of a hegemonic process rather than a static or monolithic condition.[12] In this notion of hegemony, the older idea of domination by a ruling class is rethought. The ruling group is no longer an externalized body, and is no longer exclusively class-defined; rather, a specific domination is reconceptualized as a system of internalized practices and alliances within culture.[13] One

---

[12] The notion of "the dominant"—defined by Raymond Williams ("Dominant, Residual, and Emergent," in *Marxism and Literature* [New York: Oxford University Press, 1977]) as "a cultural process . . . seized as a cultural system, with determinate dominant features: feudal culture or bourgeois culture or a transition from one to the other"—is often conflated in cultural theory with Gramsci's concept of hegemony. Indeed, Williams writes, "We have certainly still to speak of the 'dominant' and the 'effective,' and in these senses of the hegemonic" (p. 121), as if the "dominant" and the "hegemonic" were synonymous.

It is important to note, however, that in Gramsci's thought, *hegemony* refers equally to a specific hegemony (for example, bourgeois class hegemony) and to the process through which "emergent" groups challenging that specific hegemony assemble and contest the specific ruling hegemony.

[13] Gramsci's concept of hegemony integrates two poles in Marxist theories of social change. On the one hand, it goes beyond the earlier concepts of superstructure and ideology—the system of ruling ideas characteristic of a particular class group—to describe an integrated system in which the production, practice, and proliferation of those ideas are only one part. On the other hand, Gramsci transforms the Marxist concept of class rule.

Originally, *superstructure* or *ideology* referred to a set of "ruling ideas" that mirrored the economic dominance of the ruling class. In "The German Ideology" (in *Marx-Engels Reader*, ed. Robert C. Tucker [New York: Norton, 1971], p. 136), Marx writes of ideology as "ruling ideas . . . the ideal expression of dominant material relationships."

Neo-marxist theorists, however, have since greatly expanded and complicated the understanding of ideology as ruling ideas that reflect economic relations: Georg Lukács, by providing a dialectical theory of the historical novel and its historical and social context, considerably elaborated the dialectic between form and context, consciousness and history; the Frankfurt School, especially Walter Benjamin and Theodor Adorno, in theorizing culture as an area of production. Finally, the concept of structural causality

might say that hegemony is also the process by which a particular group becomes "the one" in relation to which others are defined and know themselves to be Other.

In Gramsci's discussion of the levels of the "relations of force," it is clear that the hegemony of a specific group over a series of subordinate groups is never stable or static.[14] The relation of political forces, for example, is measured in the fluctuating degrees of homogeneity, self-awareness, and organization attained by the various social classes. In *The Prison Notebooks* Gramsci describes this relation of political forces as varying and mutable: "The dominant group is coordinated concretely with the general interests of the subordinate groups, and the life of the State is conceived of as a continuous process of formation and superseding of unstable equilibria . . . between the interests of the fundamental group and those of subordinate groups—equilibria in which the interests of the dominant group prevail, but only up to a certain point."[15] By implication, the reality of any specific domination is that, although it may be powerful for the moment, its power to dominate is never absolute or conclusive. A specific domination is not static; it is a process through which a particular group overtly or covertly gains the consent of other groups to determine the political and ideological state of the society, a much more complicated process than either the imposition or the reproduction of an unmodified rule. In this sense, when a hegemony representing the interests of a dominant group exists, it is always within the context of resistance from, and compromises with, "subaltern"[16] groups. Orientalism, then, as a formation that figures the domination of one group by another, never achieves static domina-

---

with regard to ideology is posited by the French structuralist Marxist Louis Althusser, later critiqued and refined in the work of Fredric Jameson in the concept of "structure as absent cause." See, most particularly, Jameson, *The Political Unconscious: Narrative as a Socially Symbolic Act* (Ithaca: Cornell University Press, 1981), chapter 1, pp. 17–102.

[14]The "relations of force" are the complex relation of different moments or levels, including the relation of social forces to the material forces of production, the relation of political forces, and the relation of military forces. Gramsci describes these moments as implying one another reciprocally—differing in accordance with socioeconomic activity and across different countries—combining and diverging in various ways.

[15]Antonio Gramsci, *Selections from "The Prison Notebooks,"* ed. and trans. Quintin Hoare and Geoffrey Nowell Smith (New York: International Publishers, 1971), p. 182.

[16]Gramsci describes "subaltern" groups as by definition not unified, emergent, and always in relation to the dominant groups; the subaltern groups may have passive or active affiliations to the dominant political formations; they may produce new formations that assert the autonomy of the subaltern groups but are within the old framework.

tion; orientalism, as an expression of colonialism, exists always amid resistance from subaltern or emergent spaces on the discursive terrain.

Gramsci defines the subaltern classes as prehegemonic groups whose histories are fragmented, episodic, and identifiable only from a point of historical hindsight. These classes are, in Gramsci's definition, "not unified" (p. 52) and may go through different phases during which they are subject to the activity of ruling groups; they may articulate their demands through existing parties, and then may themselves produce new parties. Gramsci, however, describes a phase at which the "formations [of the subaltern classes] assert integral autonomy" (p. 52). Although what is meant by "integral autonomy" is not immediately apparent, and indeed is the subject of debate, Gramsci's definition includes some noteworthy qualifications. The condition that the significant practices of the subaltern groups may not be understood as hegemonic until they are viewed with historical hindsight is interesting, for it suggests that the some of the most powerful practices may not be the overtly oppositional ones, may not be understood by their contemporaries, and may be less overt and recognizable than others. That the subaltern classes are by definition not unified is also a key point; that is, the subaltern groups do not constitute a fixed, unified force of a single character. Rather, the assertion of integral autonomy by subaltern classes that are not unified suggests a coordination of discrete yet allied movements, each in its own not necessarily equivalent manner transforming, disrupting, and destructuring the apparatuses of a specific hegemony. In this sense the hegemonic process described by Gramsci consists of a continuously transforming and variable relationship between dissenting, intervening, and accommodating positions and practices and the current dominant for-

---

"The history of subaltern social groups is necessarily fragmented and episodic. There undoubtedly does exist a tendency to (at least provisional stages of) unification in the historical activity of these groups, but this tendency is continually interrupted by the activity of the ruling groups; it therefore can only be demonstrated when an historical cycle is completed and this cycle culminates in a success. Subaltern groups are always subject to the activity of ruling groups, even when they rebel and rise up: only 'permanent' victory breaks their subordination, and that not immediately. In reality, even when they appear triumphant, the subaltern groups are merely anxious to defend themselves (a truth which can be demonstrated by the history of the French Revolution at least up to 1830). Every trace of independent initiative on the part of subaltern groups should therefore be of incalculable value for the integral historian." Gramsci, "History of the Subaltern Classes: Methodological Criteria," in *Selections from "The Prison Notebooks,"* pp. 54–55.

mation. The independent forms and locations of cultural challenge—
ideological as well as economic and political—make up what Gramsci
calls a "new historical bloc," a new set of relations that together
embody the possibility of a different hegemony and a different balance
of power. Thus, in Gramsci's thought the concept of hegemony not
only includes the accepted meaning of hegemony maintenance but
carries the significance of hegemony creation as well.[17]

Hegemony remains a suggestive construct in Gramsci, however,
rather than an explicitly interpreted set of relations. Thus, contemporary readers face the task of distinguishing which particular forms of
challenge to an existing hegemony are significantly transforming, and
which forms may be neutralized or appropriated by that hegemony.
Some cultural critics contend that counterhegemonic forms and practices are tied by definition to the dominant culture, and that the
dominant culture simultaneously produces and limits its own forms of
counterculture.[18] Others suggest that because identifiable variation
occurs in the social order over time, as well as variations in the forms of
the counterculture in different historical periods, we must conclude
that some aspect of the oppositional forms is not reducible to the terms
of the original hegemony.[19] Still others have expanded Gramsci's no-

---

[17]Walter Adamson, in *Hegemony and Revolution: A Study of Antonio Gramsci's Political
and Cultural Theory* (Berkeley: University of California Press, 1980), reads *The Prison
Notebooks* as the postulation of Gramsci's activist and educationalist politics; in chapter 6
he discusses Gramsci's two concepts of hegemony: hegemony as the consensual basis of
an existing political system in civil society, as opposed to violent oppression or domination; and hegemony as a historical phase of bourgeois development in which class is
understood not only economically but also in terms of a common intellectual and moral
awareness, an overcoming of the "economic-corporative" phase. Adamson associates
the former, hegemony in its opposition to domination, with "hegemony-maintenance"
and the latter, hegemony as a stage in the political moment, as "hegemony-creation."
Anne Showstack Sassoon ("Hegemony, War of Position, and Political Intervention,"
in *Approaches to Gramsci*, ed. Anne Showstack Sassoon [London: Writers and Readers,
1982]) provides discussions of Gramsci's key concepts; she historicizes the concept of
hegemony and discusses the implications of some of the ways in which it has been
interpreted. Sassoon emphasizes the degree to which hegemony is opposed to domination to evoke the way in which one social group influences other groups, making certain
compromises in order to gain the consent of others for its leadership in society as a
whole.
[18]Some of the "new historicist" studies of Shakespeare and Elizabethan England
illustrate this conflation of hegemony with the dominant, suggesting that forms of
subversion are ultimately contained by dominant ideology and institutions. See Stephen Orgel, *The Illusion of Power* (Berkeley: University of California Press, 1975); and
Stephen Greenblatt, "Invisible Bullets: Renaissance Authority and Its Subversion,"
Glyph 8 (1981): 40–61.
[19]See Williams, *Marxism and Literature*, p. 114.

tion of hegemony to argue that the social field is not a totality consisting exclusively of the dominant and the counterdominant, but rather
that "the social" is an open and uneven terrain of signifying practices,
some of which are neutralized, while others can be linked together to
build pressures against an existing hegemony.[20]

I take up this last notion of expanded, or nontotalized, hegemony by
reading specific discursive incongruities and intersections as possible
sites of subaltern resistance and intervention. The orientalist situations discussed in the chapters that follow embody discursive conflicts
and collaborations that express the instability of the orientalist terrain.
This instability is illustrated in the confluences and deviations of other
discourses with orientalism and the convergences of multiple, uneven
discursive productions—such as those of gender, race, and class—not
only circumscribe sites of instability in the discourse, but also permit
the rise of new positions, practices, and alignments which are instrumental in the transformation of the prior discursive arrangements and
the generation of new conditions. Such convergences are the topic of
Chapter 2, which includes an analysis of the conflicts between British
orientalism, an emergent feminism, and representations of class and
privilege in Lady Mary Wortley Montagu's *Turkish Embassy Letters*.

Discursive instability is also produced by the relationships between
dominant and emergent formations, as well as by the multiplicity and

[20]See Ernesto Laclau and Chantal Mouffe, *Hegemony and Socialist Strategy* (London:
Verso, 1985), esp. pp. 134–45. Laclau and Mouffe interpret hegemony as a political
relation that takes place in a "field of articulatory practices." Laclau and Mouffe make
two important distinctions concerning these articulatory practices: first, they are not in
themselves sufficient to constitute hegemonic change, for it is also necessary that the
articulations take place through a confrontation with antagonistic articulatory practices;
and second, at the same time, not every antagonism determines that a hegemonic
formation will emerge. An antagonism arises when a collective subject or group finds its
subjectivity negated by other discourses and practices; this negation can be, but is not
necessarily, the basis for an antagonism. Finally, they argue persuasively that no hegemonic logic can account for the totality of the social, and that the open and incomplete
character of the social field is the precondition of every hegemonic practice. For if the
field of hegemony were conceived according to a zero-sum vision of possible positions
and practices, then the very concept of hegemony, as plural and mutable formations and
relations, would be rendered impossible.
Elsewhere ("Hegemony and New Political Subjects: Toward a New Concept of Democracy," in *Marxism and the Interpretation of Culture*, ed. Cary Nelson and Lawrence
Grossberg [Urbana: University of Illinois Press, 1988], pp. 89–104), Mouffe goes even
further, elaborating the practical dimensions of the hegemonic principle in terms of the
efficacy of contemporary social movements in the struggle for increased democratiza-
tion.

lack of closure characteristic of both dominant and emergent sites. In Chapter 3 I observe that although colonialist, capitalist, and romanticist formations intersect in the Flaubert's early work, these formations are challenged by an emergent critique in the later text *L'éducation sentimentale*. The example of the Indian scholars' critique of Anglo-American Forster criticism discussed in Chapter 4 also exemplifies dialogues between dominant and emergent positions. But it is not only difference that is represented by the debates between Indians and Anglo-Americans; it becomes clear that there is diversity among the Indian scholars as well as in the prevailing Anglo-American tradition. In Chapter 5 the utopian constructions of China by Julia Kristeva, Roland Barthes, and the journal *Tel quel*, illustrate yet another confluence of diverse discourses—feminism, semiotics, and French Maoism—that essentialize China as the Other. These theorists deploy an orientalist trope in order to critique a wide range of logics of domination, yet their arguments tend to contribute to the very logics they wish to criticize. In this sense my discussion of theorists in Paris during the 1970s suggests that discursive heterogeneity in itself is not enough to destabilize a particular hegemony. Rather, the historical circumstances surrounding interventions (in the case of Kristeva, Barthes, and *Tel quel*, I suggest that these circumstances included the events of May 1968), as well as the rhetoric and logic of these interventions, are of crucial importance. This final example of orientalism cautions us, as contemporary readers, to theorize our own positions and to scrutinize the logic through which we formulate our criticisms.

Rereading Difference, Resisting Otherness

The analysis of how nondominant races, cultures, economic groups, and sexualities are marked and figured as Other, or as the subordinated counterpart of the dominant privileged categories, has been crucial to the current project of cultural criticism. At particular moments in critical theory in the United States, criticism that makes use of the category of the Other has been powerful, illuminating, and transforming. These moments are marked by the publication of works such as Juliet Mitchell's *Psychoanalysis and Feminism* (1974), Gayatri Spivak's introduction to her translation of Jacques Derrida's *Of Grammatology*

(1976), and certainly Said's *Orientalism* (1979). These represent vital veins of scholarship that have appropriated the notions of difference and otherness from philosophical and psychoanalytic traditions, redefining them in terms of contemporary interpretive concerns.[21] Theories of colonialist discourse, feminism, ethnic studies, and deconstruction have, each in their own way, dramatically altered the objects, methods, and community of literary and cultural criticism. Studies of colonialist discourse have suggested that a coherent and dominant European colonial identity is represented and justified in terms of the subordination of non-European cultural and racial differences.[22] Femi-

[21]The categories of difference and otherness come to literary studies from other disciplines and frames of reference. *Difference*, invoked in a dualistic opposition to *the same*, or *identity*, has roots in philosophical discourse. These distinctions from Greek philosophy were recapitulated in modern Continental thinking, notably by Hegel, Heidegger, and Sartre. See G. W. F. Hegel, *Phenomenology of Mind*, trans. J. B. Baillie (London: Macmillan, 1910), particularly "Independence and Dependence of Self-Consciousness: Lordship and Bondage" (pp. 228–40). Heidegger's *mit-Sein*, or "being-with," is integral to the concept of being-in-the-world. See Martin Heidegger, *Being and Time*, trans. John Macquarrie and Edward Robinson (1962). Finally, see Sartre's discussion of the gaze of the Other and being-for-others, in Jean-Paul Sartre, *L'être et le néant: Essai d'ontologie phénoménologique* (Paris: Gallimard, 1943), esp. "Le pour-autrui," pp. 265–349.

Otherness, posited in relation to a notion of the self, is a concept borrowed from psychoanalysis. Melanie Klein is greatly responsible for elaborating Freud's initial observations of the role of the female mother as Other and for considering the consequences of otherness in identity formation, and in the division, creation, and projection of "good" and "bad" objects; see Melanie Klein, *Developments in Psycho-Analysis* (New York: Da Capo, 1952).

For Jacques Lacan, otherness is more metaphorical and less stable. He designates the "autre" with a small *a* to refer to object choices, the alter egos, or the counterpart, of the psychoanalytic subject; but, there is also the "Autre" or "grand Autre" (the capitalized *Other*), which alludes to a generalized, intersubjective field of relations. This "grand Autre" is the Other of Lacan's now famous formulation, "The unconscious is the discourse of the Other," an abbreviation of the much more complicated consequences of Lacan's rereading of Freud. For Lacan, the unconscious is structured like a language, subject to the organizing principles of condensation and displacement (like Roman Jakobson's linguistic principles of metaphor and metonymy); the psychoanalytic subject is split, both situated by language and cut off from that subject position; language is the field in which the Other speaks the subject, and through which desire for the other is enunciated, necessitated by the gap between the split-off subject and its incommensurate signifier. See Jacques Lacan, "The Function of Language in Psychoanalysis," in *The Language of the Self*, trans. with notes and commentary by Anthony Wilden (Baltimore: Johns Hopkins University Press, 1968).

[22]See, for example, Abdul R. JanMohamed, *Manichean Aesthetics: The Politics of Literature in Colonial Africa* (Amherst: University of Massachusetts Press, 1983); Christopher Miller, *Blank Darkness: Africanist Discourse in French* (Chicago: University of Chicago Press, 1985); David Lloyd, *Nationalism and Minor Literature: James Clarence Mangan and the Emergence of Irish Cultural Nationalism* (Berkeley: University of California Press, 1987);

nist analyses have likewise made use of the notion of otherness to argue that the centrality of masculine identity is signified through the objectification of woman as Other, and that the mark of otherness suppresses the representation and signifying activities of women as social subjects.[23] Various challengers of the notion of literature have conceived of difference as that which is absent from or suppressed by literary traditions, and have suggested that the acceptance of a closed and unrevised canon of texts privileges certain national cultures, as well as certain classes and genders, as producers of "high culture." This approach urges the reconceptualization of literary traditions to include not only literature by women, non-Europeans, and ethnic minorities, but also materials that might be categorized as nonliterary—scientific and historical documents, diaries, and products of mass or popular culture.[24] Finally, deconstructive literary criticism suggests that difference manifests itself as a fundamental paradox embedded in the literary figures of the text and advocates methods of reading that would shed light on these rhetorical paradoxes.[25]

---

and Patrick Brantlinger, *Rule of Darkness: British Literature and Imperialism, 1830–1914* (Ithaca: Cornell University Press, 1988). Said's *Orientalism* can be said not only to be responsible for legitimizing an area of colonialist discourse studies, but also to have initiated a questioning of scholarly assumptions in several disciplines, not the least of which is a serious ongoing interrogation of ethnographic practices within the field of anthropology. The significant debates in anthropology are represented best by two volumes: *Writing Culture*, ed. James Clifford and George Marcus (Berkeley: University of California Press, 1986); and *Anthropology as Cultural Critique*, ed. George Marcus and Michael M. J. Fischer (Chicago: University of Chicago Press, 1986). For Said's contributions to these debates, see "Representing the Colonized: Anthropology and Its Interlocutors," *Critical Inquiry* 15, no. 2 (Winter 1989): 205–25.

[23]An ever-growing body of feminist theory employs an analysis of the construction of otherness to critique rigorously the epistemological assumptions of many disciplines. See, for example, Page duBois 1982, 1988; Teresa de Lauretis 1984; Alice Jardine 1985; and Gayatri Spivak 1988a.

[24]The troubling of the oppositions between "literary" and "nonliterary" materials, and between "high" culture and "popular" culture has had consequences for a variety of works: feminist criticism interested in legitimizing genres, authors, and forms of women's writing that had been excluded from consideration by previous criteria (Gilbert and Gubar 1979, 1985; Kathryn Shevelow 1989); the growing discipline of ethnic studies establishing the scholarly value of Chicano (Marta Sanchez 1985), Asian American (Elaine Kim 1982), and African-American (Barbara Christian 1980) literatures; postmodernist challenges to modernist paradigms of culture (Hal Foster 1983); and varieties of "new historicism" emphasizing that historical, scientific, and medical documents may be of equal importance with literary texts (Leonard Tennenhouse 1986.)

[25]Jacques Derrida (1973, 1976, 1979) notes that the French verb *différer* contains both a sense of the nonequivalent, as in "to differ," as well as a sense of the same, or of a series

Although this book is clearly implicated in these critical debates about difference and otherness, I argue finally against the recuperation of any binary version of difference. For I suggest that binary constructions of difference—whether Occident and Orient, male and female, or a static concept of dominant and emergent—embody a logic that gives priority to the first term of the dyad while subordinating the second. Whether the pair is figured as a binary synthesis that considers difference as always contained within the "same," or as one that conceives of the pair as a totality in which *difference* structurally implies *sameness*—or even if difference is posited as a third term, an absolute alterity outside the structure of binaries—it is necessary to understand each of these figurations as versions of the same binary logic. Ironically, even the positing of an outside third term depends on a binary opposition between structure and nonstructure, or inside-the-binarism and outside-the-binarism; the closure and uniformity of the Hegelian dialectic is upheld. My argument for heterogeneity seeks to challenge the tradition that conceives of difference as exclusively structured by a binary opposition between two terms—represented by the orientalist logic of Occident and Orient—by proposing instead another notion of difference that takes seriously the conditions of heterogeneity, multiplicity, and nonequivalence. I suggest that the desire to classify unevenness, incongruity, and noncorrespondence in terms of binary models of difference is based on a logic inscribed by discourses of domination, and that to conform to binary difference is inevitably to corroborate the logic of domination, to underdevelop the spaces in discourse that destabilize the hegemony of dominant formations. Mine is neither a philosophical nor an exclusively literary pursuit, one that might find the ultimate otherness of discourse in language, in the interaction of the poetic with the representational. Rather, I identify heterotopic spaces from which new practices are generated at the intersections of unevenly produced categories of otherness, in the junctions, overlaps, and confluences of incommensurable apparatuses which are not primarily linguistic but practical and material.

Because logics of domination and subordination are embedded

---

of identities separated by gaps, as in "to defer." Deconstructionist literary criticism (Paul de Man 1979; Barbara Johnson 1980) explores this paradoxical quality of opposition and reversal in rhetorical and literary figures.

within binary conceptions of difference, one risks certain dangers in continuing to essentialize notions of either the Other or its foe the dominant discourse. Not only does the essentializing of otherness inadvertently valorize, by further enunciating, the powerful hegemonies it seeks to criticize, but also theories that create monoliths of managing discourses greatly underestimate other points and positions of struggle and resistance operating in a specific hegemony at any moment. The view that a dominant discourse produces and manages otherness, univocally appropriating and containing all dissenting positions within it, underestimates the tensions and contradictions within any discursive terrain, the continual play of resistance, dissent, and accommodation. Most important, this type of dominant discourse theory minimizes the significance of counterrepresentations and countercultures, and continues to subsume the resistance of emergent or minority positions to apparently dominant formations. This cannot be the case if one recognizes that locally emergent economic, sexual, and racial groups are continually resisting and contesting the homogenizing and totalizing tendencies of these so-called dominant discursive formations. For example, an interpretation of Indian history guided by the concept of a dominant colonialist discourse would represent India as having been thoroughly ruled and administered for a century and a half by British discourses, to the degree that Britain's rule can be said to have been aided by the extensive legal and administrative classification of India into forms of knowledge composed of census data, official reports, laws, histories, geographies, and encyclopedias.[26] Considering these colonialist formations as comprehensive and statically dominant, however, ignores the ongoing and quite different Indian resistances that occurred throughout the British occupation, and places the power of colonialist discourse in the hands of the colonizer. In this regard it has been the aim of contemporary radical

[26]The work of the anthropologist Bernard S. Cohn is outstanding in analyzing the British discursive management of India. Cohn fastidiously documents the modalities through which the British discourses produced India as forms of knowledge: the survey, the census, the museum, legal codes, and so on. See Cohn, "The Command of Language and the Language of Command," in *Subaltern Studies*, vol. 4, ed. Ranajit Guha (Delhi: Oxford University Press, 1985); "The Census, Social Structure, and Objectification in South Asia," in *An Anthropologist among the Historians and Other Essays* (Delhi: Oxford University Press, 1987); and "Law and the Colonial State," in *History and Power in the Study of Law*, ed. Jane Collber and June Starr (Ithaca: Cornell University Press, 1989).

historians, such as the Subaltern Studies Group, to reconstitute the histories of peasant and worker resistances, in order to displace traditional historical accounts and the official narrative through the articulation of these counternarratives.[27]

Moreover, discursively constructed positions of otherness are neither fixed nor continuous. Representations of difference and otherness are multivalent, signifying distinct meanings within particular social and historical contexts. That is, marks denoting differences in social class, race, culture, or gender may in one set of social relations be used to exclude and marginalize a social group, while in another they may be appropriated or rearticulated as marks of privilege or empowerment. For example, Stuart Hall has remarked that the designations *black* and *coloured* signify quite different things in the distinct contexts of England and the Caribbean. Hall observes that in the English system, organized around a binary dichotomy which reflects the colonizing order of "white/not-white," the terms *black* and *coloured* are more or less synonymous, whereas in the Caribbean system, where race is organized in an ascending spectrum of classifications, *black* and *coloured* denote different points on the scale rising toward the ultimate term, *white*.[28] Likewise, we will see in Chapter 4 that the signifier *Indianness* as difference serves as a multivalent hinge between the British colonialist discourse that subordinated Indians and the Indian articulation of Indianness as identity that criticized, and distinguished itself from, that colonialist discourse.

Another example of this multivalence can be found in the representation of racial and ethnic otherness in the contemporary United States.[29] Two predominant tropes figure racial difference in current discourses: "racial Others are different from the dominant majority," and the apparently opposite configuration "racial others are *like the*

[27]See Dipesh Chakrabarty, "Conditions for Knowledge of Working-Class Conditions," and Gyanendra Pandey, "Peasant Revolt and Indian Nationalism," both in *Selected Subaltern Studies*, ed. Ranajit Guha and Gayatri C. Spivak (New York: Oxford University Press, 1988).

[28]See Stuart Hall, "Signification, Representation, Ideology: Althusser and the Post-Structuralist Debates," *Critical Studies in Mass Communication* 2, no. 2 (June 1985): 91–114.

[29]The construction of "race" in contemporary American society has changed significantly since the 1950s as the result of many factors, including the civil rights movements of the 1950s and 1960s. See Michael Omi and Howard Winant, *Racial Formation in the United States: From the 1960s to the 1980s* (London: Routledge, 1986), for an analysis of this changing construction of race.

majority." Both strategies for objectifying otherness—the Other as incomprehensible and threatening, and the Other as familiar and controllable—can be used as the means of objectifying racial difference. Ironically, both models rely equally on a logic of complementarity in which racial difference is always defined in terms of a naturalized Anglo-Saxon majority or norm. These two tropes however,—the Other as different and the Other as same—are unstable representations, and can also be reappropriated by racial and ethnic minority groups. The reappropriation of these tropes is one means through which racial and ethnic minorities may challenge the existing cultural hegemony, rearticulating different versions of the same formations into social and legal arguments. For example, the Other as different has been one of the significant tropes in the discourse of civil rights (as in, "We have different histories in the United States and different degrees of access to opportunity"). Alternatively, assertions of likeness or sameness are crucial to arguments about equality ("We have different access, but we are entitled to the same opportunities"). At the same time, it is clear that the matter of racial equality has not been corrected by racial and ethnic minority groups' merely reclaiming the tropes about racial otherness, for these tropes are unstable and have been reappropriated and used differently by those who argue *against* civil rights policies ("Minorities have equal opportunity; they are already 'the same' enough"). This implies that, in terms of institutional change, although it is necessary to accomplish the wider inclusion of minorities and women in dominant formations, there are also serious limitations to the kinds of transformation this assimilating inclusion can bring; in addition to these measures, it becomes essential to recast and rethink the structures and narratives of institutions themselves in terms of a critique of the logic of sameness and difference.

In order to begin to account for and theorize the dynamics of intervention, resistance, and change within discursive formations, one may support the understanding that discourses are not closed monoliths by emphasizing the heterogeneity of both the means and the practices of representation. First, signs and objects coded as either dominant or emergent are multivalent; a sign that is in one social context part of an apparatus of exclusion may be appropriated and rearticulated as part of an enabling formation. Second, discursive formations are heterotopic, generated from different positions or spaces on the discursive terrain. Orientalism is irregularly composed of statements and restatements, contestations, and accommodations, generated from an incongruous series of writing positions; it simultaneously includes formations that may be identified as dominant as well as emergent, and challenging interventions may be articulated from a variety of uneven and unequal spaces on the terrain. In this sense, the theoretical problem facing cultural criticism is not how to fit slippage, instability, and multivalence into a conception of dominant ideology and counterideology or discourse and counterdiscourse. Rather, cultural critics might approach this question from the other direction: that is, that heterogeneities and ambivalences are givens in culture. These nonequivalences and noncorrespondences are not the objects to be reconciled or explained; they must constitute the beginning premise of any analysis.

Finally, cultural criticism that makes use of the logic of otherness must historicize and theorize its own methods and objects. This is to say that theories are produced, as are all narratives, in particular social contexts and by the particular tensions, contradictions, and pressures of that historical moment. In the final chapter I suggest that one way to explain the recuperation of orientalism by the intellectuals at *Tel quel* is to understand it as a response to their disappointment over the "failed" strikes of May 1968. French Maoism implied a judgment on the part of these progressive theorists of the late 1960s that revolution could never occur in France, and that nothing would be sacrificed if they turned their gaze toward a political utopia elsewhere. In the wake of what was judged to be a thwarted revolution, the romance with China's Cultural Revolution served as a means for some intellectuals to turn away from the still demanding struggles in France—struggles not limited to the rebuilding of a fragmented and disillusioned Left but, more important, arising from a growing racial and class stratification in France resulting from the postcolonial displacement of immigrants from North Africa, Indochina, and the Caribbean. In this sense my discussion of Kristeva, Barthes, and *Tel quel* in Chapter 5 serves as a cautionary illustration of the dangers of ahistorical literary theory, or theory that does not interrogate the circumstances of its own production and can therefore be appropriated by institutions or ideologies to justify the status quo. In this respect I wish to attach this book's discussion of heterogeneity clearly to a twofold critical project that responds to the specific context of the present. On the one hand, my discussion is conceived as an interruption of traditional orientalist and colonialist representations, and in this sense heterogeneity among categories of otherness is stressed in order to target the reductive and homogenizing aspects not only of orientalist stereotypes but also of the continued institutional production of binary theories about various social differences. On the other hand, the critique of binary conceptions of difference is also part of a discussion among scholars involved in the *critical* study of colonialism and cultural domination; it is aimed at reducing the explanatory power of the binary model of "the West and the Rest," and suggests that the prevalent model of nation-based politics may risk suppressing or precluding affiliation with positions inscribed by other valences of oppression. In this sense, this book describes heterogenous discursive terrains, not to contribute to a liberal pluralistic model of multiculturalism, but rather to emphasize that the relationships between Europe and colonized cultures are crossed by other interpellations and stratifications not reducible to the commonly held binary antagonism, and, most important, to underscore these overlapping and multiple inscriptions as moments of particular vulnerability in dominant discursive formations. By foregrounding heterogeneity I do not mean to obscure the fundamental difference of power between colonizers and colonizeds. Rather, I wish to open spaces that permit the articulation of *other* differences—themselves incongruous and nonequivalent—not only of nation and race but also of gender, class, region, and sexual preference. Thus, in understanding the logic of otherness as an apparatus that cannot but reinscribe a binary logic of domination and subordination, one must now question the continuing efficacy of using these terms in a critical analysis of power. For this reason, my ultimate aim is to challenge and resist the binary logic of otherness by historicizing the critical strategy of identifying otherness as a discursive mode of production itself.

2

Travel Narratives and Orientalism: Montagu and Montesquieu

'Tis a particular pleasure to me here to read the voyages to the Levant, which are generally so far remov'd from Truth and so full of Absurditys I am very well diverted with 'em. They never fail giving you an Account of the Women, which 'tis certain they never saw, and talking very wisely of the Genius of the Men, into whose Company they are never admitted, and very often describe Mosques, which they dare not peep into.

—Lady Mary Wortley Montagu, *The Turkish Embassy Letters*
(1717–1718)

Comment as-tu pensé que je fusse assez crédule pour m'imaginer que je ne fusse dans le monde que pour adorer tes caprices? . . . Non: j'ai pu vivre dans la servitude; mais j'ai toujurs été libre: j'ai reformé tes lois sur celles de la nature; et mon esprit s'est toujours tenu dans l'indépendance.

[How could you think me so credulous that you imagined I was in the world only to worship your caprices? . . . No: I may have lived in servitude, but I have always been free. I have reformed your laws according to the laws of nature, and my mind has always remained independent.]

—Roxane à Usbek, in Montesquieu *Lettres persanes* (1721)

Eighteenth-century portraits of the oriental world as an exotic, uncivilized counterpart of Europe were crucial enunciations of the discourses that produced representations of the European world as knowing, stable, and powerful. Travel literature performed these acts of symbolization for French and English culture; by figuring travelers in foreign lands encountering strange and disorienting customs and practices, the trope of travel allegorized the problems of maintaining cultural institutions amidst challenging othernesses, of establishing cultural standards and norms in the context of heterogeneity and difference. In this way not only did the literary theme of travel serve to express the eighteenth-century colonial preoccupation with land and empire, but also travel as a representation of territorial ambition became a predominant discursive means for managing a national culture's concern with internal social differences and change. In England these social challenges to the status quo included religious dissent, growing parliamentary control, budding industry, and a growing working class; in France the ancien régime faced nonaristocratic dissent, republican challenges to the monarchy, and peasant revolts. In other words, the utopian geographic expansion implied by travel literature addressed national anxieties about maintaining hegemony in an age of rapidly changing boundaries and territories. Yet it also regulated the social quarrels besetting the old regimes of the period by transfiguring internal challenges to the social order into fantasies of external otherness.

Lady Mary Wortley Montagu's *Turkish Embassy Letters* (1717–1718) explicitly challenge the received representations of Turkish society furnished by the seventeenth-century travel writers who preceded her. Although she writes in that tradition of letters about traveling in Turkey, Montagu distinctly sets herself apart from that tradition by criticizing the representations of women, marriage, sexuality, and customs in the travel accounts of Robert Withers, George Sandys, John Covel, Jean Dumont, and Aaron Hill. In redressing many of what she insists are the misconceptions and inaccurate representations of Turkish women propagated by these male travel writers, Montagu reports how, as a woman, she is permitted greater access to Turkish female society, and claims that her difference from these earlier writers may in fact be due to her being a woman. In this sense Montagu's position with regard to English travel writing is paradoxical, or multivalent, in a manner that the earlier travelers' accounts are not. On the one hand, some of her descriptions—written as they are from her position as wife of a British ambassador—resonate with traditional occidental imaginings of the Orient as exotic, ornate, and mysterious, imaginary qualities fundamental to eighteenth-century Anglo-Turkish relations.

At the same time, unlike the male travel writers before her, she employs comparisons that generally liken the conditions, character, and opportunities of European women to those of Turkish women. Montagu's identification with Turkish female society invokes an emergent feminist discourse that speaks of common experiences among women of different societies; in addition, Montagu's identification with the wives and mistresses of Turkish dignitaries also makes use of the existing discourse of class distinction, and an established identity of aristocratic privilege across cultures. Montagu's representations of Turkey in the *Letters* thus employ both the rhetoric of identification, most frequently in her descriptions of Turkish court women, and the rhetoric of differentiation with regard to other aspects of Turkish society in general. Indeed, Montagu's observations often invoke the rhetoric of both similarity and difference; that is, in the very act of likening Turkish and English women, Montague relies on and reiterates an established cultural attitude that differentiates Orient and Occident, that constitutes them as opposites.[1] The paradoxes of the British ambassador's wife's relation to Turkish women call our attention to the sense in which in the eighteenth century, English orientalism is not monochromatically figured through an opposition of Occident and Orient but figures itself through a variety of other differentiating discourses. The *Turkish Embassy Letters* provide a particular example of orientalist representations overlapping with rhetorics of gender and class, and of orientalism generated by differently gender-determined and class-determined positions.[2]

[1]It is interesting to note the etymology of the term *Orient*, for it bears on the discussion of eighteenth-century travel literature, the geographic figuration of otherness, as one of the earlier rhetorical frameworks of orientalist literature. From the Latin *oriens*, meaning "rising," "rising sun," or "east," the term came to mean largely all that is not the Occident, or *occidens*—"quarter of the setting sun"—from the infinitive *occidere*, "to fall down," "to set." If the Occident was the location of that geographic place on the horizon where the sun sets, then the Orient was the opposite place where the sun rises. But through a variety of social and historical turns, what began as a geographic topos became an ideological one; or to put this another way, ideological values became figured through a geographic and etymological binary opposition. In this sense, British and French knowledge of the world was represented in terms of this dualistic vision: West or East. Many other categories of definition could then be produced and ascribed according to this binary scheme: the West was the Christian land, the East was the space of infidels, heretics, pagans, and so forth.

[2]There are examples of heterogeneity among other women travel writers. In "Victorian Travel Writings," *Genre* 22, no. 2 (Summer 1987): 189–207, Susan Morgan exam-

In a rather different manner, discourses of gender, class, and orientalism also intersect in a text by a French contemporary of Montagu's, Montesquieu's *Lettres persanes* (1721). Like the *Turkish Embassy Letters*, Montesquieu's text emerges at a moment in which the discourse of orientalism is alternately destabilized, accommodated, and reinforced by a constellation of other discourses: one that constitutes women as romantic and sexual Others, as well as an emergent discourse about female independence; and a discourse about class distinction and privilege, as well as an emergent discourse of class equality. But in Montesquieu's novel, the fictional as well as the epistolary qualities work to multiply the conflicts, contradictions, and collusions between orientalism and other intersecting inscriptions. The *Lettres persanes* may conform to a traditional orientalist structure that opposes the tyranny and licentiousness of Persia to rational, civilized France. But at the same time, its ironic inversion posing the drama of Persians traveling in France and their failing rule over the harem as an allegory for French problems of rule simultaneously calls that orientalist opposition into question. In addition, the Persian wives, female slaves, and eunuchs figure significantly not merely as ornaments in the exotic harem but as "gendered" and "classed" representations; when the wives and female slaves revolt against the eunuchs and the despot, the novel's harem plot crosses orientalism with the concurrent discourses about class hierarchy and gender relations. In this sense, the orientalist opposition of France and Persia is destabilized by the ironic inversions of the two cultures and also by the novel's competing representations of gender and class struggles. The demise of the oriental despot is a plot that makes use of a sexual drama of male domination and female submission, as well as a drama of class conflicts between despot, wives, eunuchs, and female slaves. Ultimately, if we read the relationship of the master and the wives as a gendered representation of the French problem of colonial rule, or as an emblem of the relationship of unequal power between Occident and Orient

---

ines the travel writings of British women in Southeast Asia; she points out that these women writers are exceptions within the tradition of what has been monolithically termed orientalism. The orientalism of Edward Said, Morgan argues, is predominantly a male tradition, and predominantly about the Middle East. The writings of these British women writers in Southeast Asia are exceptions to this tradition, Morgan observes, and contain very different representations of the Orient, and very marked sympathy, in particular with the female population of these countries.

enunciated by the traditional orientalist frame, then the triumph of the wives and female slaves over Usbek's authority at the end of the *Lettres* provides a final narrative challenge to orientalism.

Even as we accept the general premise that orientalism is a discourse through which European institutions—literary, political, and economic—are able to generate a consistent notion of the Occident while constituting and subordinating its oriental Other, orientalist situations expressed in texts such as Montagu's and Montesquieu's illustrate that other social concerns may displace, be displaced by, or collaborate with orientalism. In other words, not only are orientalisms produced by distinct cultural and historical factors in different periods, but also the cases of Montagu and Montesquieu demonstrate that individual orientalist situations are themselves neither uniform nor without contradictions. The competing narratives of culture, class, and gender in Montagu's *Turkish Embassy Letters* serve as one example of the variety of representational forces that may complicate a particular orientalist situation. As an emblem of heterogeneity itself, Montagu's text diverges from earlier British travel writers' accounts of Turkey, and constitutes a contrast to the types of intersections to be found in Montesquieu's *Lettres persanes*, underscoring further that eighteenth-century orientalism was by no means monolithic. In focusing this chapter on two examples of early-eighteenth-century epistolary travel literature, one British and one French, I aim to explore several different narrative constructions of the relation between occidental and oriental worlds produced in the same period in order to suggest the considerable heterogeneity both between and within culturally specific orientalisms.

Thus, this chapter is concerned with the moments at which the production and the management of sameness and difference are not limited to the figuration of cultural oppositions but include representations of contrary genders and classes, or whose oriental figurations are heterogeneous by virtue of being generated from differently gender- and class-determined positions in culture. In both the British and the French examples, orientalist inscription is not a discrete operation; it comes about as the result of a multiplicity of discursive formations, dominant and emergent, conflicting and combining in the cultural fields of struggle that produce travel writings. The variety of such discourses in the eighteenth century is not limited to those that differentiate masculinity and femininity, or that separate and distinguish social classes. Along with inscriptions of mastery and slavery, racial differences, and disease and health, one discovers a spectrum of uneven representations operating both outside and within this particular orientalist terrain. I have said that the unresolved multiplicity of representational forces emphasizes how orientalism, rather than existing as an isolated, univocal discourse, takes place in a plural and mutable field of varied positions and representational practices. When one grasps this plurality and mutability as the given condition of an orientalist situation, or any situation of cultural domination, then one also identifies the destabilized moments where resistance begins and transformation becomes possible.

"So many Beautys as are under our Protection here":
The *Turkish Embassy Letters*

Lady Mary Wortley Montagu had the occasion to spend several years in Turkey beginning in 1717, when her husband, Edward Wortley Montagu, was called to serve as British ambassador there. Within her own lifetime, her literary and intellectual distinction was recognized by many writers, including Alexander Pope and his circle, and she became quite famous when the *Turkish Embassy Letters* were published the year after her death in 1763.[3] Montagu's other accomplish-

[3]Robert Halsband, editor of the *Complete Letters*, and coeditor of *Essays and Poems*, suggests that the manuscript of the *Turkish Embassy Letters* was composed from copies of letters Lady Mary had written from Turkey, and that they may have been meant for publication as a travel memoir. Halsband writes: "They are not the actual letters she sent to her friends and relations; they are, instead, a compilation of pseudo-letters, dated, and addressed to people either named or nameless. Although they are clearly an accurate record of her experiences and observations during her two-year sojourn abroad, we may still wonder to what extent they are based on real letters. Are they perhaps a travel-memoir in the form of letters (a literary genre popular since the Renaissance)?" Introduction to *Complete Letters*, pp. xiv–xv.

Before she died, Lady Mary gave a copy of the manuscript to Benjamin Sowden, implying that it had been her wish that they should eventually be published. See "Biographical Anecdotes," in Lady Mary Wortley Montagu, *Essays and Poems*, ed. Robert Halsband and Isobel Grundy (Oxford: Clarendon Press, 1977), pp. 32–33. Halsband concludes in his introduction to the *Complete Letters* that "it is certain that she intended them to be published, though not in her lifetime" (p. xvii).

ments include her essays in which she argued persuasively for a change in the treatment of women in English society in favor of recognizing women's social and intellectual virtues, as well as her significant contribution toward introducing the smallpox vaccine into England after her return from Turkey.[4]

The diplomatic presence of the Montagus in Turkey was warranted by a British commercial relationship with the Ottoman court that had begun in the late sixteenth century under Queen Elizabeth I. England imported silks, spices, cotton, soaps, oils, and carpets, while Turkey received armaments and tin. The Levant Company, founded in 1581, was one of England's most important early commercial ventures, established at the time when England was also beginning its longstanding colonial relationships with India and Africa, in the form of the East India Company and the Royal African Company. These merchant companies rose to great prominence during the seventeenth century. As a result of the Navigation Act of 1660, which resulted in England's commercial monopoly of overseas trade and transportation of goods,[5]

[4]Montagu articulates her position with regard to the sexes and declares her sympathy with the developing feminist movement in an installment of *The Nonsense of Common-Sense*, a weekly newspaper. In an essay dated January 24, 1738, Montagu responds to an essay written by Lord Chesterfield in which he advised women on how to resist various temptations, especially that of succumbing to a love affair. Montagu refutes his assumption that women must resist seduction by "filling up their time with all sort of other triffles: in short he recommends to them, Gosiping, Scandal, Lying, and a whole troop of Follys . . . as the only preservatives for their Virtue" Montagu, *Essays and Poems*, p. 131. She suggests instead "Reason or Refflection," as well as treating women "with more dignity" (p. 131).

See "Letter to Sarah Chiswell" on the subject of innoculation, *Complete Letters*, pp. 337–40; and "A Plain Account of the Innoculating of the Small Pox by a Turkey Merchant," *Essays*, pp. 95–97. Indeed, we might consider the vaccine a metaphor for cross-cultural experience. That is, Lady Mary proposed that "the best sort of the Small Pox" be introduced in small quantity—"the point of the Needle takes as much of the matter as will lye upon it"—in order to inoculate individuals against more serious fatal infection, just as twentieth-century anthropologists would later advocate some virtue in the experience of "going native" to learn more about the cultures they studied.

[5]Christopher Hill, *The Century of Revolution, 1603–1714* (New York: Norton, 1961), esp. chaps. 13 and 17, argues that the main point of the Navigation Acts was a "deliberate policy of developing the production, and monopolising the export, of colonial commodities like tobacco, sugar, cotton, dye-woods." On the labor of the colonists, Hill cites Charles Davenant, *On the Plantation Trade*, as stating that it was probably six times more profitable than labor at home, owing to slavery. "The Acts created monopoly conditions of trade with the colonies, and so increased the profits of English merchants. They mark a decisive turning-point in England's economic history" (p. 181).

and the free trade policies—affecting imported goods, re-exported products, and the slave trade—which followed the Revolution of 1688, exports and imports between England and its foreign markets tripled. By the early eighteenth century, English foreign policy decisions were being made largely to accommodate England's trading and colonial interests.

Not only did the merchant companies of the late seventeenth century enjoy the patronage of the government, but these companies, essential instruments in defeating other European trade efforts (such as Spanish, Dutch, and French commerce), were given substantial powers and privileges, including judicial and administrative power over competitors and foreign governments, as well as over the colonies themselves. The English travel accounts that accompanied the deepening of Anglo-Turkish diplomatic and commercial ties in this period form an integral part of the discourse about the colonies that depicted foreign and colonial cultures as possessing exceedingly different—and, by implication, less civilized—customs, religions, and practices from those of European society. These accounts played a leading role in establishing the terms of the relationship between European and colonial cultures. The portraits of Turkish and Middle Eastern culture as alternately violent and barbaric, slovenly and lascivious, or grotesque and incomprehensible supported and permitted an ideology that justified the cultural subordination of the foreign and colonial cultures from which profits were being extracted in the form of materials and goods, labor, and consumer markets. Included in this travel literature are accounts such as Robert Withers, *A Description of the Grand Signor's Seraglio* (1650); George Sandys, *Sandys Travailes* (1658); John Covel, *Early Voyages and Travels in the Levant* (1670); Jean Dumont *A New Voyage to the Levant* (1696); Aaron Hill, *A Full and Just*

England's monopolization of the overseas trade marked the transition to a new type of economy. Slaves from West Africa were brought to England and Jamaica by English manufacturers. Refining and finishing industries sprang up in London and elsewhere for the home market and for reexport. Between 1660 and 1700, whereas manufactured goods (other than cloth) exported to England expanded by 18 percent, exports to the colonies expanded by over 200 percent. Hill suggests that nineteenth-century industrialism might well have been impossible without the Navigation Acts. Colonial trade prepared for the industrial revolution, just as the political revolution had made possible the use of full state power for the capture and retention of monopoly colonial trade.

Account of the Present State of the Ottoman Empire (1709); as well as Montagu's *Turkish Embassy Letters*. The observations of these writers are not uniform but differ in rhetoric and style of presentation, as well as in the sorts of subjects that are discussed. It is in this tradition of travel writing that Lady Mary Wortley Montagu distinguishes herself, and to this tradition that she addresses many of her criticisms.

Robert Withers's *Description of the Grand Signor's Seraglio* attempts to establish the traveler's credibility by claiming that he had "procured admittance to the Seraglio, and by continuance many years in those parts, had time and opportunity to perfect his observations." Later in the text, however, he divulges his lack of authority by stating that "no white man can visit amongst the women." Despite this lack of experience, Withers's account is filled with the melodramatic caricatures of exotic sexuality and barbarism in the seraglio for which orientalism is so famous: the deprivation and brutalization of the Turkish women, the cruelty of the eunuchs, the ugliness of the slave girls—all of which is pointedly contradicted by Montagu in her letters. For example, Withers details a colorfully mythologized ritual in which the king selects his mistress for the evening from a display of women by dropping a handkerchief into the hand of the selected one. Montagu targets Withers's description of the ritual as an example of "the common Voyage-writers who are very fond of speaking of what they don't know" and refutes it as absolutely fictitious.[6]

Like Withers's account, which contains an admission of his lack of knowledge, Jean Dumont's *New Voyage to the Levant* is similarly marked: "We went to the Grand Signor's seraglio which I cannot describe exactly, since I was not suffer'd to go further than the Second Court."[7] Uninhibited, however, Dumont continues to extrapolate from what he does not know: "The Sultan's wives are lodg'd in a Third Seraglio. . . . I need not tell you with what severity they are guarded by the white and black Eunuchs, who never permit 'em to enjoy the least Shadow of Liberty" (p. 167). Dumont, too, records more tales of bizarre and exotic rituals, cataloguing the "lazy manner of living," con-

---

[6]Robert Withers, *A Description of the Grand Signor's Seraglio or Turkish Emperor's Court* (London, 1650), p. 110. For Montagu, see letter to Lady Mar, March 10, 1718, in *Complete Letters*, p. 383: "The Sultana . . . assur'd me that the story of the Sultan's throwing a Handkerchief is altogether fabulous."

[7]Jean Dumont, *A New Voyage to the Levant* (London, 1696), p. 165.

cubinage, and the persecution of women. Of Turkish men he writes:
"Contented with their Lot, they sit whole Days on a Sopha, without
any other Occupation than drinking Coffee, smoking Tobacco, or
caressing their wives: So that their whole Life is a continual Revolution
of Eating, Drinking and Sleeping, intermixt with some dull Recre-
ations" (p. 262). On the manners and customs of the Turks, he concludes: "I found that what they call Strength of Mind, Constancy or
Solidity, is at the bottom nothing else but a pure Insensibility and a
Weakness that is altogether inexcusable in any reasonable creature"
(p. 261).

One of Dumont's chief condemnations of Turkish men is his claim
that they enslave their women.[8] But his representation of the enslavement of women functions as an emblem for the "uncivilized" practices
of the oriental rather than as a critique of social or cultural institutions
that subordinate women. This is most evident in Dumont's portrait of
Turkish marriage, in which a thinly veiled misogyny is revealed in a
supposedly humorous barb against European women: "The men may
have four Wives and may have twenty Concubines. . . . Those who are
weary of their Wives may turn 'em away when they please, paying
their Dowry. What d'ye think, Sir, of this Custom? Is it not very
pleasant and commodious? 'Tis Pity that we have not such a Fashion
in *Christendom*; for if we had, I believe we shou'd see many *fatal* knot
unty'd" (p. 267). Dumont's quip—"Is it not very pleasant and commodious?"—does not merely condemn Turkish men; it also demonstrates a clear wish to subordinate European women. In constructing
the enslavement of women as a *sign* of Turkish barbarism, Dumont
differentiates from it the propriety of European marriage, and con-
comitantly makes the European woman a *sign* of "civilized" culture.
Dumont's humor is built on an expressed envy of the license to exploit
women; the statement suggests that the theme of female enslavement
is a male fantasy that emerges from the context of European sexual
relations rather than from any knowledge of Turkish arrangements. A
third concurrent aspect of Dumont's misogyny is the objectification of
Turkish women; in his account they are entirely sexual: "The Turkish
Women are the most charming Creatures in the World: they seem to be

[8]"There is no slavery equal to that of the Turkish Women; for a Servant may live
twenty years in a Family without seeing the Face of his Mistress," writes Dumont, *A New
Voyage*, p. 268.

made for Love; their Actions, Gestures, Discourse and Looks are all Amorous" (p. 273). In this compartmentalization he divides woman-hood into willful European women and willing Turkish women. This opposition reduces women to polar caricatures of male fear and desire, and constructs impediments to a discourse suggesting that some fe-male experiences might be shared even across cultural differences. Montagu decisively refutes this constructed opposition in her *Turkish Embassy Letters*.

As a woman, Montagu was invited into Turkish female society, and as a result she was in a particularly good position to contradict the statements of her predecessors. Her letters feature, among other ob-servations about the local culture, descriptions of pleasant occasions when she called on the wives of Turkish dignitaries or was invited to dine at the Turkish court. One particular letter to her sister (to Lady Mar, April 1, 1717) contains an elaborate representation and analysis of life among Turkish women. It is worth giving some attention to this letter, for it illustrates most aptly the ways in which Montagu's atti-tudes toward Turkish women opposed those of the seventeenth-cen-tury male travel writers, and also underscores what I described earlier as Montagu's multivalent position as an aristocratic English woman.

The paradoxes of Montagu's position are borne out in her modes of comparison, which simultaneously employ the rhetorics of identifica-tion and of differentiation in relation to Turkish women. The identi-fication that Montagu articulates between herself and Turkish women is established primarily by means of an analogy of gender, but it is also supported by an implicit rhetoric that is based on, and enunciates, an identity of social class. Montagu's comparisons with Turkish women are confined to women of only the very highest social class in Adriano-ple. Her use of identities of gender and class serve different purposes, and intersect with the discourse of orientalism in unlike ways. Mon-tagu's rhetorical assertions of identity among women are both discur-sively antagonistic to, and supportive of, the differentiating rhetorics of culture that characterize orientalism; even the rhetoric that invokes a class identity is, at the same time, built on a structure of class opposition that distinguishes aristocrats and commoners, a rhetoric of differentiation that often overlaps with and reinforces the oppositional rhetorics of orientalism.

Montagu's letter to Lady Mar begins with a detailed account of her current practice of dressing in the Turkish mode, stating that the purpose of her "full and true Relation of the Noveltys of this Place" is to awaken the "gratitude" of Lady Mar in order to urge her to write more news about England—to "let me into more particulars" about "your side of the Globe." Thus, the letter's opening establishes England and Turkey as being separated by time, distance, and culture, and this opposition is continually both posited and effaced throughout the letter. Montagu writes to Lady Mar:

> I am now in my Turkish Habit, thô I beleive you would be of my Opinion that 'tis admirably becoming. I intend to send you my Picture; in the mean time accept of it here.
> The first peice of my dresse is a pair of drawers, very full, that reach to my shoes and conceal the legs more modestly than your Petticoats. They are of a thin rose colour damask brocaded with silver flowers, my shoes of white kid Leather embroider'd with Gold. Over this hangs my Smock of fine white silk Gause edg'd with Embroidery. . . . The Curdée is a loose Robe they throw off or put on according to the Weather, being of rich Brocade (mine is green and Gold) either lin'd with Ermine or Sables. [. . .] On the other side of the head the Hair is laid flat, and here the Ladys are at Liberty to shew their fancys, some putting Flowers, others a plume of Heron's feathers, and in short, what they please, but the most general fashion is a large Bouquet of Jewels.   (*Complete Letters*, pp. 326–27)

The long passage describing her Turkish garments expresses two apparently, though not necessarily, contradictory impulses. On the one hand, Montagu provides an inventory of the fabrics, embroideries, brocades, and precious stones that she has become accustomed to wearing; the long description and analysis exhibits her familiarity with and knowledge of the Turkish female style, and the use of possessives—"my shoes," "my Smock"—rhetorically identifies her position with that of Turkish women. Indeed, the "Picture" of herself in Turkish dress to which she refers in the letter is an emblem of her high degree of assimilation into Turkish culture—a representation of a desired virtual synonymy or identity between herself and Turkish women—of which she is apparently quite proud.[9] On the other hand,

---

[9]Montagu prided herself on her immersion in Turkish culture; she learned the language, and, emblematically, had herself painted in Turkish dress. See this portrait, attributed to Charles Philips, in *Complete Letters*, pl. 5.

phrases punctuated by the comparative possessive *your* refer to English women's customs: "*your* side of the Globe," "more modestly than *your* Petticoats." These phrases rhetorically reinforce Montagu's Turkish context and her distance from English culture. A similar separation and opposition of location is stated in the distinction between "here" and "there": "and *here* the Ladys are at Liberty to shew their fancys." In other words, the rhetoric of similitude through which Montagu displays her intimate identification with Turkish women's culture relies simultaneously on stated and implied differentiations; the rhetorical act of likening herself to Turkish women ironically recalls an established separation of Occident and Orient.

Proceeding from the description of her own hair styled in the Turkish manner, Montagu goes on to admire the beautiful hair, complexion, and eyes of the Turkish women. The juxtaposition of the description of the "Turkish Ladys" with Montagu's description of herself in Turkish dress creates a structural equivalence between her position and that of Turkish women that reiterates Montagu's initial gesture of identification. This gesture implies not only an equivalence of gender but also an equivalence between the two court societies, stressing the similarity between these women's social rank and her own. Montagu rhetorically substitutes herself for a Turkish woman; the posited interchangeability enunciates an equivalence of both gender and class status. Although English and Turkish women are presented as structurally interchangeable in the juxtaposition, however, the language of the passage about hair contains superlatives that elevate the beauty of Turkish women with regard to English beauty. She writes: "I never saw in my Life so many fine heads of hair . . . every Beauty is more common here than with us. 'Tiz surprizing to see a young Woman that is not very handsome. . . . I can assure you with great Truth that the Court of England (thô I beleive it the fairest in Christendom) cannot shew so many Beautys as are under our Protection here" (p. 327). Here it is as if Montagu employs a rhetoric of differentiation—"Beauty is more common here than with us"—in order to convey a parity or equality between English and Turkish women. That is, an assertion of Turkish women's superiority in the area of physical beauty serves as an intervention that targets and challenges the implicit orientalist subordination of the Turkish to the English. Thus, in the phrase "under our Protection here," Montagu cannot avoid referring to the subordinating colonial arrangements that locate and justify her presence as part of a British diplomatic entourage in Turkey.

In the next section of the letter the argument for the advantage or superiority of Turkish women with regard to English women is even more explicitly utilized as an intervention against traditional orientalism. In these passages Montagu directly refutes the earlier travel writers' constructed accusation that Turkish women are enslaved:

> As to their Morality or Good Conduct . . . *'tis just as 'tis with you*, and the Turkish Ladys don't commit one Sin the less for not being Christians. Now I am a little acquainted with their ways, I cannot forbear admiring either the exemplary discretion or extreme Stupidity of all the writers that have given accounts of 'em. Tis very easy to see they have more Liberty than we have, no Woman of what rank so ever being permitted to go in the streets without 2 muslims, one that covers her face all but her Eyes and another that hides the whole dress of her head. . . .
>
> This perpetual Masquerade gives them entire Liberty of following their Inclinations without danger of Discovery. . . . Neither have they much to apprehend from the resentment of their Husbands, those Ladys that are rich having all their money in their own hands, which they take with 'em upon a divorce with an addition which he is oblig'd to give 'em. Upon the Whole, *I look upon the Turkish Women as the only free people in the Empire*. . . .
>
> 'Tis true their Law permits them 4 Wives, but there is no Instance of a Man of Quality that makes use of this Liberty, or of a Woman of Rank that would suffer it. When a Husband happens to be inconstant (as those things will happen) he keeps his mistrisse in a House apart and visits her as privately as he can, *just as 'tis with you*. (pp. 327–329; emphasis added)

Montagu cites the same cultural customs mentioned by the travel writers—that women go veiled in public, that they are guarded by servants—to support an entirely opposite argument. Rather than contending that Turkish women are enslaved, Montagu asserts that, owing to being veiled, they are able to enjoy even more liberties than English women. Montagu's statement that "Upon the Whole, I look upon the Turkish Women as the only free people in the Empire" is significant because of the ways in which it challenges several discourses that inform seventeenth-century male travel writing. In one respect, her statement forcefully intervenes in the orientalist discourse that proposes the enslavement of Turkish women as a *sign* for oriental barbarism. Her claim further implies that Turkish women are freer than English women, a statement that directly contradicts the anti-female discourse that is equally present in the travel writing, a discourse typified by Dumont's comment on the alleged Turkish custom of enslaving women ("Is it not very pleasant and commodious? 'Tis Pity that we have not such a Fashion in *Christendom*"). Dumont's colonialist trope of the enslaved Turkish woman is not only an orientalist construction used to condemn Turkish society as uncivilized, but also a displacement of European misogyny which disguises its European character by figuring women's subjugation in an oriental context. Montagu's assertion of the freedom of Turkish women heartily objects to the construction of women in orientalist myths, and simultaneously contradicts the exaggeration of European women's freedoms implied by Dumont's account. It is Montagu's opinion elsewhere in her writings that women in European society must be accorded more respect, more opportunities, and greater financial independence before they can even be considered as beginning to enjoy equality with men. Montagu's idealization of the liberty of Turkish women, however, which targets and challenges the male orientalist attack on European women, must also be scrutinized for its bias; her claim that Turkish women are "the only free people in the Empire" misrepresents and appropriates Turkish female experience for the purpose of defending English feminism.

The characterization of Turkish women's comportment as a "Masquerade" also assimilates Turkish culture to English terms and modes of cultural expression. The term has a particular meaning in the eighteenth-century British social and moral context. As Terry Castle explains, the masquerade was directly associated with carnivalesque practices that overturned traditional social structures, and these socially sanctioned disguises connoted sexual license as well as defiance of social and class hierarchies.[10] In the English concept of masquerade, disguises afforded an anonymity that permitted sexual and social promiscuity: masked ladies could take lovers, courtiers could pretend to be peasants, or an aristocratic lady might disguise herself as a servant girl to take a young lover from a more common class. For Montagu to call the Turkish woman's veil a masquerade is to transfer

[10]See Terry Castle, *Masquerade and Civilisation* (Stanford: Stanford University Press, 1986).

these specifically English associations to Turkish women's society, to interpret the Turkish context by means of an ideologically charged English classification, and to attribute to Turkish women a powerful ability to subvert the traditional cultural systems of sexuality and class relations. In this sense the use of the term *masquerade* does not merely confirm Montagu's identification with Turkish women; it also involves some appropriation of their position for the purpose of intervening in the male tradition of travel writing about the Orient. Implying that Turkish women are the site of a variety of subversive actions, that veiled they are protected by an anonymity that allows them sexual and social license, Montagu makes of Turkish women a sign of liberty and freedom in a manner not unlike Dumont's earlier rendering of Turkish women as a sign of enslavement and barbarism.

Montagu's paradoxical use of the rhetoric of likeness and difference challenges the established logic of orientalist travel writing in a variety of ways. Her letter to Lady Mar ends with explicit criticisms directed at the "voyage Writers" who had previously written about Turkey: "Thus you see, dear Sister, the manners of Mankind *doe not differ so widely as our voyage Writers would make us beleive*" (p. 330; emphasis added). Montagu notes, as I have remarked in the brief discussion of Withers and Dumont, that the seventeenth-century travel writers privileged a logic of differentiation in their figurations of Turkey, and that, in particular, their construction of the Orient as "different" hinged on an invention of Turkish customs regarding women as dramatically opposing English ones. Thus, when Montagu repeatedly likens English and Turkish women, her rhetoric of similitude directly contradicts the logic of difference that characterizes the observations of the male travel writers. At the same time, to a certain degree the rhetoric of identification through which Montagu displays her knowledge of Turkish women's culture inevitably restates an orientalist topos of differentiation in order to target it, ironically recalling the established separation of Occident and Orient. In this sense, on the level of rhetoric Montagu's text employs competing and fluctuating logics of similarity and difference. The use of the rhetoric of difference places Montagu's text in relation to a discourse of orientalism, whereas the rhetoric of identification expresses the critical distance of the text from orientalism, marking it as heterogeneous, divergent, and dissenting.

Other letters, such as to Lady———, April 1, 1717, describing a visit to the women's baths,[11] echo the praise of Turkish women's beauty, and extends the description of their excellence to the areas of poise, manners, and etiquette.

> I was in my travelling Habit, which is a rideing dress, and certainly appear'd very extraordinary to them, yet there was not one of 'em that shew'd the least surprize or impertinent Curiosity, but receiv'd me with all the obliging civillity possible. I know no European Court where the Ladys would have behav'd themselves in so polite a manner to a stranger. . . .
>
> The first sofas were cover'd with Cushions and rich Carpets, on which sat the Ladys, and on the 2nd their slaves behind 'em, but without any distinction of rank by their dress, all being in the state of nature, that is, in plain English, stark naked, without any Beauty or deffect conceal'd, yet there was not the least wanton smile or immodest Gesture among 'em. They Walk'd and mov'd with the same majestic Grace which Milton describes of our General Mother.   (*Complete Letters*, p. 313)

Montagu compares the manners of the "Ladys" at the Turkish court and the European courts to emphasize the "civillity" of the Turkish women. Again, there is a rhetorically established equivalence between the two groups that is based not solely on gender but also on social rank. At the same time, I cannot help but remark on a lack of parity in the physical arrangements of the scene that Montagu describes. Standing in her riding habit, thoroughly covered from her jacket to her boots, she viewed the many Turkish ladies and their slaves, who reclined against pillows and sofas, indistinguishable in their nudity. Not only is there an evident contrast between Montagu's clothed, erect singularity and the reclining, generalized nudity of the Turkish women, but also Montagu is clearly the unassimilated viewer-writer of this scene. The subjective position she occupies is not unlike that of male poets who eulogize the body of the female muse or beloved, regarding her and enumerating her many beauties: "exactly proportioned," "their skins shineingly white," "their Beautiful Hair divided into many tresses hanging on their shoulders, braided either with pearl or riband, perfectly representing the figures of the Graces"

[11]It is this letter and its descriptions of the Turkish women's baths that is presumed to be the basis for Ingres's painting *Le bain turc* (1862). Several passages from this letter were found copied in Ingres's notebooks. Norman Schlenoff, *Ingres, ses sources littéraires* (Paris: Presses universitaires de France, 1956), pp. 281–83.

(p. 324). Indeed, Montagu's reference to Milton's poetic descriptions identifies her through analogy as having powers and authorities that resemble those of the poet of *Paradise Lost*.

In another letter to Lady Mar, April 18, 1717, Montagu extravagantly praises the Kahya's lady, Fatima. Fatima becomes a good friend of Montagu's, and their visits are further described in other letters.

> I was so struck with Admiration that I could not for some time speak to her, being wholly taken up in gazing. That surprizing Harmony of features! that charming result of the whole! that exact proportion of Body! that lovely bloom of Complexion unsully'd by art! the unutterable Enchantment of her Smile! But her Eyes! large and black with all the soft languishment of the bleu! every turn of her face discovering some new charm! . . . A behaviour so full of Grace and sweetness, such easy motions, with an Air so majestic yet free from Stiffness or affectation that I am perswaded could she be suddenly transported upon the most polite Throne of Europe, nobody would think her other than born and bred to be a Queen, thô educated in a Country we call barbarous. To say all in a Word, our most celebrated English Beautys would vanish near her.   (p. 350)

Rhetorics of comparison are continued in this eulogy, for Fatima is said to be *like* a European queen, but she is also distinguished as being quite *unlike* European women in that her beauty far surpasses any European beauty: "Our most celebrated English Beautys would vanish near her." These comparisons that equate the European and Turkish court women may be understood as Montagu's further interventions in the male tradition of orientalism. If orientalism builds on and colludes with a discourse about women that divides and alienates different cultural groups of women from one another, Montagu's eulogy to Fatima's beauty represents a firm refusal to comply with this separation of occidental and oriental women.

Montagu's affectionate—and homoerotic—praise of Fatima's beauty also intervenes in the male discourse of heterosexuality that constructs divisions and hierarchies among women. In this letter and the letter about visiting the baths, Montagu's frank admiration for the physical beauty of the Turkish women underscores both situations as taking place in exclusively female society. Montagu's continual thematizing of the all-female context ironically invokes the orientalist topos of the female harem, and the specter of what Malek Alloula calls "oriental sapphism."[12] In orientalism, the female harem, forbidden to male spectators and travelers, is invented as the site of limitless possibilities for sexual practices among women. But the harem is not merely an orientalist voyeur's fantasy of imagined female sexuality; it is also the possibility of an erotic universe in which there are no men, a site of social and sexual practices that are not organized around the phallus or a central male authority. Montagu invokes, in this sense, the topos of the female harem by means of her own homoeroticism as a powerful intervention in the male discourse of orientalism. As in the letter about the visit to the baths, however, it appears that Montagu is able to articulate her affection for Fatima only by means of the established literary tradition that exists for the praise and regard of female beauty, a male tradition of courtly love poetry exemplified by the sonnets of Shakespeare, Sidney, and Spenser. Following this literary convention, Montagu takes up a posture toward Fatima that still expresses love by means of an aestheticizing and anatomizing gaze. The viewer is taken by "that exact proportion of Body," and proceeds to praise the beloved's skin, mouth, and eyes, as Petrarch would evoke the unsurpassable beauty of Laura's features. Thus, Montagu's writings about Fatima and Turkish women are ironically divided and heterogeneous. On the one hand, Montagu frames the praise of Turkish women's beauty, independence, and manners as an intervention and a challenge to the male voyage writers' subordination of Turkish women. On the other hand, occasionally, and perhaps inevitably for the eighteenth century, Montagu articulates these interventions of praise by means of male literary and rhetorical models, such as courtly love poetry, which are not without their own methods of female objectification and subordination.

It is striking that Montagu's greatest divergences from the earlier tradition of travel writing consist of letters that describe Turkish women's society and the Turkish customs surrounding and affecting women, for in other letters her perceptions regarding Turkish culture are still not far from those of her male predecessors. For example, the letter to Anne Thistlethwayte (April 1, 1717) contains many statements

---

[12]Malek Alloula, *The Colonial Harem*, trans. Myrna Godzich and Wlad Godzich (Minneapolis: University of Minnesota Press, 1986), esp. chap. 9, "Oriental Sapphism."

that coincide with the predominant British colonial discourse about foreign subjects.[13] Here "London" and "this part of the World" are explicitly distanced and separated in a manner that is left uncontested throughout the letter. In addition, Montagu frames the descriptions of Turkish life as if they were theatrical entertainment for her English reader. She writes, "A Letter out of Turkey that has nothing extraordinary in it would be as great a Disapointment as my visitors will receive at London if I return thither without any raritys to shew them" (p. 340). She then proceeds to inventory in detail the bizarre and unusual animals found in Adrianople, including camels, asses, and buffaloes. The camels are described as "never thoroughly tamed"; the asses are "to me very ugly Creatures, their heads being ill form'd and disproportion'd to their bodys"; and the buffaloes are "all black with very short hair on their Hides and extreme little white Eyes that make them look like Devils" (pp. 340–41). The qualities of these "beasts," used for plowing, carrying, and caravaning, are contrasted with the swiftness and spirited elegance of horses, which "are not put here to any Laborious Work, nor are they at all fit for it" (p. 341). Indeed, Montagu characterizes the camels, asses, and buffaloes as lower species than the horse, and more physically suited to difficult labor.

> I have a little white favourite that I would not part with on any terms. He prances under me with so much fire you would think that I had a great deal of courrage to dare Mount him, yet I'll assure you I never rid a Horse in my life so much at my command. My Side Saddle is the first was ever seen in this part of the World and gaz'd at with as much wonder as the ship of Columbus was in America. Here are some birds

---

[13] I have chosen not to discuss the entire question of the letters' addressees, their reception, and so on, for this would take me far afield from the focus of the chapter, namely, that orientalism overlaps with discourses of gender and class, and that these concurrent discourses may contest and displace orientalism. It is clear, however, that the different subject matters, as well as the treatment of those matters, in Montagu's letters must also be influenced by the addressees of the letters—their gender, class, occupation, and relation to Montagu. In this sense Montagu's letter to Alexander Pope, April 1, 1717, contains extensive discussion of classical literature, Turkish poetry, and the problems of translation, and the letter to Abbé Conti, May 17, 1717, a comparative discussion of the church and religion; whereas the letters to her sister Lady Mar address none of these subjects, dealing instead, as I have shown, with matters of female society—the customs, behavior, and dress—and the relation of Turkish female society to women in her own English society.

held in a sort of religious Reverence and for that reason Multiply prodigiously: Turtles on the Account of the Innocency, and Storks because they are suppos'd to make every Winter the Pilgrimage to Mecha. To say the truth, they are the happiest Subjects under the Turkish Government, and are so sensible of their priveleges they walk the streets without fear and gennerally build in the low parts of Houses. Happy are those that are so distinguish'd; the vulgar Turks are perfectly perswaded that they will not be that year either attack'd by Fire or Pestilence. I have the happyness of one of their Sacred nests just under my chamber Window.   (p. 341)

The world described in this letter is composed of an orderly chain of being ranging upward from beasts of burden, to birds, to horses, to Turks, to Englishmen. Just as the coarse "black" beasts of burden are contrasted with the "white" prancing horse, so, too, does Montagu's letter imply a distinction between the Turks, with their bizarre animal superstitions, and the English, with their more refined, rational tastes. Montagu's text accepts the topos of civilized culture as adherence to natural order and hierarchy; that she rides her horse sidesaddle is an emblem of the English command over and domestication of animals, while in contradistinction the "vulgar Turks" ("vulgar" being presumably a reference to their class as well as their cultural location) honor turtledoves and storks, granting them religious power, improperly elevating animals over humans. Not only does Montagu's portrait of the Turks' "unnatural" worship imply that they are less civilized than the English, but her descriptions of the natural hierarchy of beasts and horses might itself be understood to contain an allegorical defense of the "natural order" of colonialism. The colonial allegory is further dramatized in the image of Montagu's sidesaddle, which is viewed by a group of Turkish observers "with as much wonder as the ship of Columbus was in America." Finally, the characterization of storks as "the happiest Subjects under the Turkish Government" offers a metaphor of birds and humans that further allegorizes, and moralizes, the necessary and happy subjection of one group to another.

Just as Montagu's *Letters* occasionally resonate with the dominant British orientalist discourse, so the social context that produces *The Turkish Embassy Letters*—the diplomatic presence of Montagu's husband, Ambassador Wortley Montagu, in early-eighteenth-century

Turkey—locates her text as part of England's colonial discourse about Great Britain's foreign commercial interests and colonies. For this reason it is appropriate to consider Montagu's *Turkish Embassy Letters* as part of the tradition of British travel writing about Turkey. Yet, quite evidently, Montagu's text occupies a dissenting position in the tradition; particularly on the questions of Turkish women's society and the treatment of women in Turkey, Montagu's *Letters* directly refute the perspectives, rhetorics, and themes of her orientalist predecessors' writing in that tradition. The conflicted relation of *The Turkish Embassy Letters* to orientalist travel writing—it is within the tradition yet critical of it—illustrates that orientalism does not make up a unified and dominant discourse, and that orientalist logic and statements often exist in a climate of challenge and contestation.

An emergent feminist discourse provides Montagu with the language, arguments, and rhetoric with which to interrogate traditional travel writing about the Orient while furnishing her with a critical position from which to write. Montagu's interventions in the orientalist tradition are primarily articulated in a feminist rhetoric and take place in the moments when her text refutes the constructed topos of the enslavement of Turkish women. In addition, a residual discourse about class and social rank supports Montagu's rhetoric likening Turkish and English court women; indeed, Montagu's praise of the civility, refinement, and politesse of aristocratic Turkish women may make use of this rhetoric of class identification even more than it expresses a belief in solidarity among women of different cultures. What I have characterized as Montagu's shifting of the rhetoric of identification and differentiation is indicative of the location of her text at an intersection of orientalism, feminism, and representations of class and social rank. Montagu employs the rhetoric of identification between women of the Turkish and English courts as a means of intervening in the differentiating rhetoric of orientalism; the shift in rhetoric brings into conflict the figuring apparatus of orientalism and of discourses about gender and class. The contentious relationship between Montagu's text and the earlier travel writings concerning the subject of Turkish women illustrates that orientalism is not exclusively figured through an opposition of Occident and Orient, but figures itself through the formations of gender and class as well. It illustrates that distinct discourses may collude and overlap, but also, more important, that the crucial means for contesting and displacing one discourse may derive from the rhetoric and writing position of other concurrent ones.

Voyages imaginaires: Lettres persanes

The seventeenth- and eighteenth-century French tradition of travel literature contains its share of accounts that were the by-products of French colonial ventures in the Caribbean, India, West Africa, and North America, and missionary activities in China.[14] These accounts can be considered analogues of the seventeenth- and eighteenth-century English travel writings discussed previously in this chapter. Yet the French tradition of orientalism differs from the English in an important respect: in the eighteenth century the French figure of the Orient is marked as a fictional site, and more elaborately drawn from a literary tradition. Whereas the English writings directly accompanied the British diplomatic and commercial contacts with the Turkish and Levantine Orient, the Orients of Montesquieu, Diderot, and Voltaire were more frankly imagined, more decidedly literary. The French figuration of the oriental harem as an exotic world of sexual and despotic license had a different status in French culture than Robert Withers's travelogue representation of the oriental harem did in England, owing to distinct national conditions, but primarily because the French conception of the Orient as Persia, Egypt, and the Ottoman Empire largely predated the extension of French colonialism to that

[14]Between 1630 and 1640, under Louis XIII, Cardinal Richelieu sought to build France's strength on the Continent by setting up a system of colonization through privileged companies. The Compagnie des Indes later built France's first colonies in India; the Compagnie des 100 Associés developed trade with Canada. Under Richelieu's command, merchants settled Martinique and Guadeloupe, St. Kitts, Grenada, the Grenadines, and St. Lucia; he sent pioneers to Réunion and l'Ile de Bourbon and reinforced colonies in Madagascar and Guiana.

Under Louis XIV Colbert developed Richelieu's colonial and trade policies. In 1664 he commissioned the Compagnie des Indes occidentales and the Compagnie des Indes orientales. The first was to settle both the Americas and the Caribbean; the second to colonize Madagascar and dominate trade with China. In 1670 he created the Compagnie du Levant to import silk and cotton from Asia Minor. Despite this limited trade with the Middle East, however, French colonialism during the seventeenth and eighteenth centuries focused on North America, Africa, and the Caribbean. It was not until 1798 that Napoleon's France attempted to colonize Egypt and other parts of the Middle East.

region. The English travel accounts about the Orient accompanied the deepening of Anglo-Turkish diplomatic and commercial ties that began in the late sixteenth century under Queen Elizabeth I, but the French orientalism of the same period prefigured the more extensive French economic and military intercourse with the Middle East that began in the early nineteenth century under Napoleon Bonaparte, with the invasion of Egypt in 1798, and his efforts to establish a military alliance with Iran as an instrument of anti-British and anti-Russian policies.[15]

This is not to imply, however, that France was not also gripped by the desire for empire and the *mission civilisatrice*. French colonialism in the Americas, in West Africa and the Caribbean, and to a smaller extent in India was well under way by the eighteenth century, and colonial ambition was piqued by continental competition as the French trailed the British and the Dutch in the struggle for empire under Louis XIV. In this sense, the literary figure of the Orient portended an as yet undeveloped relationship for France; the Orient became the French sign of desire for unconquered, uninfluenced territories in the context of a race for colonies among the European continental nations. Thus, in the French literature travel is allegorized to a greater extent—it is a geographic metaphorizing of the French nation's encounter with the non-French world—and the Orient is an imaginary figuration of *ailleurs*, of the *au-delà*. For France in the eighteenth century the Orient becomes the imagined site for the realization of colonial ambition.

At the same time, the travel literature of Diderot, Voltaire, and Montesquieu figured social elements that were marginal to, and that contested, the social structures of the ancien régime.[16] There were

[15]On the importance of Napoleon's campaign in Egypt to the tradition of orientalism, see Said, *Orientalism*, esp. chap. 1, sec. 3. For an account of Napoleon's use of Iran for anti-British and anti-Russian policies, see Hasan-e Fasa'i, *History of Persia under Qajar Rule*, trans. Herbert Busse (New York: Columbia University Press, 1972).

[16]By ancien régime, I mean the feudal organization of old French society that prevailed roughly from 1600 to 1750. The predominant economic base of the ancien régime was the rural agriculture economy. It was a rooted, stable society with very little or no class mobility or redefinition, society being organized in terms of the *seigneurie*—a group of landed estates owned and under the jurisdiction of the *seigneur*—and administered by the *intendants*, and the *manses* (tenured farms) worked by the *mainmortables* (serfs), peasants, or indentured farmers. During the seventeenth century 19.5 million, out of France's 20 million people remained bound to the land, plot, hut, cottage, or *quartier* where they grew up, according to Pierre Goubert, *The Ancien Régime: French Society, 1600–1750*, trans. Steve Cox (New York: Harper and Row, 1973). The old France was

internal and external challenges to the stability of feudal France—nonaristocratic republican elements, antimonarchical forces, peasant revolts, the beginnings of small industry—which necessitated some migration and different roles for women and men, in addition to increasing continental competition from other colonial powers such as England, Spain, and Holland. In travel literature these pressures are registered and represented by and in the foreign space of an imagined Orient. Just as English novels based on the fiction of travel—such as Defoe's *Robinson Crusoe* (1719) and Swift's *Gulliver's Travels* (1726)—portrayed England's internal social and political struggles in the displaced and imaginary locales of Crusoe's island, or the lands of the Lilliputians, Brobdingnag giants, and Laputans, so too did the eighteenth-century French *voyages imaginaires* become the means through which internal domestic challenges to social order could be figured and emplotted as foreign challenges, although it is apparent that the nature of the internal struggles was determined by different forces and factors in the English and French situations. Voltaire's representations of the social injustices of a thinly disguised ancien régime in the faraway worlds of *Zadig* (1747) and *Micromégas* (1752), or Montesquieu's wives, eunuchs, and oriental despots in the *Lettres persanes*, employ the theme of travel to signify the desire for empire, as well as to veil the more urgent preoccupations with the diminishing stability and coherence of the national culture itself. Thus, not only does the literary topos of travel express the French preoccupation with land and empire, but travel as a representation of imagined territorial expansion becomes an available discursive means of registering and regulating the domestic culture's concern with internal social differences and change during the ancien régime.[17] In this sense both dominant and

characterized not by unrest, social mobility, and popular migration (as was the case by the mid-nineteenth century) but by stasis.

For a thorough demographic description of the ancien régime, see Goubert, *L'Ancien Régime*. Other studies of life during this period include Marc Bloch, *Les caractères originaux de l'histoire rurale française*, 2 vols. (Paris: Armand Colin, 1952, 1956); Fernand Braudel, *Civilisation matérielle et capitalisme* (Paris: Armand Colin, 1967); and Natalie Zemon Davis, *Society and Culture in Early Modern France*. Alexis de Tocqueville, *L'ancien régime et la révolution* (Paris: Michel Levy 1856), offers a political analysis of the ancien régime from the standpoint of the dismantling of its institutions after the French Revolution of 1789.

[17]In a sense I am responding to a question posed by Louis Althusser in *Politics and History: Montesquieu, Rousseau, Hegel, and Marx*, trans. Ben Brewster (London: New Left

emergent discourses of class and gender interrupt and disfigure the orientalizing genre of travel literature in France, as they do in Montagu's *Turkish Embassy Letters*. Yet the constellation, arrangement, and interplay of these discourses are quite different in the French instance than in the English example.

On one level Montesquieu's *Lettres persanes* is a text that proposes an orientalist structure in which Persia is the constructed opposite of France: the tyranny of the Persian harem contrasts with French representative government; the cruel instinct of the Persian master and his eunuch guards opposes French rationalism and law; and the confined chastity of the Persian wives counters the freedom and infidelity of French women. Composed of letters exchanged between two fictitious Persian travelers and their wives and eunuch guards at home, Montesquieu's text displaces internal French struggles into oriental characters and onto oriental spaces. The letters describe France from an invented "foreign" viewpoint of Persian travelers, and in this gesture they produce an Orient overtly fictionalized to elucidate the Occident they portray; the visitors, Rica and Usbek, record their observations of French social and political institutions, the church, the relations between men and women; interspersed among these letters are those that concern the intrigues and passions of the *sérail* (seraglio) that Usbek has left behind, providing a picture of the eunuchs' frustrations and the wives' ultimate revolt.

On another level, however, the text also offers a variety of challenges to this orientalist structure of opposition. The various means of "staging" Persia are exposed in Rica's letters, which thematize the theatricality and artifice of culture, and the "logic" of binary dependence and compatibility that informs the oppositional relationship between the French and the Persians is thus continually undermined.

Books, 1972), p. 75, at the point where he discusses Montesquieu's idea of despotism: "If the Persian does not exist, where does a French *gentilhomme*, born under Louis XIV, get the *idea* of him?" Despotism is Montesquieu's postulation of evil, lawlessness, the lack of order that continually threatens the structure of feudal monarchy; it is not based on knowledge of the Persian system of governance but is a representation of the perceived threats to social order, cloaked in foreign guise.

As Alain Grosrichard writes concerning the eighteenth-century concept of oriental despotism: "What makes it possible in effect to think the concept of despotism is less the reality of a *political regime* than the irrepressible part of the imaginary on which all *political power* rests. Despotism is the concept of a fantasm." Grosrichard, *La structure du sérail: la fiction du despotisme asiatique dans l'occident classique* (Paris: Seuil, 1979), p. 40.

Most important, the binarism of Occident and Orient is ultimately challenged by the subplot of the wives' revolt. The relationship between the despot and his wives and slaves is not merely an emblem of the tyranny of a ruler over his subjects; it also emblematizes the very topos of orientalist domination. When this relationship is inverted by the conclusion to the novel, in which Usbek's wives successfully revolt against his rule, a number of different themes of mastery and rule are negated, including, most pointedly, that of orientalism itself. In this sense the dominant discourse of class hierarchy that figures the black and white eunuch harem guards as representations of the French *intendants* and nobility reinforces the orientalizing structure of the novel to the degree that the eunuchs never cease to be instruments of the master's power over the wives, or indeed to facilitate his power over the eunuchs themselves. In contrast, the emergent discourse of gender that portrays the wives as the revolutionary force that finally overthrows the master succeeds in challenging key assumptions and positions that are cornerstones to orientalism. Although the eunuchs' plot and the wives' plot develop and work together throughout the *Lettres*, they ultimately diverge and contradict each other as either plot supports or contradicts the orientalist themes.

The *Lettres* narrate the story of how a culture discovers and defines itself through imagined cross-cultural contact with a "foreign" Other. The fictional device that displaces the Persian travelers in France provides an occasion for a lively critique of French society on subjects as diverse as language, religion, law, education, sexual roles, and government; at the same time, the Persian criticisms of France reflect ironically on the invented oriental world from which they have supposedly come (this "Persia" itself being a thinly veiled metaphor for France). Rica's letters, in particular, are filled with this sort of self-reflexive commentary on French society, and in this sense they exemplify the orientalist logic that defines an eighteenth-century French world in terms of oriental otherness while critically commenting on the asymmetrical opposition of Persia and France. In *lettre* XXX, to his friend Ibben at Smyrna, Rica describes his reception by the inhabitants of Paris:

> Lorsque j'arrivai, je fus regardé comme si j'avais été envoyé du ciel: vieillards, hommes, femmes, enfants, tous voulaient me voir. Si je sor-

tais, tout le monde se mettait aux fenêtres; si j'étais aux Tuileries, je voyais aussitôt un cercle se former autour de moi.[18]

[When I arrived, they looked at me as though I had been sent from Heaven: old men and young, women and children, they all wanted to see me. If I went out, everyone perched at the windows; if I was in the Tuileries, I experienced immediately a circle gathering around me.]

Twentieth-century anthropologists have recorded similar experiences in which an ethnographer, crowded by staring "natives," enters another culture to do fieldwork. In the context of eighteenth-century Parisian society, Rica, the proto-anthropologist in Persian garb, is strikingly visible; he is marked by his difference, and his dress codes him as other, foreign, outré. "Enfin, jamais homme n'a tant été vu que moi" (In short, never was anyone as seen as much as I was), he writes (p. 104). He finds portraits of himself in Paris shops; his image is multiplied, distributed, and circulated everywhere. The Parisians' fascination with the exotic exposes a fascination with difference based on a preoccupation with defining sameness, an anxiety about the consistency and the cohesion of French identity in an age of rapidly mounting colonial ambitions. But paradoxically, although Rica is often, as letter writer, in the anthropologist's role of describing the French natives, he does not study their cultural otherness; rather he finds himself in the position of being the object studied by the Parisians.

Fittingly, when Rica decides to "go native," to give up his Persian clothing and to dress like a European, he finds he is ignored. "Libre de tous les ornements étrangers, je me vis apprécié au plus juste . . . car j'entrai tout à coup dans un néant affreux" (p. 105) (Free of all foreign ornament, I found myself assessed more exactly . . . for all at once I fell into a terrible state of nonexistence). People no longer stare at him; he falls into oblivion. It is the cultural costume, the representation of difference, which is the French fetish. When someone announces that Rica is Persian, he reports: "J'entendais aussitôt autour de moi un bourdonnement: 'Ah! ah! monsieur est Persan? C'est une chose bien extraordinaire! Comment peut-on être Persan?' " (p. 105) (I would hear a buzz around me: "Oh! oh! Is he Persian? What a most extraordinary

---

[18]Charles Louis de Secondat, Baron de Montesquieu, *Lettres persanes* (Paris: Gallimard, 1973), p. 104. All quotations are from this source.

thing! How is it possible to be Persian?"). In this sense Rica's cultural difference is like a costume or mask that is attributed to him by French society. The Persian must assume the costume constructed for him or fall into nonexistence. As Rica is encircled by Parisian observers, his costume provides a mark of difference around which the Parisians can position themselves. Yet without his exotic garb, Rica cannot be objectified as Other. The circle has no central object, and the crowd lacks cohesion, perspective, and point of view. Without invented signs of visible otherness, sameness fails to locate itself. "Comment peut-on être Persan?" is indeed the question, for although it is possible to occupy the position of either the French or the exotic, the same or the different, it is not possible, within the world represented in the *Lettres*, to be other than either of the two categories of the opposition. Rica's only choices are visibility as an exoticized object that exists only in contrast to occidental orthodoxy or invisibility in his disguise as a Frenchman. In the world of the *Lettres*, the subjective presence of Persians is inconceivable; thus it is the paradox of his being Persian yet not being adorned as an exotic object that initiates the Parisians' incredulous query, "How is it possible to be Persian?"

Rica is a complex figure, for he is a central voice and authority who presents French customs, attitudes, and society, as well as an invented foreigner, the means through which the French text stages its critique of French culture. The paradox of Rica's authoritative position (as author of the letter) and his ultimate disempowerment (as masked fiction, as constituted Other) foregrounds the fundamental irony in Montesquieu's text. Rica's letter thematizes the use of the oriental in the process of French cultural identification and self-regard, and at the same time the letter is an example of this appropriation; it suggests that the *Lettres persanes* is not a simple orientalist text but more precisely a text that both discloses and comments on the eighteenth-century French invention of the Orient.[19] That is, the *Lettres persanes* does not simply "colonize" the oriental; the text also criticizes cultural appropriation by means of the manner in which it inverts and destabilizes the very categories of observer and observed, ruler and ruled, or

[19]Suzanne Pucci, in "Orientalism and Representations of Exteriority in Montesquieu's *Lettres persanes,*" *Eighteenth-Century* 26 (1985): 263–79, also suggests that in its representations of exteriority the novel is a fiction about, rather than an example of, the European appropriation of the Orient.

persan and *parisien*. The inversion of the Persians and the Parisians—
throughout a text that has as a very clear theme the identification of
France through the discovery of its foreign Other—calls into question
the orientalist binary logic on which the making of Others is founded.
Furthermore, although a story of the Persians' cultural adaptation and
conversion is being told, the epistolary form of the novel undermines
the continuity of this familiar plot. Not only do the multiple perspectives of the letters disrupt any simulation of continuity or duration, but
there are many lengthy digressions in the *Lettres persanes* that impede
the progress of the conversion plot: the fable of the Troglodytes, the
quotation of other letters within letters, the story of Zulema, and so
on. Thus, the text represents a fiction in which the orientals Rica and
Usbek are projected as being Other to the occidental, but the very
process of this displacement is foregrounded and ultimately criticized
by the irony and the epistolary nature of the text itself.

At the same time that the novel represents France from the "oriental" point of view, it also depicts an "oriental world" in the portrait of
the Persian harem offered by the letters from Usbek's wives and the
eunuch guards. These letters describe the intrigues and crises that take
place in the harem during Usbek's absence. Thus, Montesquieu's
novel of letters is often described as containing two parallel stories:
one of Usbek's and Rica's travels to Paris, and the other of the despot's
eventual loss of authority and the revolt of his wives in the harem.[20]
But even as the representation of the Persian world presents a French
image of its cultural Other, it also allegorizes the problems and tensions of eighteenth-century France: the oriental despot is a figure for
Louis XIV; the harem hierarchy of white and black eunuch guards is an
analogy for the roles of the nobility and the *intendants*; and the wives in
revolt are a figure for the peasantry during the regency of Philippe
d'Orléans following Louis's death in 1715. In the sense that the first

[20]See, for example, Robert O'Reilly, "The Structure and Meaning of the *Lettres persanes*," *Studies on Voltaire and the Eighteenth-Century* 67 (1969): 91–131, and Aram Vartanian, "Eroticism and Politics in the *Lettres persanes*," *Romanic Review* 60 (1969): 23–33.

The notion of two stories should not be applied too literally, however. It is merely a
critical device to allow the discussion of two different impulses in the novel, for the two
stories are not so easily distinguished. Throughout the letters of Rica and Usbek, the two
stories overlap and intersect at different junctures. For example, some of Usbek's letters
to his wives and to the eunuchs can be considered as contributing to the "first story,"
others to the "second story."

story–second story structure erects a binary relationship in which the oriental world is subordinated as a metaphor for French political problems, this binary relation is itself instrumental to the orientalism of the novel. But to the degree that the second story about the despot's overthrow interrupts and disallows a satisfactory closure of the portrait of foreign visitors in Paris depicted by the first story, the orientalizing structure is troubled and rendered more complex. Indeed, it is apparent that the heterogeneous conflicts invoked in the portrait of the harem bring a variety of narrative, logical, and rhetorical challenges to bear on the orientalism of the novel.

Figuring Orientalism: Slavery, Marriage, Sapphism

In the discussion of Rica's *lettre* XXX, I have suggested that the first story stages Persian culture as a means of commenting on French institutions and practices; this staging of Persia enunciates a binary relationship of complementarity between the French and oriental worlds that is characteristic of French orientalism, and in this sense the first story epitomizes the logic of the orientalist topos. But this binary logic is not restricted to the cultural opposition of France and Persia; it is reiterated by several additional figures invoked by the first story—in particular the institutions of slavery and marriage. During his stay in Paris, Usbek writes continually to his wives and eunuch slaves. In these letters the relationship between master and slave, as well as the marriage relationship between husband and wife, is represented as an emblem for despotism, or the absolute rule over one party by another.[21] The relation between the despot Usbek and members of his harem appear in the first story as analogies for French political tyranny

[21]Despotism, in this sense, is the extreme tyranny of one over others. Montesquieu distinguishes despotism from democracy or monarchy: in a democracy, property and even relative wealth are guaranteed by the law; in a monarchy, the nobility and clergy are protected by a recognition of their privileges; but under despotism, there is no hereditary order, no nobility.

Grosrichard, *Structure du sérail*, p. 59, suggests that for Montesquieu, despotism is "the monster of monarchy," the internal possibility of disorder that may potentially erupt. "But then it stops being a specifically distinct form of government, and one might conceive of monarchy and despotism as being each a part of the other." In this sense despotism is the Other of the French political system, figured in the Orient of Persia.

and rule, and are the principal vehicles for Montesquieu's attack on the despotic tendencies in the French system of government. Yet, if French rule is understood to extend to foreign territories under France, then the relationships between Usbek and his slaves and wives also serve as emblems of orientalism as colonial rule; in this sense the challenges to the institutions of slavery and marriage in the narratives of Usbek's declining rule and the wives' representations of female homosexuality in the harem provide implicit critiques of orientalism itself. The second story's narratives intervene in the first story's orientalism by complicating its binary logic of ruler and ruled with the more heterogeneous and multidirectional conflicts between the master, the eunuchs, and the wives, and by ultimately concluding the novel with the wives' triumph over the master.

Rica's and Usbek's letters about Parisian life are interrupted throughout by others from Persia: from friends, from various eunuch guards, and from Usbek's wives Roxane, Fatme, Zashi, and Zélis. These letters reveal that within the structure of the harem, a hierarchy exists in which Usbek dominates both the eunuchs and his wives; in his absence the wives answer to the eunuchs, who are the representatives of the despot's will.[22] The eunuchs are enslaved by the master, and are commanded to exercise the master's power in his absence; yet they are essentially without their own power. In this sense their castration is a physical sign of their enslavement, and of their political impotence within the *sérail*. Just as the eunuchs feel sexual desire but lack the ability to act on this desire, so too do they have the illusion of exercising political power and yet, upon being commanded by the master, realize that they have no power of their own. In *lettre* IX, the Premier Eunuque offers to a friend Ibbi, a poignant description of his life in the harem:

Lorsque mon premier maître eut formé le cruel projet de me confier ses femmes, et m'eut obligé, par des séductions soutenues de milles menaces, de me séparer pour jamais de moi-même . . . j'espérais que je

[22]The *Lettres* portray the harem as a hierarchical system, in which Usbek is master of the eunuch slaves, and the slaves control the behavior of Usbek's wives. Locating these relationships—of slavery and of sexual domination—in the oriental harem displaces the responsibility for these systems of oppression from France. The slave trade that brought West Africans to work for the French on the sugar plantations of the Caribbean islands, and the political and social inequality of women to men in eighteenth-century France, are concealed by this orientalist displacement.

serais délivré des atteintes de l'amour, par l'impuissance de le satisfaire. Hélas! on éteignit en moi l'effet des passions, sans en éteindre la cause; et bien loin d'en être soulagé, je me trouvai environné d'objets qui les irritaient sans cesse. J'entrai dans le sérail, où tout m'inspirait le regret de ce que j'avais perdu: je me sentais animé à chaque instant . . . pour comble de malheurs, j'avais toujours devant les yeux un homme heureux.   (*Lettres persanes*, p. 62)

[When my first master conceived the cruel project of entrusting his wives to me, and had compelled me, by inducements backed by innumerable threats, to be forever separated from myself . . . I hoped that I would be free of love's seizures owing to my powerlessness to satisfy them. But alas! they eliminated the effects of my passion, but not their cause; and far from finding relief, I found myself surrounded by scenes which continually aroused them. On entering the seraglio, where everything made me regret what I had lost, I felt excited all the time . . . to my greater misfortune, I had a happy man permanently before my eyes.]

Within the structure of the harem, the domination of the slave by the master is sexually coded in the castration of the eunuch, literally forever separated from himself—"me séparer pour jamais de moi-même." The eunuch's divided person, and his lack of sexual means, excludes him from the social institutions of marriage, family, and generation; in this way his sexual misfortune emblematizes a social and political impotence.[23] Furthermore, as the eunuch's letter makes clear, the castration does not render him asexual; it does not eliminate sexuality and desire from his person. The eunuch is plagued by the

[23]The eunuch's social exclusion is a characterization of the political exclusion and impotence of the nobility, which began during the reign of Louis XIV and continued during the regency. Indeed, although *L'esprit des lois* was adopted by Enlightenment thinkers as liberal political philosophy, it must not be forgotten that Montesquieu wrote his critique of despotism from a position within a troubled and disenfranchised nobility. As Louis Althusser points out in *Politics and History*, Montesquieu had a very particular understanding of republicanism based on ancient models that placed "free men" at the forefront, and the multitude of artisans and slaves in the shade. He would have the people deprived of all direct power but grant them the right to choose representatives. Montesquieu did not want this "common people" (*bas-peuple*) to have power.

Althusser writes that "in denouncing depotism, Montesquieu is not defending against the politics of absolutism so much as *liberty in general* as the *particular liberties* of the feudal class, its individual security, the conditions of its lasting survival and its pretensions to return in new organs of power to the place which had been robbed from it by history." Althusser, *Politics and History*, p. 83. Therefore, on the most overt level, the *Lettres persanes* moralizes: despotism is the sure road to popular revolutions. "*Princes, avoid despotism if you would save your thrones from the people's violence*," paraphrases Althusser (p. 85).

memory of having once been whole and unseparated, and this memory is aroused by the company of the wives, and further by living with the fact of his master's continual satisfaction. In the harem world described in the *Lettres*, castration coexists always with an idealized memory of possession and power; it is the mark of a state of lack which is characterized by desire that can never be fulfilled.[24]

For the eunuchs, Usbek represents self-possessed masculinity and sexual identity. His political mastery is also symbolized by his sexual status, that is, by his noncastration, and by his sexual right to possess the wives. The apparent possession of himself and his wives creates Usbek's phallic role in the harem, but Usbek's mark of masculine potency, his "phallus," is purely symbolic; it is not denoted or determined by the mere presence of sexual organs.[25] Rather, the phallus functions here as a socially constructed and conferred mark of masculinity, and is itself a signifier for the desire for masculine self-possession and its social and symbolic significance.[26] In this sense, Usbek and the eunuchs alike desire phallic potency; absolute mastery and self-possession eludes them all. By placing Usbek away from the harem, and then recounting the story of his declining power and authority there, the novel further reinforces that even the master himself does not possess the phallus; his sexual and political rule is precarious, and he is no longer the principal authority around which the harem is organized.

[24]The desire for the lost state of wholeness may be a figuration of the aristocrat's nostalgia for the feudal estate and the untroubled autonomy of the noble classes during the ancien régime.

[25]Grosrichard argues, citing Ancillon's "Traité des eunuques" (Treatise on eunuchs, 1707), that traditionally eunuchs were organized into four classes, characterized by different degrees of physical castration: "those who were born such, those from whom everything was removed, those rendered sterile, and those types of men who were so unsuitable or of such a frigid temperament that they were incapable of procreating." Grosrichard, *Structure du sérail*, p. 190.

[26]I use the term *phallus* according to its development in the work of Jacques Lacan. The phallus is not the penis; it is the symbolic signifier of desire and the mark of subjectivity in that it includes within its definition both the desire for self-possessed subjectivity and its impossibility. In Lacan's rereading of Freud's oedipal process, the castration is symbolic and takes place when the subject is named and enters the social-linguistic field, identifying with the masculinity of the symbolic social arrangements and disidentifying with the femininity of the imaginary prelinguistic domain. In Lacanian theory no subject ever possesses the phallus; it is mythical, contradictory, and impossible. See Jacques Lacan, "The Agency of the Letter in the Unconscious, or Reason since Freud," in *Écrits*, trans. Alan Sheridan (New York: W. W. Norton, 1977).

Despite the structure of the *sérail*, which would seem to offer the despot absolute power, Usbek is portrayed in an increasingly vulnerable position as the novel progresses. Many of his letters betray a sense of geographic isolation and a suspicion that his rule is weakening at home. For example, in *lettre* CXIII Usbek writes about flux, change, and the eventual decay of life, as if he is anxious that even the most permanent structures may include their own destruction. He seems to suspect the decline of his authority in the harem even before the eunuchs report it to him. And in *lettre* CXIV an argument against the virtues of polygamy as a means for increasing population exposes Usbek's fears about not satisfying his wives.[27] As early as the second letter Usbek is writing to the Premier Eunuque Noir in order to maintain his troubled rule over the harem. In other words, the novel begins with Usbek's rule endangered by his absence, and with his commands and threats to the eunuchs expressing an anxiety about his waning dominance.

> Tu les sers comme l'esclave de leurs esclaves. Mais, par *un retour d'empire*, tu commandes en maître comme moi-même, quand tu crains le relâchement des lois de la pudeur et de la modestie.
>
> Souviens-toi toujours du néant d'où je t'ai fait sortir, lorsque tu étais le dernier de mes esclaves, pour te mettre en cette place, et te confier les délices de mon coeur: tiens-toi dans un profond abaissement auprès de celles qui partagent mon amour; mais fais-leur, en même temps, sentir leur extrême dépendance.   (p. 52; emphasis added)
>
> [You should serve them (the wives) as if you were the slave of their slaves. But, by a reversal of authority, you are master of them like myself, whenever you fear a relaxation of the laws of chastity and modesty.
>
> Always remember the nothingness from which I elevated you, when you were the lowest of my slaves, and that I put you in this post and entrusted to you my heart's delights: humiliate yourself profoundly before the women who share my love, but make them simultaneously aware of their absolute dependence.]

Usbek maintains his rule over the eunuch slaves through threats and reminders of their powerlessness; and by means of his control over the

[27]Usbek writes in *lettre* CXIV: "I think of a good Muslim as an athlete doomed to compete without respite, who is soon weakened and overcome by his initial efforts, and languishes on the very field of victory, lying buried, so to speak, beneath his own triumphs. . . . It is to this state of debility that we are always reduced by the large number of wives we have, which is more likely to wear us out than to satisfy us" (pp. 259–60).

eunuchs, he attempts to rule his wives.[28] But even though the eunuchs are the executors of Usbek's will over the wives, they are indeed slaves, as Usbek is quick to remind them. In some ways they inhabit even lower rungs of the ladder of harem hierarchy because, under Usbek's orders, they must also serve the wives.

The slaves' impotence is signified not only by their castration but also by their lack of names; whereas Usbek, his friends, and his wives are all named in the letters, many of the eunuchs are referred to only by their rank and color (Premier Eunuque Blanc, Premier Eunuque Noir, and so on). The eunuchs themselves are not a homogeneous group of equal standing, for not only are there black and white eunuchs, but among these groups there are "first" and "second" eunuchs. Alain Grosrichard argues that the difference in color is also a mark of a division of labor in the harem: "The white eunuchs are the officers of the seraglio, and they command and administer according to a very strict hierarchy, or they serve as preceptors who look after the seraglio's children. The black eunuchs, on the other hand, specialize in guarding the harem; they watch over the entrances and exits. The white eunuchs flank the despot, doubling as his shadow. The blacks are at the sides of the wives, never letting them out of their sight."[29] This coded system of rank among the eunuchs—a highly competitive group *among* whom there is scarce and diminishing power to be shared by many—reinforces the parallel between the eunuchs and the nobility and *intendants* under the French monarchy.

The passage quoted from *lettre* II also establishes the analogy between the topoi of despotism and slavery and the relations of ruler and subjects, master and slaves. This analogy is enunciated by Usbek's use of the expression "un retour d'empire" to convey the sense of a transfer of command over the wives from Usbek to the eunuch. On the one hand, this expression signifies a shifting of power from Usbek to the eunuch—indeed, a "return" of power and masculinity to the castrated slave. But, on the other hand, "un retour d'empire" also carries the sense of a reversal of empire, a reversion of dominions to another rule, perhaps home rule. The power to command the wives is equated with the rule of territorial empire. Not only does the double valence of the

[28]Threats occur in other letters as well. For example, in *lettre* XXI Usbek writes to the Premier Eunuque Blanc: "And who are you but lowly instruments, which I can break at will; who exist only insofar as you know how to obey; who are only in the world to live under my laws, or to die as soon upon my order" (p. 87).

[29]Grosrichard, *Structure du sérail*, p. 185.

expression convey Usbek's anxiety about the security of his rule—in that it portends the end of the novel where there is a reversal of authority and the "ruler" becomes the "ruled"—but also the choice of the word *empire* reinforces an analogy with the themes of slavery and colonial rule.

The use of *empire* to describe the rule of the wives in the harem emerges also in *lettre* IX. After having described the frustration that results from his castration, the Premier Eunuque singles out one last source of pleasure:

> Je me souviens toujours que j'étais né pour les [les femmes] commander; et il me semble que je redeviens homme, dans les occasions où je leur commande encore. . . . Quoique je les garde pour un autre, le plaisir de me faire obéir me donne un joie secrète: quand je les prive de tout, il me semble que c'est pour moi, et il m'en revient toujours une satisfaction indirecte: *je me trouve dans le sérail comme dans un petit empire*; et mon ambition, la seule passion qui me reste, se satisfait un peu.   (p. 63; emphasis added)

> [I never forget that I was born to command them (the wives), and it seems to me that I become a man again on those occasions when I give them orders. . . . Even though I guard them for someone else, the pleasure of making them obey gives me a secret joy. When I deny them everything, it is as if I do it for myself, and indirectly it gives me satisfaction. *The seraglio is for me like a small empire*, and my desire for power, the only passion that remains mine, is to some extent satisfied.]

Deprived of social and sexual status by his master, the eunuch is able to "become a man again" when he commands the wives. Several significant equations are contained in the eunuch's remarks. First, he echoes his earlier formulation that masculine station is provided and signified by the subordination of the wives; that is, possession of the phallus in the harem is essentially a socially conferred position. But in addition, for the eunuch in the absence of the master, the harem becomes for him "a small empire"; that is, the wives are equated with territories and masculinity is conflated with colonial rule. This portrait of the eunuch guard as petty oppressor, in which his own subjugation is converted into the will to subordinate the wives, renders the eunuchs as a class of people somewhat like the colonial French—the groups of settlers and military sent abroad, many of whom had been unprivileged commoners in France, but who were suddenly and ar-

bitrarily powerful among the Caribbean, Canadian, and Indian populations over whom they ruled.

The eunuch's social exclusion, however, is often also interpreted as
a characterization of the political exclusion of the nobility and *intendants* during the reign of Louis XIV, and continuing through the regency. But whether the Persian eunuch's plight is interpreted as an
allegory for French colonials or for the noble and middle classes within
French society itself, what is most notable about the figure of the
eunuch is the discrepancy, the lack of signification, between the eunuch's "class" status and his actual access to power. The eunuch is the
instrument of the master, with the ability to command the wives for
him; but he also possesses less collective power and a less stable
position with regard to the master than do the wives. For unlike the
wives, who have some, if limited, social and sexual means of negotiat-
ing with Usbek, the eunuch has none. Furthermore, unlike the wives,
the eunuch feels competitive with his fellow eunuchs, and he is not
inclined to join with them—or with the wives—in revolt against the
master; or perhaps in his singular impotence he is too attached to and
dependent on the structure of the harem for social status. Despite his
enslavement and subjection to the master's rule, he believes in the
fiction of limited power he is granted over the wives; therefore he
colludes with the master rather than objecting to his own enslavement.

Thus, the class tensions of French society become figured in the
Persian harem in terms of the eunuch's castration, his rank in the
hierarchy, and, most interesting, in terms of his relation to the master
and his power over the wives. But if we note the textual conflation of
masculine potency with imperial power, and consider the slavery of
the eunuchs to be not only an analogy for despotic rule but a metafigure for colonialism or orientalism itself, then the degree to which
the eunuchs accommodate the rule of the master is significant. It
suggests that the class drama that is figured through the eunuch story
never completely intervenes in or reverses the orientalist logic embodied in the master-slave relationship. Just as the eunuchs continue until
the end to uphold Usbek's rule, and are not willing to disturb the
structure of tyranny on which the harem is built, so too the narrative of
the eunuch's dissatisfaction does not truly challenge the narratives of
mastery, tyranny, or orientalism for which the topos of slavery stands.

Although the eunuch plot complicates the binary logic and structure of the first story's orientalism, the narrative about slavery ultimately corroborates and sustains orientalism's logic and its figures.

The wives, like the eunuchs, are also subordinated by the harem structure and subject to the will of the master. Unlike the eunuchs, however, the wives revolt against Usbek, and the narrative about the wives' triumph reverses and intervenes in the binary logic of the novel's orientalism. The sexual domination of the wives by Usbek is first evident in the letters in which wives are characterized as property—"ornement," "trésor"—kept for the honor of the husband: "Qu'une femme est malheureuse . . . ornement inutile d'une sérail, gardée pour l'honneur, et non pas pour le bonheur de son époux!" (p. 59) (How unhappy a wife is . . . a useless ornament in the seraglio, kept for the honor, not the happiness of her husband!), writes Fatme, one of the wives, to Usbek in *lettre* VII. *Lettre* XXVI, in which Usbek writes to his newest wife, Roxane, also reiterates the proprietary ownership of the wife by the husband; he characterizes the husband's right of sexual access to the wife as the "mastery of that treasure that you defended so steadfastly" ("pour me rendre maître de ce trésor, que vous défendiez avec tant de constance!"; p. 95). In the world imagined in the *Lettres*, the Persian "marriage" is represented as the relationship emblematizing the mastery over women by men. As in Jean Dumont's *New Voyage to the Levant*, the oriental marriage is constituted as a sign for both the enslavement of women and the barbarism of the oriental world. In the *Lettres*, marriage also serves as a metafigure for orientalism itself.

Marriage, or the subordinated relationship of women to men, is a significant emblem of social hierarchies in general during the early eighteenth century. In the essays "The Reasons of Misrule" and "Women on Top" in *Society and Culture in Early Modern France* (1975), the historian Natalie Zemon Davis suggests that the festivals in which symbolic reversals of the sexual and social roles of women and men occurred constituted regular intervals of relief from the traditional order; these inversions were a social and cultural means of deferring actual disorder or real redistributions of power in family and political life. One implication of Davis's argument is that the relationship of men and women was, in this period, a privileged symbol of social hierarchy that came to represent a variety of hierarchical relationships:

the relation of the colonial power to the colonies on the one hand, or of sovereign to citizenry on the other. In this sense the wives' actions at the end of Montesquieu's novel may have constituted a multivalent metaphor of rebellion that contributed to the postponement of actual revolutions to the degree that it figured a successful fictional revolution.

In the discussion of Usbek's relation to the eunuchs, I remarked earlier that Usbek's letters express his evident anxiety about the security of his rule at home. But the sense of the precariousness of his rule is even greater in terms of his relations with his wives. In *lettre* XXVI Usbek attempts to reestablish his authority over Roxane by renarrating the tale of his physical pursuit of her during the early days of their marriage:

> Deux mois se passèrent dans ce combat de l'amour et de la vertu. Vous poussâtes trop loin vos chastes scrupules: vous ne vous rendîtes pas même, après avoir été vaincu: vous défendîtes jusqu'à la dernière extrémité une virginité mourante: vous me regardâtes comme un ennemi qui vous avait fait un outrage, non pas come un époux qui vous avait aimée. . . . Je n'avais pas même une possession tranquille; vous me dérobiez tout ce que vous pouviez de ces charmes et de ces grâces; et j'étais énivré des plus grandes faveurs, sans avoir obtenu les moindres.   (pp. 95–96)

> [This struggle between love and virtue lasted two months. You carried the scruples of chastity too far: you did not surrender, even after you had been conquered; you defended your dying virginity to the very end; you considered me an enemy who had inflicted an outrage on you, not as a husband who had loved you. . . . I did not even have a tranquil possession of you: you deprived me, as far as you could, of your charms and your grace, and I was swooning from the greatest favors, without having obtained the lesser.]

In Usbek's narration of the consummation, Roxane first attempts to stab him, and then for the succeeding two months resists his advances. After the physical penetration takes place, she still does not surrender, but defends her "virginité mourante" until the end by withholding her own desire. In Usbek's retelling, Roxane's terror is evident, yet she appears to have practiced one potent form of resistance: what Usbek wants to construe as Roxane's modesty is her means of refusal. To disallow Usbek "une possession tranquille," to refuse willing or passionate participation, is her only weapon of re-sistance. As if acknowledging his lack of total possession, in *lettre* XXVI Usbek substitutes a narrated conquest of Roxane for the actual conquest he has never attained. In the novel's final letter, *lettre* CLXI, written during the wives' revolt, Roxane articulates this means of resistance to Usbek. She declares that although she submitted to his physical demands, she had always withheld herself and had sought her pleasures elsewhere; she is triumphant in announcing her decep-tions and betrayals: "Oui, je t'ai trompé; j'ai séduit tes eunuques; je me suis jouée de ta jalousie. . . . Comment as-tu pensé que je fusse assez crédule pour m'imaginer que je ne fusse dans le monde que pour adorer tes caprices?" (p. 350) (Yes, I deceived you. I seduced your eunuchs, outwitted your jealousy. . . . How could you have thought me so credulous as to imagine that I was in the world only in order to worship your caprices?]. Roxane ultimately escapes Usbek's tyranny by articulating her dissimulation, displacing his assumptions that she has always been his possession.

Lettres CXLVII through CLXI record the story of the revolt: the eunuchs' letters report the wives' growing defiance to Usbek; Usbek's letters order the guards to stop the transgressions and order his wives to obey; ultimately, the wives' letters to Usbek refuse to recognize his authority and declare their independence from him. The wives' acts of rebellion include quarreling, disobeying the eunuchs, and indulging in gaiety and infidelity; but the transgressions most forcefully con-demned in the eunuchs' reports to Usbek are the implied erotic rela-tionships between the wives and their female slaves. In both *lettres* IV and CXLVII female homoeroticism is introduced as one of the most serious violations of the rules of the harem. Usbek's wife Zéphis writes to him to ask that her slave Zélide not be taken from her. She alludes to the eunuch's reports of illicit homoeroticism, and offers an explanation of the eunuch's suspicions:

> Il veut, à toute force, m'ôter mon esclave Zélide, Zélide qui me sert avec tant d'affection, et dont les adroites mains portent partout les ornements et les grâces. Il ne lui suffit pas que cette séparation soit douloureuse; il veut encore qu'elle soit déshonorante. Le traître veut regarder comme criminels les motifs de ma confiance: et parce qu'il s'ennuie derrière la porte, où je le renvoie toujours, il ose supposer qu'il a entendu ou vu des choses, que je ne sais pas même imaginer.   (p. 55)

[He is determined to take my slave Zélide away from me, Zélide who
serves me so affectionately, and whose deft hands perform beauty and
grace everywhere. It is not enough for him that this separation should be
painful; he wants it to be dishonorable as well. The brute wants to
regard the motives for my trust as criminal; and because I always send
him outside the door and he gets bored, he dares to assume that he has
heard or seen things that I could not even imagine.]

Zéphis's letter not only registers that female homoeroticism is regarded as a most serious transgression of harem laws, but it also
provides an analysis of how that transgression is constituted. Zéphis's
explanation of the eunuch's accusations suggests that female homosexuality has a history in the cultural text and imagination of the
harem: whether as a pleasurable fantasy for voyeuristic eunuchs or,
conversely, as an imagined threat to the master's rule and to the
structure of the harem, the topos of sapphism already exists as a
constructed opposition to the required licit heterosexual fidelities of
the wives that sustain the harem hierarchy. Furthermore, in emphasizing that the eunuch is always kept outside the door, she implies that
he has particular motives for fabricating his accusations. As *lettre* IX
records, the eunuchs feel continual frustration—placed as they are
among the women they desire yet cannot touch, and in the shadow of
the master's satisfaction and his access to the wives, which the eunuchs envy. The imagined locus of female homosexuality—a site that
the eunuchs are forbidden to enter or even to gaze into—is the perfect
emblematic figure for the eunuch's frustration, and for his castration.
Finally, the possibility, whether practiced or imagined, of a nonhet-
erosexual female society not organized around the master's phallus
threatens the ultimate subversion of the institution of marriage and
fidelity to the master so essential to the structure of the harem. The
eunuch's accusations against Zéphis and Zélide, and his insistence on
separating the two women, illustrate the powerful force of this specter
on the imagination of those most invested in, and dependent on, the
harem structure.

Therefore, at a later point the reported incident of one of the wives,
Zachi, sleeping with her slave fills not only the eunuchs but also Usbek
with panic and dread. They believe that the acts and practices they
previously had only imagined have come to pass; it is the beginning of
the end. In *lettre* CXLVII the Grand Eunuque reports to Usbek:

Les choses sont venues à un état qui ne se peut plus soutenir: tes femmes se sont imaginées que ton départ leur laissait une impunité entière: il se passe ici des choses horribles. . . .

J'ai trouvé Zachi couchée avec une de ses esclaves, chose si défendue par les lois du sérail.   (p. 337)

[Things have arrived at an unendurable state of affairs; your wives have come to think that your departure meant complete impunity for them. Horrible things are happening here. . . .

I found Zachi in bed with one of her slaves, which is absolutely forbidden by the laws of the seraglio.]

The "choses horribles" he reports would seem to refer to homosexuality among the wives. But the acts themselves remain unspecified as if to allude to sexual excesses in general: "a universe of *generalized perversion* and of the *absolute limitlessness of pleasure*," as Malek Alloula describes the locus of the seraglio in orientalist literature.[30] That is, the reporting of "choses horribles" may be purposefully ambiguous so as to allude to a variety of unnamed things—not only forms of female sexuality that are neither dependent on nor organized around men but also the possibility of other sexual acts and practices that are unimaginable, deviant, polysexual, which also break the laws of the *sérail*.

Thus, the figure of sapphism—constructed as the most powerful threat to the sexual economy of the harem—is instrumental to the masculine discourse on the necessary discipline and containment of the wives. In her final letter to Usbek, however, Roxane reappropriates this figure of female homosexuality and through it articulates the power of the wives' rebellion. She declares in *lettre* CLXI that she has confounded and "remade" the harem laws, alluding to the sign of sapphism to deliver the last potent blow to Usbek: "J'ai su, de ton affreux sérail, faire un lieu de délices et de plaisirs. . . . Non: j'ai pu vivre dans la servitude; mais j'ai toujours été libre: j'ai reformé tes lois sur celles de la nature; et mon esprit s'est toujours tenu dans l'indépendance" (p. 350) (I knew how to turn your terrible seraglio into a place of delightful pleasures. . . . No: I may have lived in servitude, but I have always been free. I have reformed your laws according to the laws of nature, and my mind has always remained independent). In announcing to Usbek that she has remade his laws according to "celles de la

---

[30]Alloula, *The Colonial Harem*, p. 95.

nature," Roxane ventures an ironic reversal that renders the wives' diverse pleasures among themselves as natural while the supposedly licit heterosexual fidelity that is demanded of the wives is cast as unnatural.[31] Her proclamation of having remade the harem into "un lieu de délices et de plaisirs" alludes to the notion of sexual transgressions among the wives, knowing this to be a powerful weapon against Usbek. As if to goad his imagination further, she stops short of specifically naming these acts and pleasures; the specter of female homosexuality may be even more powerful when it remains unnamed. Her defiguring of the topos of marriage reminds him that the husband's hold over the wife is a wholly uncertain one. The revolt of the wives, with its images of female transgression, ends the novel; Roxane has the last word, and her statement of her independence and the failure of Usbek's authority are the final motifs of the novel.

In this sense, although the novel may conform to a logic that constitutes Persian tyranny as the opposite of French rationality, this orientalist binarism is challenged in several ways. On one level, the fictional device of placing Usbek and Rica in Paris inverts the roles of *persans* and *parisiens*, and throughout the novel the allegorizing of the French court in the oriental figure of the harem parodies the orientalist logic. On another level, orientalism as despotic and colonial rule is thematized in the domination of the eunuch slaves, the wives, and the female slaves in the harem, and is thus further challenged by the inversion of hierarchy that results from the wives' rebellion. The narrative conflicts of the Persian harem plot disrupt the binary logic of this orientalist projection, recasting the initial orientalism of the novel. As I have suggested, however, the heterogeneous class and gender narratives bear different relationships to the orientalist framework. Although the class narratives that figure the French nobility and *intendants* in the harem eunuchs compete with the orientalist narrative of the novel, in portraying the eunuchs as remaining loyal to the master,

[31]Roxane's declaration of her ultimate freedom from Usbek's mastery, and of her own sources of pleasure, echoes an earlier statement by Zélis in *lettre* LXII: "However, Usbek, don't imagine that your present situation is happier than mine. Here I have enjoyed countless pleasures unknown to you. My imagination has worked continually in order to realize their value. I have lived while you have stagnated. . . . Although you keep me imprisoned, I am freer than you" (p. 161). Both Roxane and Zélis taunt Usbek that they have invented other means of pleasure—pleasures he could not offer them and to which he does not have access.

the class narratives do not displace the topoi of either despotic rule or, ultimately, orientalism. The eunuchs bitterly feel the suppression of their potency and power by the master, yet they inevitably comply with Usbek's rule by attempting to administer the wives, as the French nobles and *intendants* ultimately taxed and administered the peasantry. Yet the gender narrative that represents peasant unrest in the wives' anarchy challenges the theme of rule by portraying the wives as victors over the master's tyranny. The final images of the novel are of an exclusively female community not organized around a male authority or symbolic phallus. The wives' plot is not only a dramatic representation of female challenges to a patriarchal system but also a narrative of peasant class struggle figured in terms of female sexuality and gender. If we accept the harem as a metaphor for orientalism as colonial rule, then the wives' revolt constitutes a gendered narrative critique of that topos of rule. Thus, in Montesquieu's *Lettres persanes*, as in Montagu's *Turkish Embassy Letters*, the tensions between orientalism and the numerous challenges from competing narratives demonstrate that orientalism is not univocal or discrete but rather that orientalist logic often exists in a climate of challenge and contestation from other distinct yet intervening narratives.

3

Orient as Woman, Orientalism as Sentimentalism: Flaubert

La femme orientale est une machine, et rien de plus; elle ne fait aucune différence entre un homme et un autre homme. Fumer, aller au bain, se peindre les paupières et boire du café, tel est le cercle d'occupations où tourne son existence. Quant à la jouissance physique, elle-même doit être fort légère puisqu'on leur coupe de bonne heure ce fameux bouton, siège d'icelle. Et c'est là ce qui la rende, cette femme, si poétique à un certain point vue, c'est qu'elle rentre absolument dans la nature. . . .

C'est nous qui pensons à elle, mais elle ne pense guère à nous. Nous faisons de l'esthétique sur son compte.

[The oriental woman is a machine, and nothing more; she doesn't differentiate between one man and another. Smoking, going to the baths, painting her eyelids and drinking coffee, such is the circle of occupations which make up her existence. As for physical pleasure, it must be very slight since they cut off that famous button, the very place of it, quite early on. And for me, this is what renders this woman so poetic, that she becomes absolutely one with nature. . . .

We are thinking of her, but she is hardly thinking of us. We are weaving an aesthetic on her account.]

Gustave Flaubert, "Lettre à Louise Colet," *Correspondance* (1853)

Traveling through Egypt in 1853, Flaubert wrote to his mistress, Louise Colet, about the courtesan Kuchuk-Hânem, describing her thus in order to assure Colet that she had no reason for jealousy. This unsettling description of "la femme orientale" is paradigmatic of the intersections of and collusions between several nineteenth-century French discourses, not only of orientalism and romanticism but also of race and industrial capitalism. Like the passage from Flaubert that begins Chapter 1—the young adulterer's comparison of Emma Bovary's shoulders with those of Ingres's odalisque—the evocation of Kuchuk-Hânem also conflates an eroticized female figure with a stylized orientalist iconography. On one level, Flaubert's use of orientalist and romantic motifs in the description of Kuchuk-Hânem aestheticizes and elevates a narrative that ultimately subordinates the woman as a sexual object; on another, allusions to the romantic topos of woman as artistic muse obscure the depoliticization of the history of French colonialism in Egypt and North Africa in a tale made innocent of the occidental writer visiting an exotic courtesan. Furthermore, the equation of the oriental woman with the highly prized object of industrialized society, the machine, not only dehumanizes the woman as technology, rendering sexual pleasure the surplus value for which the "femme/machine" is exploited, but also classifies her as racially Other: as machine she is not "human," that is to say, not European; she does not fatigue, does not possess self-consciousness or consciousness of others. "Kuchuk-Hânem" is not merely a *locus* of orientalism but is represented across a multiplicity of discourses and social relations. She is not a singular object but is variously and heterogeneously projected as at once sexual enchantress, productive machine, and racial inferior. The site of "la femme orientale" responds to a variety of cultural anxieties. Kuchuk-Hânem is a masculine fantasy of pure erotic service in the industrialized age of French imperialism: she generates sexual pleasure, yet she is impassive, undemanding, and insensate herself; her oriental mystery never fails to charm, her resources are never exhausted.[1]

[1]The nature of the letter as correspondence between Flaubert and Colet is also relevant. Flaubert constitutes Kuchuk-Hânem as the fiction of the woman who has no needs to satisfy. Although ostensibly reassuring Colet that the Egyptian woman means nothing to him (because his relationship with her is merely sexual), Flaubert also derides Colet, implying that Colet is, by contrast, too jealous and demanding. Furthermore, in arguing that the Egyptian woman's insensibility makes her completely different from Colet, a French woman, Flaubert attempts to make Kuchuk the sign and object of exchange between the two occidental correspondents. In constructing women as ma-

To what cultural anxieties can we say this particular phantasm of the oriental woman responds? In the early nineteenth century France faced a crisis of national identity. The instability of the regimes oscillating between revolution and reaction after 1789; the crisis of class definition in the bourgeois age of rapid industrialization; the changes in family, gender, and social structure in a time of urbanization and emigration—all of these factors shook and destabilized the old regime. There was a new and urgent desire to refigure "the nation," to imagine new forms of national community as well as coherent emblems of that community rather than relying on the older models of religion, monarchy, and dynasty offered by the ancien régime. Benedict Anderson has argued that the modern concept of the nation-state, born in late eighteenth-century Europe with the development of print capitalism, was a historically specific means of imagining social community in response to the erosion of religious and dynastic "verticalities."[2] Flaubert's texts are relevant to the nineteenth-century French project of imagining community, for they ironically parody stories about this desire for forms and emblems of the new French nation. For example, the "sentimental education" of Frédéric Moreau and Charles Deslauriers is very much an ironic allegory for French disillusionment and the search for national identity in the period between the July Monarchy and the failed revolutions of 1848. But Flaubert also observes the French preoccupation with figuring the nation in *L'éducation sentimentale* (1869) and many of the other texts that constitute (and mock) the standard norms of French culture by constructing oppositions between central sites and the margins, between bourgeois figures and their antifigures. In addition to the oriental woman, which may be Flaubert's antifigure par excellence, a variety of nineteenth-century antifigures—the adulteress, the decadent, the barbarian, the warring mercenary, the prostitute—are situated at the margins of plots, at odds with the social order. They imply, through contrast, the coherence of figures celebrated as emblems of French orthodoxy: the man of letters, the bourgeois doctor, the industrialist, the landowner,

---

chines, however, Flaubert makes Colet (as addressee, as witness) complicit in her own degradation as a woman, and an uneasy accomplice to his exploitation of Kuchuk-Hânem.

[2] Benedict Anderson, *Imagined Communities: Reflections on the Origin and Spread of Nationalism* (New York: Verso, 1983), esp. chaps. 2 and 3.

the military officer. Ironically, figuring otherness in order to situate a coherent national bourgeois identity, as Flaubert does, textualizes the desires of French nationalism in an age of instability, as much as this textualizing contributes to, and further determines, the convention of establishing national identity in the projection of otherness. In this sense Flaubert's oriental woman is an antifigure that articulates by negation a profile of desired traits for the nineteenth-century French bourgeois community: as she is insensate, vulgar, and licentious, they are sensitive, bourgeois, and discreet.

Although the desire to locate and identify coherent standards for the national community was partly the result of conflicts between classes and ideologies within the unstable nineteenth-century French state, the concurrent tendency to figure French national identity in terms of "oriental" differences was rooted in French colonial activities: the social and economic intercourse with the French North African colonies of Algeria, Morocco, and Tunisia served to shift and recast the rhetorical modes and logic of existing discourses, inserting different terms for expressing these new concerns with national identity. Nineteenth-century orientalism provided a means of displacing, while obliquely figuring, both domestic instability *and* colonialist conflicts; orientalism supported a coherent notion of the "nation"—"the one"— while subsuming and veiling a variety of other social differences in the figuration of the Orient as Other.[3] But just as Flaubert's use of the metaphor of the machine to describe Kuchuk-Hânem betrays not only an orientalist concern with Egyptian women but also a fascination with industrial production, the orientalist narratives that attempt to

[3]See Jean-Claude Berchet, ed., *Le voyage en Orient: Anthologie des voyageurs français dans le Levant au XIXe siècle* (Paris: Robert Laffont, 1985), an anthology of nineteenth-century French travel literature about the Orient. French orientalism at that time included quite diverse literatures, ranging from travel narratives (Chateaubriand's *Itineraire de Paris à Jérusalem, et de Jérusalem à Paris*, Nerval's *Voyage en Orient*, and the journals of Maxime du Camp), to the poetic images of the Orient in the verse of Lamartine, Rimbaud, and Baudelaire, to orientalist novels such as Loti's *Aziyadé* and Flaubert's *Salammbô*.
   The topos of the Orient seized the imagination of nineteenth-century French painters, too: Delacroix painted Arabian battle and hunt scenes, Gérôme depicted Muslims at prayer, and Ingres's paintings portrayed oriental bathers, odalisques, and slaves. The Orient evoked in nineteenth-century literature and art was alternately a powerfully consuming unknown, a forbidden erotic figure, a grotesquely uncivilized world of violence, and a site of incomprehensible difference. In all senses the Orient was always a richly literary space, a place where French culture could inscribe its various myths and preoccupations by invoking imaginary, and culturally different, Others.

project many kinds of social differences in the image of a single Orient register the displacement of these contiguous concerns—with colonialism, race, class, and gender—in the employment of particular rhetorics and motifs.

The role of the Orient in Flaubert's work has been noted in a number of studies of both Flaubert and orientalism.[4] In particular the *Voyage en Orient* (1849–1852), an account of Flaubert's travels through Egypt and the Middle East, and *Salammbô* (1862), his novel set in Carthage after the First Punic War, occupy influential positions in the French tradition of orientalism. I depart, however, from interpretations of Flaubert's orientalism that view his orientalist texts strictly as expressions of French interest in the Orient, just as I depart from traditional literary discussions of Flaubert that would treat his corpus as if it were a single, aesthetically uniform object of study. I observe instead that, particularly from the standpoint of orientalism, Flaubert's work consists of a heterogeneous, uneven set of texts in which the oriental figures are bound up with—and may reanimate some of the structuring themes of—other discourses. On the one hand, his texts enunciate a multiplicity of discourses; even in my brief discussion of Kuchuk-Hânem it is clear that the figure of the Egyptian courtesan is produced at a complicated nexus of distinct contradictions. It is really not possible to isolate a single determining factor. The representation of Kuchuk-Hânem as oriental is figured through the discourse about women as much as the representation of her as woman is figured through the capitalist metaphor of the machine; the diverse constructions are inextricably conjoined. On the other hand, the discursive site represented by Flaubert's corpus is also heterogeneous to the degree that we can also identify uneven formations—what we might call dominant figures and emergent critiques of those figures—among the Flaubertian texts. The relationship between these dominant and emergent moments comes to light in the discussion of the differences between the articulation of orientalist logics in the early texts and in the parodic destabilizing of orientalism that emerges in the later *Éducation senti-*

---

[4]See Said, *Orientalism*; as well as Jean Bruneau *Le "conte oriental" de Gustave Flaubert* (Paris: Denoël, 1973); Richard Terdiman, *Discourse/Counter-Discourse: The Theory and Practice of Symbolic Resistance in Nineteenth-Century France* (Ithaca: Cornell University Press, 1985); and Naomi Schor, *Breaking the Chain: Women, Realism, and the French Novel* (New York: Columbia University Press, 1985).

mentale. As I shall suggest, orientalism is targeted in *L'éducation* as being symptomatic of the regressive topos of sentimentality; orientalism as sentimentalism is parodied as a posture of subjective and cultural instability. Thus, my discussion of Flaubert treats the unevenness and reflexivity of his work as an example of discursive multivalence in French orientalism; not only is orientalism a means of figuring a diversity of concerns with social difference, but also the texts are divided and polyvocal, containing orientalist postures as well as critiques of those postures.

The Descending Woman: Kuchuk-Hânem and Salammbô

We find the portraits of Kuchuk-Hânem in the *Correspondance* and the *Voyage en Orient*, written during Flaubert's travels to Egypt and the Middle East between 1849 and 1851; Kuchuk-Hânem is said to be the model for the Carthaginian woman in *Salammbô*, which he wrote after returning from his travels. One of the principal figurations of both Kuchuk-Hânem and Salammbô makes use of the topos of the descending woman. The trope of descent commences rhetorically with a distancing of the oriental woman as elevated and remote, while performing a simultaneous immediacy, rendering her close through particularized descriptions of physical and ornamental details; in this sense the trope of descent is paradoxical, a means through which the oriental woman is represented as both transcendent and material, virginal yet eroticized. Tracing the descending woman through *Salammbô* and the *Voyage en Orient* allows me to remark on how the figure both thematizes and upholds ambivalence, and leads me to make some observations about the relationship between this ambivalence and the repetition of the topos.

Flaubert's novel concerns the Carthaginian priestess Salammbô, and Mâtho, the leader of the North African mercenary army, who falls in love with her. Salammbô, the daughter of the Carthaginian ruler Hamilcar, is betrothed by her father to a rival leader. In the story of Mâtho's impossible desire for Salammbô, the oriental woman is distanced as forbidden and inaccessible and yet objectified as the prize or bounty in Mâtho's war against Carthage. The Barbarians' efforts, under Mâtho's leadership, to penetrate barricaded Carthage, to puncture the city's aqueduct, and to steal the sacred veil of Tanit are concurrent with Mâtho's growing desire for the virgin priestess; the simultaneity of the two conquest themes contributes to the figuration of the oriental city of Carthage as the woman, Salammbô, while the cultural and historical alterity of Carthage as the Orient is figured in the sexual alterity of Salammbô as woman. Salammbô as "oriental woman" is a complicated representation of intersecting inscriptions: she is a forbidden object of desire as well as a material object of exchange, the barricaded city and the virgin priestess, the infinite beauty of *la nature*, and the sacred, violent oriental world. She is a fiction of European man's Other, represented as the seducer and recipient of Mâtho's desire, as the prey and object of men's social exchange in war, and as a metonym for the wealthy city of Carthage, which starves its mercenary children.

Two separate descriptions of Salammbô's descents emblematize her ambivalent function in the novel as eroticized woman and as object of exchange in war. The first occurs when she enters the courtyard where the mercenary soldiers are feasting at her father's house in his absence. During the feast the soldiers have proclaimed the injustices of the Carthaginian republic, which has neglected to pay them for their labor during the war against Rome. They curse Hamilcar's wealth and power and kill the sacred fish of the Barca family.

> Enfin elle descendit l'escalier des galères. Les prêtres la suivirent. Elle avança dans l'avenue des cyprès, et elle marchait lentement entre les tables des capitaines, qui se reculaient un peu en la regardant passer.
> Sa chevelure, poudrée d'un sable violet et réunie en forme de tour selon la mode des vierges chananéenes, la faisait paraître plus grande. Des tresses de perles attachées à ses tempes descendaient jusqu'au coins de sa bouche, rose comme une grenade entr'ouverte. Il y avait sur sa poitrine un assemblage de pierres lumineuses, imitant par leur bigarrure les écailles d'une murène. Ses bras, garnis de diamants, sortaient nus de sa tunique sans manches, étoilée de fleurs rouges sur un fond tout noir.[5]

> [Finally she came down the galley staircase. The priests followed her. She proceeded through the cypress avenue, and walked slowly between the tables, where the captains stood back a little as they watched her pass.]

[5]Gustave Flaubert, *Salammbô* (Paris: Garnier Flammarion, 1961), p. 12.

Her hair, powdered with mauve sand, was piled up like a tower in the style of the Canaanite virgins and made her appear taller. Ropes of pearls fastened to her temples fell to the corners of her mouth, rose red like a half-open pomegranate. On her breast was a cluster of luminous stones, iridescent as lamprey's scales. Her arms, adorned with diamonds, were left bare outside a sleeveless tunic, starred with red flowers on a black background.]

In the full passage from which this excerpt is quoted, Salammbô is described in a vertical descent from her hair to her mouth, her breasts, her arms, and finally her ankles. The descriptive gaze of the narrator anatomizes, particularizes, and sequesters isolated parts of Salammbô. The gems of her costume are an ironically conspicuous display of her market value as an object, her significance as Hamilcar's daughter. The attention to the "perles," "pierres lumineuses," and "diamants" of Salammbô's dress mark her as the embodiment of Hamilcar's hoarded wealth, the war chest desired by the mercenaries as she enters the scene. And yet the narration remains at a distance from her; the narrative gaze does not penetrate into the interior of Salammbô but remains fixed on the jewels, textures, and fabrics of her dress. Salammbô, although described in particulars, is not a character in the immediate world of the novel as others might be, but rather a represented figure that calls attention to itself as representation—unknowable, eccentric, and extravagant to the narrator and the soldiers. Salammbô is compared to "un tour," "une grenade," and "une murène"; while the metaphors attempt to capture her, she is nonetheless rendered quite strange by these comparisons. The metaphor of the tower evokes height, but the comparison renders the woman excessively tall and unfamiliar, as if dwarfing the men below. Salammbô is paradoxically distanced and isolated, objectified and desired by the narrative description. "Salammbô" is a figure for ambivalence; she is concrete and worldly, like her gems, but she has a remote, unworldly aspect that resists possession and referentiality.

In a second passage Salammbô descends to greet her father when he returns to Carthage from the war.

Salammbô descendait alors l'escalier des galères. Toutes ses femmes venaient derrière elle; et, à chacun de ses pas, elles descendaient aussi. . . .

Hamilcar s'arrêta, en apercevant Salammbô. Elle lui était survenue après la mort de plusieurs enfants mâles. D'ailleurs, la naissance des filles passait pour une calamité dans les religions du Soleil.   (pp. 139–140)

[Salammbô was then descending the galley staircase. All her women came behind her; and at each step she took, they took one also. . . .
   Hamilcar stopped when he saw Salammbô. She had arrived unexpectedly after the death of several male children. Besides, the birth of daughters was regarded as a calamity in the religions of the Sun.]

The two descents—the one before the mercenaries, Mâtho, and Narr'Havras, the other before Hamilcar—indicate two valences of the representation of Salammbô as oriental woman. In the first passage she is a remote, inaccessible erotic object; in the second, as she greets her father, she is a material object of exchange, useful only to Hamilcar as wealth to barter. In the first she is beloved, sought, and desired; in the second she is a disdained possession to be exchanged for the best price. The objectification of Salammbô as material property is particularly evident when Hamilcar receives the rumor that his daughter may have lost her virginity to the leader of the Barbarian tribes. Hamilcar's rage at imagining his daughter's violation mixes with his anger over the theft of the sacred veil, as well as his indignation that his properties and riches have been mismanaged in his absence: "Malgré ses efforts pour les bannir de sa pensée, il retrouvait continuellement les Barbares. Leurs débordements se confondaient avec la honte de sa fille" (p. 153). (Despite his efforts to put them out of his mind, he continually thought about the Barbarians. Their debauchery was conflated for him with his daughter's shame). For Hamilcar, his daughter's alleged rape is equal to his discovery that property has been stolen from his home. It is the combined effect of acknowledging all of his losses—his material loss of possessions as well as the loss of ownership of Salammbô, which the hypothetical violation represents to him—which moves Hamilcar to accept the command of the Carthaginian armies against the Barbarian tribes. When Hamilcar enlists the aid of the Numidians, he offers his daughter as bride to the Numidian king Narr'Havras, saying, "En recompense des services que tu m'as rendus, Narr'Havras, je te donne ma fille" (In exchange for your services, Narr'Havras, I give you my daughter). Narr'Havras's gratitude is described: "[Il] eut un grand geste de surprise, puis se jeta sur ses mains qu'il couvrit de baisers" (p. 235) ([He] made a great gesture of surprise and then threw himself on his hands, which he covered with kisses). In the economy of war, Salammbô is the prize, the bounty, which is bartered and exchanged between men. Although "ses mains" is somewhat ambiguous in its reference, it is presumably Hamilcar's hands that Narr'Havras kisses; the man is granted the possession of the woman when he kills for another man; through the exchange of Salammbô, the two men are erotically united.[6] Salammbô is described as being "calme comme une statue, semblait ne pas comprendre" (p. 235) ("calm like a statue, seeming not to understand"). She is the token whose receipt seals the contract whereby the Numidians promise to kill for the Carthaginians.

The descending oriental woman appears also in the *Voyage en Orient*, in a description of Flaubert's first encounter with Kuchuk-Hânem. Just as Salammbô's two descents embody twin valences of the "oriental woman," this descent, too, is a means of both eroticizing and materializing the oriental woman, of simulating a progression that charts her movement from being a distanced erotic image to being an immediate and particularized anatomy, under the mastering gaze of the narrator-observer.

> Sur l'escalier, en face de nous, la lumière l'entourant et se détachent sur le fond bleu du ciel, une femme debout en pantalons roses, n'ayant autour du torse qu'une gaze d'un violet foncé.
> Elle venait de sortir du bain, sa gorge dure sentait frais, quelque chose comme une odeur de térébenthine sucrée. . . .
> Ruchiouk-Hânem est une grande et splendide créature, plus blanche qu'une Arabe, elle est de Damas; sa peau, surtout du corps, est un peu cafetée. Quand elle s'asseoit de côté, elle a des bourrelets de bronze sur ses flancs. Ses yeux noirs et démesurés, ses sourcils noirs, ses narines fendues, larges épaules solides, seins abondants, pomme.[7]

[6]In a most interesting manner, in *La femme dans les romans de Flaubert: mythes et idéologie* (Lyons: Presses Universitaire de Lyon, 1983), Lucette Czyba associates the reduction of Salammbô as an object of exchange with the homoeroticism of war. Czyba suggests that the sadism of war in *Salammbô*, may be the obverse aspect of erotic bonding between men. Both male *eros* and *thanatos* have the common characteristic of excluding women from a closed society of men; the two parts of the war economy are compatible and mutually productive.

[7]Gustave Flaubert, *Oeuvres complètes de Gustave Flaubert*, vol. 10 (Paris: Club de l'Honnête homme, 1973), pp. 487–88. The name "Kuchuk-Hânem" appears variously and inconsistently in the *Voyage* and the *Correspondance*.

[On the staircase, facing us, with the deep blue of the sky illuminating her, stood a woman in pink trousers, with nothing around her torso but dark violet gauze.

She had just come out of the bath, her firm bosom smelled fresh, something like the odor of sugared turpentine. . . .

Ruchiouk-Hânem is a tall, splendid creature, whiter than an Arab, as she is from Damas; her skin, especially on her body, is a bit coffee colored. When she sits nearby, she has small bronze bulges on her flanks. Her eyes are black and inordinately large, her eyebrows black, flared nostrils, large solid shoulders, abundant breasts, like apples.]

Like Salammbô in her first entrance, Kuchuk-Hânem is paradoxically distanced and rendered immediate, simultaneously inaccessible and eroticized. The violet gauze around her torso is the detail on which this ambivalence turns; the gauze is at once a reference to female modesty and the initial distance between the narrator and the oriental woman (as a parodic representation of the veil that ensures female modesty in Muslim societies), as well as a signifier of eroticism and sexual accessibility, to the extent that the transparent fabric is the only detail mediating the distance between them. As with the descents of Salammbô, the Egyptian woman enters the narrative gaze from an elevated position on the staircase; the distance and elevation render her exotic and strange. There is an allusion to her height as well in "[elle] est une grande et splendide créature." It is not simply her height, however, that marks her as different: she is called a "créature," as if she were another species, not human but animal. Furthermore, her eyes are "noirs et démesurés," and their color and scale seem to make them icons of her difference. After she descends the staircase, the perspective from which the Egyptian woman is regarded changes suddenly to a disturbingly immediate one; now the writer emphasizes her otherness not through the use of distancing metaphors but through the intimacy of the physical and sensual detail in the descriptions of her race and sex. In "quand elle s'asseoit de côté, elle a des bourrelets de bronze sur ses flancs," the perspective of close proximity is utilized both to aestheticize her image and to reduce her anatomized particulars; the very details—"ses sourcils noirs, ses narines fendues, larges épaules solides, seins abondants, pomme"—work to privilege the artist's eye while constituting Kuchuk-Hânem as fragmented object. The description of her skin color—"plus blanche qu'une Arabe . . . sa peau, surtout du corps, est un peu cafetée"—enunciates a further dimension of the oriental woman's ambivalence. If, as Christopher Miller suggests, the construction of "blackness" as the negation of "whiteness" is a nineteenth-century trope fundamental to the invention and positioning of the French race, then the "mixed," ambivalent color of Kuchuk-Hânem's coffee-colored skin undoes this constructed opposition, calls the stability of "whiteness" into question. Miller discusses an analogous ambivalence in Baudelaire's poems to Jeanne Duval, his Creole mistress of many years, noting that in the poem "Les Ténèbres," the line "C'est Elle! noir et pourtant lumineuse" (It's she! black and yet luminous) underscores this ambivalent relationship of darkness and light, in which "elle" figures as the hinge between polar opposites of black and white. For Baudelaire, "la dame créole" is also a figure for racial instability, signifying that races are not pure (that, as Miller observes, everything is "créole"), that colors cannot be fixed but are implicated one within the other.[8]

The trope of descent performs a physical elevation and subordination of the oriental woman. Rhetorically it figures her as at once modestly virginal and erotically alluring; Salammbô's transcendence is signified by the priests who accompany her, while her material value is evidenced by the gems and fabrics of her dress. In addition, Flaubert's oriental woman is racially ambiguous: "bronze"—not "white," but not "black" either. In this sense Flaubert's topos of the oriental woman is fundamentally ambivalent, a characteristic of the colonialist stereotype on which Homi K. Bhabha has remarked.[9] Bhabha argues that the process of ambivalence is central to the colonialist construction of otherness, which vacillates between a reference to what seems to be accepted knowledge and a contradictory space that challenges this reference and makes it necessary to both fix and repeat it. The descending woman in Flaubert signals this irreducible ambivalence.

[8]See Miller, *Blank Darkness*, chap. 2.
[9]See Bhabha, "The Other Question." Bhabha outlines a more psychoanalytically defined argument for the fundamental "ambivalence" underlying the stereotype of otherness. He suggests that the stereotype (for example, the duplicitous Asiatic or the licentious African), is like the fetish described by psychoanalysis, "between what is always 'in place,' already known, and something that must be anxiously repeated. . . . For it is the force of ambivalence that gives the colonial stereotype its currency: ensures its repeatability in changing historical and discursive conjunctures" (p. 18).

To the degree that the narrative never succeeds in fully mastering or containing her, the oriental woman exceeds narrative and resists objectification; the narrative must thus repeat the trope of descent in the attempt to arrest and contain this excess. Like the name Kuchuk-Hânem, which occurs inconsistently in *Voyage* and *Correspondance*—appearing as Ruchuk-Hânem, Ruchiouck-Hânem, and then Kuchuk-Hânem, as if, despite anxious repetition to ensure its fixity, the name can never be arrested in an identical form—the topos of the descending oriental woman is repeated variously, with different nuances, different emphases. In his discussion of colonialist discourse, Bhabha suggests a convincing analogy between the colonialist stereotype and the psychoanalytic fetish: like the scene of fetishism, the colonialist construction of otherness includes both a reactivation of the material of original fantasy (for fetishism it is the anxiety of castration and sexual difference, for colonialism the condition of racial difference and the absence of racial purity) and a normalization of that difference in terms of a fixing of the fetish object. But rather than identifying an exclusively psychoanalytic ambivalence, as Bhabha would have it, in my reading of the "oriental woman" I locate ambivalence not only in the psychic shuttling between disavowal and fetishism, but also in the unsettled, multiple social conditions that inform the nineteenth-century discursive site on which she is inscribed: not only in the encounter with racial difference that comes from French colonial contact with the Algerian or the Egyptian, but also in the undeniable economic stratification that widens with industrialization, as well as the irrepressibility of sexual difference thrown into new relief by dramatic shifts in the patriarchal social order. These heterogeneous and uneven conditions render the oriental woman a heterogeneous, unstable signifier, in excess of what can be objectified or singularized, and therefore necessitating and inspiring repetition. It is in this sense that the descent of the oriental woman is narrated at least three times in Flaubert's works, as if repetition could fix its ambivalence or arrest the fundamental excess of the spectrum of otherness.

French Barbarians in *Salammbô*

Salammbô takes place in 240 B. C., after Carthage's loss to Rome in the First Punic War, and at the moment in which the various North African tribes employed as mercenaries by Carthage revolt against the Carthaginian republic; the novel describes the wars between Carthage and these Barbarian tribes. Although *Salammbô* evokes a world that is historically and geographically different from nineteenth-century France, it is not difficult to recognize similar imperial themes: just as Carthage had been a commercial republic competing with Rome for markets and empire in the western Mediterranean, so too was early-nineteenth-century France an emerging commercial force, threatening and being threatened by Great Britain. Napoleon's defeats by the British echo Carthage's repeated defeats, under Hamilcar and then his son Hannibal, in the First (264 B.C.), Second (218–201 B.C.), and Third (149–146 B.C.) Punic Wars. Moreover, the decline of Carthage had been due as much to its losses to Rome as to the revolt of the Barbarian tribes of North Africa, just as the instability of France after its international losses in the period of bourgeois revolt (1830) was shaken further by the workers' revolts during the revolutions of 1848.

Yet, although one would expect Flaubert to figure France as its western antecedent the Roman republic, Rome is conspicuously absent from *Salammbô*, which focuses strictly on the civil war between Carthage and the Barbarians.[10] The French narratives of imperialism and revolution are displaced in the "oriental" plot of the Carthaginian war. In the sense that *Salammbô* represents the Barbarians as subjugated members of the empire, these tribes simultaneously figure both internal and external threats to French bourgeois society in the mid-nineteenth century: on the one hand, the volatile and emergent French working class, whose concerns erupted in 1848, and on the other hand, the North African colonies violently encountered by French armies in the 1830s and 1840s. The extreme brutality of the battle scenes in *Salammbô* alienates the slaughter of the rioting masses of 1848 onto a very distant historical setting, while at the same time the location of the violence in North Africa curiously "confesses" the French colonial activities in North Africa and Egypt during the first

---

[10]In *Improvisation sur Flaubert* (Paris: Editions de la Différence, 1984), p. 117, Michel Butor suggests that Carthage is "the hidden face of Roman antiquity" at once denied and suppressed by Rome, the precursor of France, and yet signifying Rome, and, by implication, France. In the sense that Carthage is the oriental Other of Rome, the Other of Christianity and classical antiquity, the absenting of Rome decenters Rome as the place of western origin and presents the French tale in oriental disguise.

half of the nineteenth century. The French occupation and military subjugation of Algeria in the 1830s and 1840s, which included systematic massacres of the native populations, is defamiliarized in the portrait of Carthage's commercial and military exploitation of the nomad peoples outside the walls of the city. Internal class violence and external colonialist violence are thus thematized in the novel, but the responsibility for those deeds is lifted from France when the violence is detoured into the oriental world of Carthage and the surrounding Barbarian tribes. A world of war—determined by commercial greed and the desire for empire, and dependent on the occupation of other lands and other peoples—is made remote by the exotic, defamiliarized context of *Salammbô*.

Even though the apparent center of the novel is the story is Mâtho's romantic quest for Salammbô, the novel is filled with themes of war: the violent subjugation of many races by the Carthaginian republic; the penetration of the walled-in city; war as a system of alliance and enmity among men. The drama that juxtaposes two powerful warring factions against each other looms large: both the Carthaginians and the Barbarians are involved in a frenzy of violence; each group disapproves of the other's violence, and does not recognize that the other community's "barbarism" is thoroughly reflected within its own side. The rhetoric used to describe the two factions equates one with the other; in so doing the novel foregrounds the process by which one group's violence is at once denied and expelled in the image of a threatening and degraded Other. This process of denial and expulsion further alludes to the displacement of French violence—from the massacres in North Africa as well as the suppression of the working-class revolts in 1848—in the novel's own fiction of a historically distant Orient.

The dynamic by which one group is constituted as Other to the hegemonic culture is represented in the description of the nomad peoples who live just outside the walls of Carthage. This description occurs in the context of the Barbarian tribes' approach to the fortifications, as if the perceptions characterized the attitude of the Barbarians toward the nomadic tribes; the passage contains an inventory of the various means by which a group is classified and constituted as Other, or as "outside." The same logic for constituting otherness is then repeated in the passages describing the Barbarians' attitude toward the Carthaginians, and in turn the Carthaginians' construction of the Barbarians.

> Il y avait en dehors des fortifications des gens d'une autre race et d'une origine inconnue—tous chasseurs de porc-épic, mangeurs de mollusques et de serpents. . . . Leur cabanes, de fange et de varech, s'accrochait contre la falaise comme des nids d'hirondelles. Ils vivaient là, sans gouvernement et sans dieux, pêle-mêle, complètement nus, à la fois débiles et farouches, et depuis des siècles exécrés par le peuple, à cause de leurs nourritures immondes.   (pp. 60–61)

> [There were outside the walls people of another race and of an unknown origin—all hunters of porcupines, eaters of shellfish and snakes. . . . Their huts, of mud and seaweed, clung to the sides of the cliff like swallows' nests. They lived there, with neither government nor gods, in disorder, completely nude, simultaneously feeble and wild, and for centuries ostracized by the people because of their impure foods.]

The nomads are described as "d'une autre race," a difference and an exteriority underscored by their position outside the walls of Carthage, and "d'une origine inconnue," beyond Mâtho's people's territory of information and outside their historical narratives of origin. Their dwellings are made of materials that are coded as primitive and natural. They eat prohibited foods considered "immondes" and wild: porcupines, shellfish, snakes. Hayden White discusses the cultural function of the "savage" as a "technique of ostensive self-definition by negation. . . . If we do not know what we think 'civilization' *is*, we can always find an example of what it is not."[11] In a complementary observation, Mary Louise Pratt notes the particular ethnographic tropes that characterize the reports of European anthropologists encountering "primitive" native cultures.[12] This description of the nomads as "sans gouvernement et sans dieux, pêle-mêle, complètement nus," evokes the tropes of lawlessness, sin, and nakedness, used throughout the eighteenth and nineteenth centuries for constituting the "primitive" as a state of uncivilized nature, prior to language,

[11]Hayden White, "The Forms of Wildness: Archaeology of an Idea," in *Tropics of Discourse* (Baltimore: Johns Hopkins University Press, 1978), pp. 150–96. See also "The Noble Savage Theme as Fetish" in the same volume.

[12]Mary Louise Pratt, "Fieldwork in Common Places," in Clifford and Marcus, *Writing Culture*, pp. 27–50.

religion, and law. In this sense, the novel foregrounds the rhetorical operations for constituting difference and thus thematizes the displacement of French "barbarisms" into a novel about oriental Barbarians.

Carthage's violence toward the Barbarians is described in sensualized, particularized detail, as are the Barbarian tortures of Carthaginians. Both sides are grotesque and "barbaric," neither more so than the other. The rhetorical equality of the descriptions of the two warring groups suggests that one group's sadism is reflected in the brutality of the other; they are twin images of reciprocal violence, aggressively and narcissistically bound each to the other. Carthage's torture of the Barbarians is described:

> Les deux milles Barbares furent attachés dans les Mappales, contre les stèles des tombeaux; et des marchands, des goujats de cuisine, des brodeurs et même des femmes, les veuves des morts avec leurs enfants, tous ceux qui voulaient, vinrent les tuer à coups de flèche. On les visait lentement, pour mieux prolonger leur supplice: on baissait son arme, puis on la relevait tour à tour; et la multitude se poussait en hurlant. . . .
> Puis on laissa debout tous ces cadavres crucifiés, qui semblaient sur les tombeaux autant de statues rouges.   (p. 184)

> [The two thousand Barbarians were attached to the stelae of the tombs in the Mappalian quarter; and merchants, kitchen scullions, embroiderers, and even women—the widows of the dead with their children—all who would, came to kill them with their arrows. The arrows were aimed slowly at them, in order to prolong their torture, lowering the weapon and then raising it in turn; and the multitude pressed forward howling. . . .
> Then all these crucified corpses were left upright, looking like so many red statues.]

The description records in telling detail the carnality of the Carthaginians' sadism: that the torturers include women and children, that they aim their arrows slowly, that the corpses are left standing as monuments to their bloody demise—all these details signify the extremity and excess of the Carthaginians at war. The acts of the Barbarian troops are likewise described in painful detail:

> Les hommes y vinrent ensuite, et ils les suppliciaent depuis les pieds, qu'ils coupaient aux chevilles, jusqu'au front, dont ils levaient des cou-

ronnes de peau pour se mettre sur la tête. . . . Il envenimaient les
blessures en y versant de la poussière, du vinaigre, des éclats de poterie:
d'autres attendaient derrière eux; le sang coulait et il se réjouissaient
comme font les vendangeurs autour des cuves fumantes.   (p. 241)

[The men came next and tortured them from from their feet, which
they cut off at the ankles, to their foreheads, from which they took off
crowns of skin to put upon their own heads. . . . They envenomed the
wounds by pouring into them dust, vinegar, and fragments of pottery;
others waited behind them; blood flowed, and they rejoiced like vin-
tagers around steaming vats.]

Like the Carthaginians, among whom gleeful merchants make profits
by selling arrows to the crowds, the Barbarians who put vinegar and
irritants in the soldiers' wounds are described as being as joyful as
wine makers. The narratives in both passages treat each community's
sadism, and in the detailed descriptions of the extravagance of their
acts, both factions are implicitly condemned; both sets of torturers are
unmoved by their own violence and the suffering of others. Similar
descriptions of brutality are also present in the descriptions of the
slaughter of soldiers and workers during the June battles of 1848 in
L'éducation sentimentale; this parallel suggests that the battles scenes in
Salammbô are thinly veiled statements about the failures, and loss of
human life, in 1848, whereas the location of these battles in a historically distanced North Africa reveals the preoccupation with, and
unsuccessful denial of, the French massacres in North Africa. As an
allegory of the battles between the French workers and the bourgeois
army in 1848, neither faction is privileged; in *Salammbô* the workers'
revolts are as cynically condemned as they are in *L'éducation sentimentale*. The novel levels the two sides in the conflict between Carthage
and the Barbarians, making each equally barbaric, as if confirming that
nationalism and war depend not only on the displacement of one's
own barbarism onto another community but also on the inability to
recognize the other community's crimes as similar to one's own. Ultimately, the manner in which Carthage constitutes the Barbarians as
sacrilegious and violent and the Barbarians consider Carthage to be
cruel and hoarding are themselves emblems of the process by which
the oriental world of *Salammbô* is produced, and enjoyed as a spectacle
of displaced "barbarism," by the novel itself.

Oriental Motifs and Sentimentalism: *L'éducation
sentimentale*

I have suggested that Flaubert's corpus contains a variety of texts for
which oriental difference is the structuring trope, but within which
other kinds of social differences are figured and elaborated. These
texts reflect the shifting and antagonistic nature of the nineteenth-
century culture in which they were produced, and which they, in turn,
helped to produce. As cultural products Flaubert's texts are inscribed
by a variety of discursive formations, just as a multiplicity of ideological strains compete within the culture; in this sense the orientalism in
Flaubert's texts is divided and plural, expressing a variety of often
contradictory concerns. For example, Flaubert may have traveled to
and written about the Orient as an attempt to escape from bourgeois
society and to find a position from which to criticize French society; the
appearance of the Orient in his work is thus one representation of
cultural self-criticism, of an antibourgeois position.[13] But the figurations of the oriental otherness in Flaubert's texts equally textualize—
even if only to parody—the cultural preoccupation with defining a
coherent national identity, and a bourgeois identity, at a moment
when stability was being challenged by class dislocations during and
following the revolutions of 1848, by changing definitions of gender
and family in a time of accelerated industrialization and urbanization,
and by encounters with racial difference in colonial North Africa. Like
the unsettled nineteenth-century cultural moment of which it is a
product, Flaubert's work expresses a variety of contradictory ideologies, articulated by both dominant and emergent discursive formations. Moreover, in addition to the multiplicity of ideological positions
represented, the narrative styles of the texts are themselves ironic and
divided in complex ways. In *L'éducation sentimentale* (1869), for example, the "style indirect libre," for which Flaubert is so famous, merges
narratorial and subjective modes to achieve the greatest elimination of
distance between narrator and character.[14] The result is a subtly ironic

[13]This interpretation of Flaubert's orientalism is offered in Terdiman, *Discourse/Coun-
ter-Discourse*, pt. 2, chap. 5.

[14]The discussions of Flaubert's style are many. For particularly lucid explications, see
Roy Pascal, *The Dual Voice: Free Indirect Speech and Its Functioning in the Nineteenth-Century
European Novel* (Manchester: Manchester University Press, 1977); and Dominick La-
Capra, *"Madame Bovary" on Trial* (Ithaca: Cornell University Press, 1982).

narrative that in one description preserves the subjective perspective of Frédéric's thoughts as it simultaneously represents a narratorial commentary and critique of that perspective through mimicry of Frédéric's idiom, and through the ironic juxtaposition of different contexts in which this idiom occurs. Thus, whereas Frédéric has a penchant for oriental symbols, and orientalism is present in *L'éducation* as an aspect of Frédéric's world, at the same time we see that the orientalist posture that associates the Orient with eroticism is established in the narrative as Frédéric's posture; and as a mark of Frédéric's sentimentalism the use of the oriental motif is mocked, parodied, and ultimately criticized.

Oriental motifs—a painting of a Turkish odalisque by Ingres, a Chinese parasol, an Egyptian tarboosh—occur in a number of Flaubert's novels as fragments of an exotic world elsewhere, references to oriental contexts eccentric to the scenes in which they are invoked. These motifs accompany, and come to characterize, the young man's erotic interest: Léon imagining he finds in Emma's shoulders "la couleur ambrée de l'*Odalisque au bain*," the harpist playing "une romance orientale, où il était question de poignards, de fleurs et d'étoiles" during Frédéric's first sight of Madame Arnoux; or the "chaînette d'or" between the ankles of Salammbô seen by Mâtho when she first approaches the group of soldiers. As fragments they quote from the detailed iconographies of other orientalist texts which associate certain motifs with the Orient: nude slaves, daggers, gold ankle chains. They are incomplete, partial quotations, and their fragmentary nature underscores their standing as marks of incompletion, and hence as marks of desire. For example, in *Madame Bovary* (1857), Léon's imagining of Emma's shoulders as those of the Turkish odalisque in Ingres's painting does not refer to a woman in a Turkish harem. In imagining Emma as Ingres's subject, Léon expresses his desire by invoking an already established association of the oriental and the erotic; the erotic relationship of present lover and absent beloved, and eroticism as the transgression of prohibition and taboo, are expressed in an oriental motif. In addition, Léon's desire for Emma portrays desire as consisting of the quotation of cultural signs; the metaphor of Emma's shoulders as those in Ingres's painting is twice distanced—itself a quotation of an orientalist painting. It signifies orientalism in order to signify erotic desire. Just as Emma learns her posture of desire from popular novels, Léon casts this moment of his desire in an orientalist, and equally literary, mode.[15] Ironically enough, Ingres never traveled to North Africa or the Near East, but acquired the colors and textures for his bathers, odalisques, and Islamic interiors from the eighteenth-century letters of Lady Mary Wortley Montagu and Montesquieu's *Lettres persanes*.[16] In the sense that Ingres received his Orient from literary sources, it is a literary Orient that he painted, and Léon's notion of desire is as literary as that of Emma. The oriental motif is the distinguishing mark of sentimentalism in Flaubert, a sentimentalism that longs for a memory of earlier innocence, an impossible union, a lost wholeness in which European culture is faithfully reflected in its oriental Other. This paradigm of sentimentalism, represented by the oriental motif, is exemplified, critically observed, and ultimately mocked by the cited motifs in *L'éducation sentimentale*.

The oriental motif, though perhaps not central to *L'éducation*, emerges nonetheless as the mark that characteristically expresses and initiates Frédéric's erotic desire. The first time Frédéric meets Madame Arnoux aboard the steamboat, a harpistis playing an oriental ballad. The narration of this scene begins: "Il la supposait d'origine andalouse, créole peut-être" ("He imagined her to be of Andalusian origin, maybe Creole"), which establishes the figuration of Madame Arnoux as exotically Other as Frédéric's perceptive mode. The passage describing the oriental melody, though undesignated by a pronoun as belonging to Frédéric, continues his romantic idiom and postures. The throbbing of the boat's engine is so noisy that the harpist must play even louder to compensate: "les battements de la machine coupaient la mélodie à fausse mesure; il pinçait plus fort: les cordes vibraient, et leur sons métalliques semblaient exhaler des sanglots et comme la plainte d'un amour orgueilleux et vaincu" (The throbbing of the engine punctuated the melody as an uneven accompaniment; he plucked harder, the strings vibrated, and their metallic sounds seemed to plaintively cry out the sad story of a proud, defeated love).[17] Fré-

[15]That Emma takes her particular notion of romantic desire from the clichés of popular novels and from the songs she sang in the convent as an adolescent has been noted by many critics, including Victor Brombert, *Flaubert* (Paris: Seuil, 1971); Jonathan Culler, *Flaubert: The Uses of Uncertainty* (Ithaca: Cornell University Press, 1974); and Tony Tanner, *Adultery in the Novel* (Baltimore: John Hopkins University Press, 1979).

[16]Stevens, *The Orientalists*, p. 17.

[17]Gustave Flaubert, *L'éducation sentimentale* (Paris: Garnier Flammarion, 1969), p. 41.

déric's adulterous desire for Madame Arnoux is signified, as is Léon's in *Bovary*, by the quotation of fragments from orientalism; not only is the ballad a fragment, an emblem of incompletion and desire, but in this image the Orient of its origin is also associated with a lost, threatened past. Frédéric's impossible passion for Madame Arnoux is personified in the sobbing sounds of the plucked notes as the musician attempts to be heard over the engine noises. In this image the narrative observes Frédéric's conflation of several kinds of censorship and prohibition: the noises from the engine impinge on the delicate sounds of the ballad, just as the bourgeois Arnoux obstructs Frédéric's passion for Arnoux's wife and, even more grandly, as western industrial society supersedes an earlier oriental age of plenitude and sensuality. Frédéric's plight is dramatized as that of a lost oriental civilization. Desire is figured in a typically romantic opposition: an earlier temporality is juxtaposed with a corrupted present, an unknown plenitude opposed to a known world. The oriental ballad is already tortured and sad; from the first moment, Frédéric's desire for Madame Arnoux is characterized as one of loss and impossibility. His idealization of Madame Arnoux is continually cast as an exaggerated drama about loss, and is underscored by the hyperbolic language used to express his infatuation: "Plus il la contemplait, plus il sentait entre elle et lui se creuser des abîmes. Il songeait qu'il faudrait la quitter tout à l'heure, irrévocablement, sans avoir arraché une parole, sans lui laisser même un souvenir!" (p. 43) (The longer he gazed at her, the more he felt the opening of abysses between the two of them. He reflected that he would have to leave her soon, irrevocably, without having drawn a single word from her, without leaving her a single memory of himself!). The intensity of Frédéric's desire is represented by the growing enormity of the abysses he imagines opening between them; the moment of contact with her is framed entirely by the inevitable subsequent separation. The narrative critically observes Frédéric creating his sublime sentiment for Madame Arnoux by dramatizing her inaccessibility in the inversion of two moments: the future in which Madame Arnoux is gone is substituted for the present moment of contact. She is constituted as already lost, the moment of contact thoroughly desired because it is irrevocably past. The oriental motif is the mark under which Frédéric's sentimentalizing hyperbole takes place.

The oriental motif occurs at other moments in the novel as well. Frédéric's passion for Madame Arnoux is continually associated with travel to distant oriental lands: he imagines that he and Madame Arnoux will travel to "des pays lointains . . . au dos des dromadaires, sous le tendelet des éléphants" (p. 101) (faraway countries . . . on the backs of camels, under canopies atop elephants), and he dreams of her "en pantalon de soie jaune, sur les coussins d'un harem" (p. 102) (in yellow silk pants, on pillows in a harem). Later, a bawdy party attended by Frédéric and his young friends takes place in "moresque" rooms, where Hussonet speaks the now typical conflation of the erotic and the oriental by suggesting "un raout oriental" (p. 105) (an oriental orgy). When he is not able to attend Madame Arnoux's birthday party, Frédéric selects for her "une ombrelle . . . en soie gorge-pigeon, à petit manche d'ivoire ciselé, et qui arrivait de Chine" (p. 112) (an umbrella . . . of iridescent colored silk, with a small handle of carved ivory, which had come from China). The motifs are all heterogeneous fragments: camels and elephants, bits of Moorish interiors, a Chinese silk parasol. They are incomplete allusions to disparate orientalisms, and their fragmentary qualities as motifs call attention to their importance as signifiers, and as marks of desire. Furthermore, the orientalist texts themselves, to which these motifs refer, also represent postures of incompletion, ultimately sentimental paradigms that constitute the invented Orient as a sublime ideal, a lost otherness, a time and space removed from the occidental world. The oriental motif calls attention to itself as a signifier that, in effect, does not signify except to signify orientalism (a larger tradition of postures of incompletion). It is an emblem of the desire to signify desire, as if the structure and character of desire were—as Lacan suggests[18]—a perpetual series of linguistic

[18]Lacan's notion of the "signifying chain" is perhaps most clearly articulated in "Agency of the Letter in the Unconscious, or Reason since Freud," in *Ecrits*, pp. 146–78.

Lacan's subject is situated in and by language, language being the most determining structure in the Symbolic, or social, realm. He discusses signification in the Symbolic as a process in which every signifier corresponds not to a signified but to another signifier: "No signification can be sustained other than by reference to another signification" (p. 150). Desire inheres in the chain of signifiers, and more particularly in the incommensurability of word and thing, the failure of metaphoric similitude, and the determined succession of metonymic associations. "It is in the word-to-word connexion that metonymy is based" (p. 156). The metonymic structure, or the connection between signifier and signifier, "permits the elision in which the signifier installs the lack-of-being in the object relation, using the value of 'reference back' possessed by signification in order to

and social postures of incompletion, which does not find its completion in objects but renews itself in the signification of other desiring postures. That the novel represents desire as inhering in the metonymic substitution of one signifying posture for another is echoed in Frédéric's voyage from one love interest to another: from the infatuation with Madame Arnoux to the desire for Rosanette to the interest in Madame Dambreuse. Frédéric's love choices parallel his efforts to rise into the society of the haute bourgeoisie. He wishes to signify himself and his social standing by the possession of women from particular classes (or women possessed by other men of particular classes); his efforts are unsuccessful, and the progress of his desire is the repeated substitution of one woman for another, or one signifying posture for another. Indeed, in a single day, he visits all three women, going from one residence to the next, and on the day of the fateful rendezvous with Madame Arnoux on rue Tronchet, Frédéric makes love with Rosanette "dans le logement préparé pour l'autre" (p. 307) (in the accommodations prepared for the other).

After Frédéric has deserted Rosanette, spurned Madame Dambreuse, and refused finally to consummate his love with a much older Madame Arnoux, the novel ends with his "atrophie sentimentale" (p. 394) (sentimental atrophy). The Revolutions of 1848 have given way to the installation of Louis Napoléon in 1851. It is not only the young men in the novel who do not achieve their ambitions; their society also fails to realize the ideals of equality and liberty, lost first in 1789 and now again in 1848. Frédéric's disillusionment in love corresponds to the political disillusionment after the virtual restoration of the old structures of wealth and privilege during the Second Empire. The failure of the revolutions and the betrayal of revolutionary ideals by the bourgeoisie is most poignantly figured when Frédéric witnesses the death of his working-class friend Dussardier at the hands of Sénécal, a former revolutionary turned *agent de police*. Frédéric's long desire for and pursuit of Madame Arnoux is one model of sentimental idealism observed throughout the novel, but the novel also draws an analogy between Frédéric's education in love and the political education of the French society which has suffered two thwarted efforts at revolution-

---

invest it with the desire aimed at the very lack it supports" (p. 164). The signifier—in this case the oriental fragment—becomes an index of inaccessibility to totalization, or wholeness, the desire for which it repeatedly motivates.

ary social change. Frédéric's love quest, a process of desire already marked by the loss of the object, is compared to the failure of the revolutions of 1848 to achieve the egalitarian society previously desired and lost in 1789.[19] In this metaphor of the young man's sentimentalism and his society's aspirations, the revolution and its political idealism are judged severely.

The oriental motif that marks Frédéric's and Deslauriers's reminiscence of the bordello at the end of the novel provides the final commentary on the oriental figuration of erotic desire. The two friends' remembrance of their first visit to a house of prostitution in 1837 is introduced by an explanation of how the woman who ran the house had come to be called "la Turque": many people believed her to be a Muslim from Turkey, and as this "ajoutait à la poésie de son établissement" (p. 444) (added a bit of poetry to her establishment), she was from that point known as "la Turque." Hearsay embellished the house with an exotic flair, endowing it with an intriguing erotic quality: "Ce lieu de perdition projetait dans tout l'arrondissement un éclat fantastique. On le désignait par des périphrases: 'L'endroit que vous savez,—une certaine rue,—au bas des Ponts.' " (p. 445) (This dangerous place enjoyed a remarkable reputation in the whole district. People referred to it with circumlocutions: "You know the place I mean . . . a certain street . . . below the Bridges"). Frédéric and Deslauriers recall that the townspeople would use euphemisms when speaking of the house of prostitution. Ambiguous, nonreferential phrases such as "l'endroit que vous savez" were used to signify the prohibited site of sexuality. The oriental motif of "la Turque" does not refer to the woman who manages the house (indeed, she does not appear in their reminiscence), nor does not it refer to Turkey; "la Turque" is the periphrasis, a turning or deferring of meaning, used by the young boys to signify the plenitude of unknown women and sexual practices within the house of prostitution. It is also the motif under which Frédéric and Deslauriers reconstitute the adolescent position of curiosity, still uninterrupted by failure and disillusionment. The remembered scene has value as a reconstructed moment of pure idealism and innocence:

[19]For a discussion of historical representation in Flaubert's novel and Marx's *Eighteenth Brumaire of Louis Bonaparte*, see Hayden White, "The Problem of Style in Realistic Representation: Marx and Flaubert," in *The Concept of Style*, ed. Berel Lang (Philadelphia: University of Pennsylvania Press, 1979), pp. 213–22.

Frédéric presents a bouquet "comme un amoureux à sa fiancée" (p. 445) (like a lover to his fiancée), and, flustered by the presence of so many women, he ultimately flees. He leaves the establishment of la Turque a virgin, still inexperienced, with all desire and all disappointment ahead of him. The irony of this final scene, in which Frédéric and Deslauriers invoke a lost moment of plenitude, is punctuated by their final declarations: "C'est là ce que nous avons eu de meilleur!" (p. 445)(That was the happiest time we ever had!). In a characteristically romantic strategy, the two friends perform a dialectic of presence and absence, rhetorically substituting a constructed past—"c'est là"—for their fallen, corrupted present states. The invocation of the house of la Turque as the place where they had their happiest times replaces their condition of loss with a reconstituted plenitude of adolescent virginity. The novel portrays Frédéric in an endless repetition of these desiring postures, marked by the oriental motif as an unsignifying signifier of incompleteness. This final use of the motif suggests Frédéric's ultimate failure to change; although older and more weary—having lived under Louis Philippe, through the revolutions, and now under Napoléon III—Frédéric invokes once more the adolescent oriental motif to recall an earlier state of desire.[20]

The scene in which Frédéric reminisces about the house of la Turque exposes his invention of oriental exoticism as sentimentality. In a sense, the scene offers us a retrospective critique of orientalism within the Flaubertian corpus itself, whereas the earlier descriptions of "la femme orientale" in *Voyage*, *Correspondance*, and *Salammbô* more vividly exemplify the orientalizing posture that both desires and debases its culturally and sexually different object. To the degree that orientalism and sentimentalism are equated in *L'éducation*, the narrative criticizes the ultimate delusion and romanticism of the orientalist posture. It is as if the various texts in the oeuvre of the author were themselves different orientalist moments on a continuum in which, to ever greater degrees, the narrative calls attention to orientalism as a posture, and ironically contextualizes that posture. With *L'éducation*, the orientalist

---

[20]On the failure of romanticism, the prolonging of youth, and the end of the bildungs-roman, in *L'éducation sentimentale*, see Franco Moretti's discussion of the novel in *The Way of the World* (London: Verso, 1987). On Frédéric's systematic pursuit of failure, and his refusal to mature, produce, or develop, see Pierre Bourdieu, "The Invention of the Artist's Life," trans. Erec R. Koch, *Yale French Studies* 73 (1987): 75–103.

imagery is no longer performed by the narrative but is instead mocked as a function of the protagonist. In the final reminiscence of a reconstituted ideal moment under the signifier "la Turque," the utility of the oriental motif as sentimentalism is illustrated, just as the reminiscence emphasizes how the oriental motif indeed fails to signify throughout the novel. The narrative's use of the oriental motif to signify Frédéric's sentimentalism is appropriate because the individual paradigm of sentimentalism is structurally similar to the cultural paradigm of orientalism: each substitutes an invented otherness for a present condition of failed self-possession or unstable cultural identity.

4

Orientalism as Literary Criticism: The Reception of E. M. Forster's *Passage to India*

"A Mohammedan! How perfectly magnificent!" exclaimed Miss Quested. "Ronny, isn't that like your mother? While we talk about seeing the real India, she goes and sees it, and then forgets she's seen it."

E. M. Forster, A Passage to India (1924)

I don't myself like the phrase "the real India." I suspect it. It always makes me prick up my ears. But you can use it if you want to, either for the changes in her or for the unchanged. "Real" is at the service of all schools of thought.

E. M. Forster, "India Again" (1946)

In 1975 one of the more noted Indian literary critics of E. M. Forster, Vasant A. Shahane, edited a volume of essays by Indians on Forster's famous novel *A Passage to India* (1924). In the introduction to *Focus on Forster's "A Passage to India"* Shahane explains that the primary justification for the collection of essays was "to project an Indian critic's image of Forster's *A Passage to India* after about fifty years of its impact on this country and the English-speaking world. What is basically important in this approach is *the Indianness of the native point of view*, its process of evaluation and its validity."[1] The importance of Shahane's notion lies not so much in an emphasis on a *unified* Indian point of view, for in fact the collection can be interpreted as a heterogeneous emblem of diver-

[1] Vasant A. Shahane, ed., *Focus on Forster's "A Passage to India": Indian Essays in Criticism* (Bombay: Orient Longman, 1975), p. xiii; emphasis added.

sity among Indian critics of this period, with essays ranging from a study of the symbolism of the cave, to a criticism of the novel's representation of race relations in India, to a stylistic analysis of the speech of the Indian characters in the novel. Rather, I believe that the significance of Shahane's articulation of "Indianness" inheres in its description of an opposition between the points of view of Indians and those of the Anglo-American intellectuals who had historically constituted the English literary tradition. It is a powerful opposition to the degree that it poses the notion of a native point of view over and against the ruling British perspective that traditionally considered India a colorful backdrop to the central British drama, and Indians as peripheral objects to be colonized and scrutinized rather than as possessing a point of view themselves. Indianness, in this sense, is proposed as an oppositional category, a means of articulating a position that is at once essential and eccentric to the English literary tradition. As Gauri Viswanathan argues, in *Masks of Conquest: Literary Study and British Rule in India* (1989), the institutionalization of English literature in India was a vehicle of British rule, and part of the imperial mission of educating colonial subjects in the literature and thought of England. The teaching of an English literary canon to Indian subjects had the unique role of justifying imperial rule to its subjects by inculcating assumptions of the superiority of western aesthetic principles and the complementary inferiority of the "impure" traditional literatures of the East. This ideological construction was supported, in concrete practical terms, by the distinctly separate formations of English literature in England and in India, by the exclusivity of the former institution and the subordination of the latter. Viswanathan points out that a gap existed between the functions and uses of literary education in its English and Indian contexts, manifested in different uses of the same curricula and the different values accorded to the various literary genres, as well as in the marginalization of the work of certain orientalist scholars such as William Jones in the context of Indian educational policy and the simultaneous elevation of these same scholars in British educational culture.[2] It is as a critical counterpoint both to the function of English

[2]Gauri Viswanathan, *Masks of Conquest: Literary Study and British Rule in India* (New York: Columbia University Press, 1989). Viswanathan discusses the relationship between the institutionalization of English in India and the exercise of colonial power, as well as between the processes of curricular selection and the impulse to dominate and control.

literature as an instrumental part of the British imperializing mission and to the closed elite superiority of the institution of English literary studies in England that Shahane's notion of the Indian point of view must be read and understood.

Shahane's comment is at once both obvious and subtle. On the face of things, it logically proposes that Indians ought to write about a novel that purports to be about India, and that what Indians can observe about *A Passage to India* would necessarily be different from what other English speakers would find in it. As such, it calls attention to what postcolonial intellectuals such as Gayatri Spivak and Radha Radhakrishnan have distinguished as the difference between "representation" as "speaking for" a cultural and political locality and the "re-presentation" of an object, as in literary, artistic, or philosophical discourses.[3] In other words, Shahane's comment points out that *who* is speaking may deserve as much attention as *what* is being said. At the same time, by foregrounding the history of an exclusion of Indian contributions as Indian, Shahane's volume both disrupts and alters the exclusivity of the English literary tradition itself. The Indian intervention into a tradition that subordinates and objectifies Indians transforms the set of conditions that regulates the range of possible articulations in that tradition: the criteria for inclusion and exclusion, the relationship of British scholar and Indian object of study, the question of what constitutes scholarly topics and scholarly inquiry. With these transformations, the discursive terrain on which English literature is constructed shifts; the fixed exclusivity of its structures is interrupted and displaced.

I begin this chapter with Shahane's articulation of "the Indianness of the native point of view" to stress that although the tradition of British orientalism includes many texts that establish the centrality of British power and identity through the literary construction of India and Indians as Other, the discourse of orientalism does not consist solely of univocal British-generated narratives. As we have seen in the previous chapters, discursive inscription and domination are hardly uni-

---

[3]See, for example, Gayatri Spivak's "Can the Subaltern Speak?" in *Marxism and the Interpretation of Culture*, ed. Cary Nelson and Lawrence Grossberg (Urbana: University of Illinois Press, 1988); and Radha Radhakrishnan, "Toward an Effective Intellectual: Foucault or Gramsci," in *Intellectuals: Academics/Politics/Aesthetics*, ed. Bruce Robbins (Minneapolis: University of Minnesota Press, 1990).

form, but operate through a variety of unequal apparatuses at different moments. Heterogeneous, rather than homogeneous, orientalism includes a variety of positions, not only articulations of orientalist formations, but critiques of these formations as well. If the field includes that set of British texts in which the Indian is constituted as the ruled Other of the British ruler, it also includes the Indian textual responses provoked by and implicated in these texts. The discussion by Indian critics of Forster's controversial novel, and indeed all Indian criticism in English, must be considered as bearing a significant, if not paradoxical, relationship to the British-dominated institution of English literary study. Although some of the Indian work may be interpreted as reproducing traditional English ideas about literary aesthetics and genre, a significant portion of this scholarship cannot be dismissed as merely a quiescent colonial counterpart to the British literary tradition; rather it is one of the possible locations of significant challenges to the colonial hegemony that characterizes that tradition. I am not suggesting, by restricting my focus to the Indian debates in English about English literature, that it is the Indian relationship to the dominant formations of British institutions that legitimizes these articulations, nor that all contestations of these formations must be made within spaces recognized by the official discourse, for we can certainly locate equally, if not more important, insurrectionary and "subaltern" activities that occurred in spaces "outside" the British gaze.[4] My point is rather that the debates between the Indian and Anglo-American literary critics about *A Passage to India* provide a particularly illustrative example not only of the heterogeneity characteristic of discursive fields but, more particularly, of the dynamic process of intervention, dissent, and accommodation between emergent and dominant positions through which discursive formations are transformed. These debates ultimately illustrate that discursive hegemony is neither fixed nor monolithic, but that any existing hegemonic relationship exists in the context of ongoing conflicts and pressures from a variety of locations.

I begin with Shahane to signal, too, that this chapter is not primarily

[4] I am thinking here of the work of the historians of the Subaltern Studies Group, whose project is discussed further in the conclusion to the book, and the activities of worker and peasant rebellions to which these historians give their attention. See Guha and Spivak, *Selected Subaltern Studies*.

about the novel *A Passage to India* but about the intervention of Indian criticism on that novel, and the role that the Indian critics had in shifting the tradition of British orientalism. If I offer a brief discussion of the narrative of the novel, it is only to suggest some of the reasons why *A Passage to India* became a social link and literary nexus of British and Indian concerns, and how it both contributed to and broke with orientalism. In previous chapters I have considered a variety of texts— letters, travel narratives, and journals as well as novels—to propose heterogeneity as a method, to suggest that an accentuation of the heterogeneity that pervades the discourse of orientalism is one means of resisting its domination, its managing tropes. In this chapter I discuss another heterogeneous object—literary criticism—rather than reiterate the singularity of the novel-centered or author-centered study so characteristic of much literary criticism.

British Orientalism and *A Passage to India*

India lay at the core of the British imperial strategy in the late nineteenth and early twentieth centuries, "the brightest jewel in the imperial crown."[5] The British presence in India produced over a century and a half of orientalist literature—including journals, letters, novels, and stories—explicitly recording the British experience there. This literature arose from the circumstances of British rule and administration, which, since the eighteenth century, had placed British soldiers, missionaries, and civil service officers in India; at the same time, these writings contributed to and determined possible models for representing and developing British-Indian relations.

Like the French examples considered in the previous chapters, Lady Mary Wortley Montagu's *Turkish Embassy Letters* and Forster's *Passage to India* are also expressions of a complex plurality of concerns raised

[5]See Eric Hobsbawm, *The Age of Empire, 1875–1914* (New York: Random House, 1987), chap. 3. Hobsbawm gives credence to the explanation that British expansion can be accounted for in part in terms of the British need to defend the land and maritime routes to India; as India was the core of British strategy, this required control of the short sea routes to the subcontinent (Egypt, the Middle East, the Red Sea, the Persian Gulf, and south Arabia) and the long sea routes (Cape of Good Hope, Singapore). India was essential to the British economy; 60 percent of British cotton exports went to India and the Far East, between 40 and 45 percent to India alone (pp. 68–69).

by the histories of British encounters with the non-European world. Having been produced, however, by independent and unequal sets of social and historical pressures and circumstances, French and British orientalisms are clearly characterized by different literatures, and by distinct relationships between literary representations and the social situations that produce those representations. Even though both French and British orientalisms are products of European colonial encounters with non-Europeans, the French tradition does not often directly represent French colonial situations. Rather, the allegories about otherness in French orientalism tend to be literary figurations that detour or displace the problems of colonial encounter; in effect, colonialism is often not named or addressed. Furthermore, the French tradition frequently alludes to the literary figures and iconography of an Orient drawn from the previous literary tradition of orientalism, even if the narratives are associated with actual travels to the Middle East or Asia. For example, even though Flaubert's orientalist novel *Salammbô* emerges at a specific moment of French colonial expansion and war, and makes oblique, defamiliarized references to these cir- cumstances, the novel does not explicitly record the history of the French presence in Egypt or Algeria; contemporary violence is dis- placed and rendered historically Other in the dramatization of the Punic Wars. In this sense, French colonialism is often buried beneath literary representations of the Orient as temporally remote, or fictions of a distanced and imaginary oriental world. The British literature, by contrast, while including its own poetic images of the Orient as an exotic past, also contains an important body of writing that explicitly records the contemporary British experience in the colonies; this is particularly true in the case of British narratives about the rule and administration of India. Furthermore, we might observe that the French and British orientalist traditions differ with regard to the narra- tive representations of the gendered relationship between the subject and object of orientalism. Whereas Flaubert's figuration of the Orient as an eroticized woman makes use of the rhetoric and narrative struc- ture of masculine romantic desire, the British stance toward India may be generalized as being narrated, in contrast, in terms of a paternalistic metaphor that figures the colonial power as the father and the oriental object as his child, underdeveloped and in need of British protection.

Much of the British literature about India documents the experiences of authors who lived as Anglo-Indians themselves, and portrays situations contemporaneous with the authors' lifetime.[6] Missionaries, colonial administrators, members and officials of the Indian Civil Service, and their wives, wrote about India as if its people were caught in a primordial past imagined as anterior to their own society before its evolution to civilization; they represent the British presence there as a high and holy mission to save souls and to deliver the Indians from pagan sexuality. Often the poetic melancholy of the exile and misfit dominates these works, contributing to the romantic self-characterizations of the Anglo-Indians as an aristocratic culture displaced among a savage, confusing, encroaching people. In "A Real Life City" (1888) Rudyard Kipling, who may represent the foremost exemplar of the British imperial position with regard to India, writes of the Bengalis' inability to manage their own city:

> The damp, drainage-soaked soil is sick with the teeming life of a hundred years, and the Municipal Board list is choked with the names of natives—men of the breed born in and raised off this surfeited muckheap! . . . They can put up with this filthiness. They *cannot* have feelings worth caring a rush for. Let them live quietly and hide away their money under our protection, while we tax them till they know through their purses the measure of their neglect in the past. . . . Surely they might be content with all those things without entering into matters which they cannot, by the nature of their birth, understand.[7]

Kipling's invective carries out several characteristic rhetorical strategies. The language used to describe the Bengalis condemns them by attributing to them qualities of the nonhuman (for example, "breed"), while also, more significantly, physically and linguistically distancing them from the narrator's position, which is contemporary whereas they are mired in the past, healthy whereas they are sick, and singular

---

[6]See Benita Parry, *Delusions and Discoveries: Studies on India in the British Imagination, 1880–1930* (Berkeley: University of California Press, 1972); Allen Greenberger, *The British Image of India: A Study in the Literature of Imperialism, 1880–1960* (New York: Oxford University Press, 1969); Philip Mason, *The Men Who Ruled India* (London: Jonathan Cape, 1985); Michael Edwardes, *Bound to Exile: The Victorians in India* (London: Sidgwick and Jackson, 1969).

[7]Rudyard Kipling, "A Real Life City," first published in *Pioneer*, March 2, 1888; quoted in Parry, *Delusions and Discourses*, p. 212. For a discussion of twentieth-century assessments of Kipling as a spokesman for British imperialism, see Benita Parry, "The Contents and Discontents of Kipling's Imperialism," *New Formations*, no. 6 (Winter 1988): 49–63.

whereas they are the multitude. Thus, not only is the narrating subject of the passage constituted as untouched and removed from the land, which is "damp," "drainage-soaked," and "sick," but also the independence and singularity of the narrative viewpoint is distinguished from the condition of the Bengali multitude, which is "teeming," and who are so numerous that the list is "choked with the names of natives."

The British narratives feature several persistent tropes through which Indians are figured: at times the Indians are represented as incomprehensible, erotic, and lawless; at others they are portrayed as unsophisticated and childlike. Two examples from an early-twentieth-century moment of the tradition illustrate how both figurations serve a similar orientalist function of constructing the culturally different as Other in order to signify British culture as central, stable, and coherent. On the one hand, a district officer of the Indian Civil Service (I. C. S.) writes in 1924: "We are here to govern India as delegates of Christian and civilized power. We are here as representatives of Christ and Caesar to maintain this land against Shiva and Khalifa."[8] On the other hand, Sir Andrew H. L. Fraser, a former lieutenant governor of Bengal, writes in *Among Rajahs and Ryots* (1911) of his fond acquaintance with Indian country people, as opposed to educated urban Indians:

> Often in the evening they would come round . . . telling me stories of their daily life or old legends connected with the country, and acquiring that kindly familiarity with a British officer which camp life induces, and which is so valuable in the administration of India. . . . The simplicity of the country people, their confidence in the officers whom they learned to trust, their patient endurance of the severest trials, and their deep gratitude for all that was done for them, made an impression on our minds which will never be effaced.[9]

Fraser's description stresses the intimacy and familiarity between the British officers and the country people and praises the Indians for their simple, trusting behavior. For him, Indians are not wild and uncontrollable but rather agreeably comprehensible and in need of British

[8]Al. Carthill [Calcraft-Huntingdon], *The Lost Dominion* (London: Blackwood, 1924), p. 236.

[9]Andrew H. L. Fraser, *Among Rajahs and Ryots* (London: Seeley, 1911), pp. 89–91.

compassion and protection. These narrative voices of the missionary, the protector of British dominion, and the sympathetic I.C.S. officer all form parts of a discourse that figures Indian otherness to construct British subjectivity, elaborating a logic of binary complementarity in which Indian subservience becomes a signifier for British superiority. Whether India is figured as a primitive culture to be civilized or as an inferior culture to be protected, both representations of India refer to, and signify, the necessary roles of British savior and guardian. Above all, the British representations of India and Indians establish as British the position of narrative agency or subjectivity; the Indian people, landscapes, and images occupy the position of objects brought into focus by the British subject's point of view. What becomes accepted as Indian life is the textual product of British viewing and scrutiny.

Although the binary relationship of British narrating subject and Indian object of description is the rule, occasionally a mutual regard between Briton and Indian is implied. Some of the British accounts are punctuated by passages that, in acknowledging the Indian scrutiny of the British, constitute British subjectivity in relation to an anxiety about, or a consciousness of, the Indian gaze. Inasmuch as Indian objectivity is rendered by the British subject's gaze, British subjectivity is constructed as being dependent on recognition by the Indian. For example, the narrator of Y. Endrikar's *Gamblers in Happiness* (1930) represents an awareness that he may be the object gazed upon when he writes of attending church for the express purpose of being seen by Indians: "I go on principle in India to show that I am not ashamed of my religion. . . . In England I confess I take a holiday."[10] Endrikar finds it necessary to represent the ruling race in relation to what he projects the expectations of the Indians to be. Because he understands the Indians to be deeply religious, he thus imagines that Indians may be apt to judge the British as much less spiritual than themselves in spite of their regular church attendance. In other words, the Englishman comprehends himself and his own subjectivity through seeing himself as existing for the Other, understanding himself as being seen by the Other. This formation is echoed in Sir Evan Maconochie's *Life in the Indian Civil Service* (1926):

[10]Y. Endrikar, *Gamblers in Happiness* (London: Heath Cranton, 1930), p. 155.

> To the raiyat the visit of a "saheb" or a casual meeting with one has some of the qualities of excitement, which a great statesman once attributed to a circus, in the case of his English counterpart. It will be talked of for days over the village fire and remembered for years. The white man will be sized up shrewdly and frankly. So take heed unto your manners and your habits! The day is fast approaching when many villages will have their wireless set, and the Patel and his family will drive off in their bulging Ford to the nearest cinema, and then the villager will have more to think about and be far less attractive to meet.[11]

Like Endrikar, Maconochie also reveals an anxious consciousness of the Indian gaze in his description of how the entire village will "size up" the British visitor "shrewdly and frankly." Maconochie further associates this ability to view the British discriminately with the development of modernization and the introduction of products of industry into the Indian village. His association of Indian subjectivity with industrialization and westernization articulates the colonialist ideology which proposes that western imperial policy is responsible for "educating" India, that modernization is the eventual by-product of the British occupation of India, and that this modernization is made possible through contact with the West. Another version of this ideology is the notion that it is western liberal humanism that engenders an independent Indian gaze and subjectivity, indeed that English education permitted the growth of Indian nationalism by providing Indians with the tools to question colonial authority.[12] This progressive structure of development is itself an ideological narrative that continues today to subordinate countries and communities of the Third World to the modernizing West.[13] Beneath the colonialist ideology of Maco-

[11]Even Maconochie, *Life in the Indian Civil Service* (London: Chapman and Hall, 1926), pp. 48–49.

[12]For a most persuasive critique of this colonialist discourse about Indian development, see Gauri Viswanathan's analyses of Bruce McCully's *English Education and the Origins of Indian Nationalism* (1942) and David Kopf's *British Orientalism and the Bengal Renaissance* (1969), in *Masks of Conquests*.

[13]Interesting work has been done in anthropology to examine the ideological content and agenda of the "discourse of development." See, for example, Arturo Escobar, "Discourse and Power in Development: Michel Foucault and the Relevance of His Work to the Third World," *Alternatives* 10 (Winter 1984–85): 377–400. On the narrative of development, and its function in aesthetic and political discourses of representation that subordinate localities, as well as ethnic and class minorities, see David Lloyd, "Genet's Genealogy: European Minorities and the Ends of Canon," in *The Nature and Context of*

nochie's statements, however, is a more interesting rhetorical fluctu-
ation, a linguistic tremor that registers the shift from an earlier formation—of knowing British subject and known Indian object—to
another formation in which British omnipotence gives way to anxiety
and Indian impotence is refigured as a powerful and constitutive
authority. Whereas India previously served as spectacle for the colonizing viewer, in Maconochie's description it is the British "saheb"
who is rendered as "circus," as the viewed object of study.

As we have seen, then, although British orientalist discourse about
India begins with the British construction of the Indian as silent, non–
English-speaking Other, ultimately, by the twentieth century, this
discourse posits Indo-British relations as an exchange in which British
and Indians reciprocally construct one another, each subject position
existing within the context of the other, dependent on the recognition
of the other. These later British articulations of Indian scrutiny and
judgment express a British consciousness of the Indian as subject, and
express in the discourse the vulnerability of British rule in the hegemonic relationship between colonizer and colonized. British anxiety
about the Indian as subject reveals an implicit acknowledgment of
Indian subjectivity, despite the discourse's overt exclusion of Indians
from subject positions. The pressure built up by Indians on the structures of exclusion—not simply at this small space opened up in the
literary discourse, but at all levels of the social text where Indians were
subordinated or ignored—is registered by this anxious notion of Indian subjectivity embedded within the British writings about Indians.
Ironically, the English-language representation of Indians as subjects
under colonial rule constitutes one of the occasions through which
Indian writing subjectivity in English is admitted; it is with an analogous irony that I consider the Indian Forster criticism as one example
of the emergent Indian position embedded within the British-dominated discourse of English literature itself.

In the tradition of British orientalism, E. M. Forster's *Passage to India*
figures prominently as both a turning point in the tradition itself and a
nexus of critical attention. Although the centrality of Forster's novel to
the literature of British imperialism is indubitable, the purpose of my

Minority Discourse, ed. Abdul JanMohamed and David Lloyd (Oxford: Oxford University Press, 1990).

discussion is not to render Forster's novel as an exemplary representation of the tradition. Rather, what makes *A Passage to India* interesting, indeed atypical of the tradition, is the vigor and heterogeneity of the literary debates the novel aroused, and the fact that it continued to be the focus of both English and Indian criticism throughout the 1950s, 1960s, and 1970s. There were other novels, such as the journalist Edmund Candler's *Abdication* (1922) and the I.C.S. missionary Edward Thompson's *Indian Day* (1927), which portrayed the Indian predicament sympathetically and even went so far as to be critical of British imperialism and the attitudes of the Anglo-Indians; these novels, however, cannot be said to have had an equal impact on Anglo-American and Indian literary audiences. Although some of this attention by both Anglo-American and Indian critics to *A Passage to India* may have been due to Forster's status as a successful novelist and member of the Bloomsbury group, the timely and unique qualities of the novel's drama also played a role. The Indian protagonist, Dr. Aziz, falsely accused of raping a visiting Englishwoman, Adela Quested; the evocative and poetic descriptions of the Indian landscape and climate; and the tripartite novel's controversial ending section, "Temple," in which the Hindu ceremony of Gokul Ashtami is described in detail: all these elements mark *A Passage to India* as different from other novels about India. Cultural misapprehensions, dramatized through the cross-cultural friendships between the Indian Aziz and the Englishman Cyril Fielding, and between the Muslim Aziz and the Christian Mrs. Moore, further distinguish the novel. In short, the central drama of Adela's false accusation of Aziz thematizes the misapprehension of India and Indians by the British, and the Indians' continual misreading of the intentions of the British and the portrait of the ensuing hysteria among the Anglo-Indians may be interpreted as constituting a strong indictment of the British imperial posture. Furthermore, the novel departs from traditional characterizations of Indo-British relations in the emphases it places on Indian characters, culture, and religion, as well as on friendships between Britons and Indians.

Yet, although the novel differs from the traditional British literary attitude toward India, it also responds to, and is situated within, this very tradition, and thus retains particular residues of the British narrative tradition about India. The fluctuations in narrative perspective provide some illustrations of the novel's ambivalent relation to the earlier stances of British orientalism. Throughout the novel, there are many moments when the narrative perspective shifts to include the points of view of both the English and the Indian characters, accomplishing, on the level of narration, a dissolution of the oppositional relationship between British and Indian elements. Although this narrative technique challenges the customary relation of British narrator and Indian object of description, the narrative perspective at times returns to a position outside the drama, a position culturally coded as British and distinctly non-Indian. For example, in these descriptions of Aziz the narrative perspective is similar to one inherited from earlier British orientalism:

> Like most Orientals, Aziz overrated hospitality, mistaking it for intimacy, and not seeing that it is tainted with the sense of possession. It was only when Mrs. Moore or Fielding was near him that he saw further, and knew that it is more blessed to receive than to give.

> Suspicion in the Oriental is a sort of malignant tumor, a mental malady, that makes him self-conscious and unfriendly suddenly; he trusts and mistrusts at the same time in a way the Westerner cannot comprehend. It is his demon, as the Westerner's is hypocrisy.[14]

In both passages the narrator generalizes Aziz's emotionality as a racial and ethnic trait. In these cases the narrator assumes the British orientalist posture inherited from the previous tradition, while at other times the narrative calls attention to the paradoxical status and location of the narrator.

An example of the paradoxical situation of the British narrator of Indian scenes occurs during the description of the Hindu ceremony in the last section of the novel:

> Hindus sat on either side of the carpet where they could find room, or overflowed into the adjoining corridors and the courtyard—Hindus, Hindus only, mild-featured men, mostly villagers, for whom anything outside their villages passed in a dream. They were the toiling ryot, whom some call the real India. Mixed with them sat a few tradesmen out of the little town, officials, courtiers, scions of the ruling house. Schoolboys kept inefficient order. The assembly was in a tender, happy state unknown to an English crowd.   (pp. 283–84)

[14]E. M. Forster, *A Passage to India* (New York: Harcourt, Brace and World, 1924), pp. 142–43, 279–80.

The narrative describes a Hindu ceremony from which all but Hindus are excluded, and underscores this exclusivity with several deictic markers: "Hindus, Hindus only" and "a tender, happy state unknown to an English crowd." The situation of description foregrounds the paradox that the narrator must be at once absent as excluded non-Hindu, yet present as narrative witness of the ceremony. The very marking of this paradox foregrounds and thematizes the narrative problems of a British novel about India and Indians, and confesses the structural limitations of the British subject's ability to render Indians as other than objects of description. The Indian in a British novel is always marked by British presence, and rendered by means of British observations. This is expressed later in the same scene when an inscription to honor a Hindu supreme being is "composed in English to indicate His universality," and "consisted, by an unfortunate slip of the draughtsman, of the words, 'God si love'" (p. 285). Not only does this presence of English in a gathering of "Hindus, Hindus only" draw attention to the pervasive extent of British rule, but also the miscomposition "God si love" is a comic emblem of two cultural misunderstandings, the rendering of the Hindu concept into English and the Indian appropriation of this Anglicized rendition. The predicament of ambivalence described in this scene is echoed in the many instances of cultural misinterpretation that fill the novel: the Englishwomen cannot understand Mrs. Bhattacharya's inviting them to her home at a time when she will not be there; Aziz mistakes Fielding's remark about "post-impressionism" as a condescension; Adela misunderstands Muslims when she asks Aziz if he has more than one wife, and then tragically misconceives Indians when she hallucinates the attack in the cave; Aziz mistakes the facts of Fielding's marriage; and so on. The novel contains an assortment of anecdotes that record the misinterpretation of the one culture by the other, and in this portrait of Indo-British misreadings, the problematic western representation of the Orient is pointedly thematized.

But the text of the novel alone does not explain the status of *A Passage to India* as a turning point in British orientalism. Its importance is rather to a great extent the result of the way the novel has been constituted and appropriated by a variety of schools of criticism. Since *A Passage to India* has attracted criticism from British, North American, and particularly Indian commentators, the reception of the novel has been marked by a relationship in which the Anglo-American and the Indian literary traditions mutually construct each other by commenting on this text that links and emblematizes a variety of both groups' national concerns. The attention of the Indian scholars has contributed to the novel's singular prominence in the field of English literature; at the same time Forster's novel has offered an occasion for Indians to enter the discourse and has been an important vehicle for certain kinds of Indian critical visibility.

Orientalism and Anglo-American Forster Criticism

It is noteworthy that one of the first significant dialogues between Indian and British intellectuals should occur in the discussion of a British novel, which in itself represents one of the patterns of British rule and Indian accommodation: the Indian acceptance of the condition that this dialogue take place in the English language and deal with English texts. Forster's enigmatic novel about Indo-British misunderstanding became a locus of these dialogues not only because it was a British novel that represented with sympathy the Indian position in Indo-British relations, and one of the first to feature an Indian protagonist, but more practically because its publication coincided with an increase in the number of Indians entering the discipline of English literature. Functioning as a "rupture" in the British representations of Indians, *A Passage to India* provided an occasion for Indian entry into what had previously been a British-dominated tradition. The Indian scholarship about the Forster novel is situated, and so marks itself, within the context of British and North American critical work; indeed, every Indian critic writing on *A Passage to India* writes in English and addresses or responds to previous work by British and American figures in Forster criticism (and, quite often, also by Forster himself). In this sense, the Indian commentary is always defined in relation to the presence of Anglo-American criticism; the dialogues of dissent and accommodation within the field of Forster criticism reproduce the larger "dialogues" of British power, occupation, and administration, and Indian subjugation, noncooperation, and independence.

At the risk of oversimplification, it may be useful to characterize some of the historical patterns particular to the execution of British rule and the development of Indian independence, and relevant to the tensions and dissensions present in the Indian debates about *A Passage to India*. The British came to power in India in the eighteenth century by defeating the Mughal princes who had ruled since the sixteenth century, and through turning the instability of Mughal control to the British advantage. One of the primary means by which the British continued their economic control over ever larger portions of India while securing and expanding cultural control over the people was through a rigorous anglicization of the Indian landlord and merchant-banker classes; for the classes of Indians who eventually aided the British in establishing regional controls over India in the eighteenth and nineteenth century were schooled in the extensive legal, administrative, and educational system imposed by the British. After the Great Mutiny of 1857, however, the British redirected these efforts to rule through anglicization of the Indians, and in order to maintain British rule paid more attention to what they understood to be the traditional Indian system of caste and privilege. Eric Wolf argues that although the Mutiny was defeated, the violent outbreaks of the 1850s brought a sudden realization that the British control over India was tenuous, and the rulers "abandoned the idea of reforming India through the application of English liberal ideas, and strove instead to strengthen what they regarded as Indian traditions."[15] There arose what Francis Hutchins has called an "attempted orientalization of British rule." This orientalization presumed that "Indians could not be changed, and furthermore that the superiority of the British character presented no obstacles to a full understanding of Indians." This policy advocated separation and hierarchization of the British and Indians. As Englishmen constructed a myth of their own omniscience, there also evolved the myth of the "real India." This was conceived of as "the ancient India of the countryside; and of retainers and dependents of British power, of princes, peasants, and minority groups. Indians who lived in cities, engaged in business and the professions, who were not dependent on British favor, without an interest in preserving for themselves a privileged position guaranteed by British might, were desig-

[15]Eric Wolf, *Europe and the People without History* (Berkeley: University of California Press, 1982), pp. 251–52.

nated as 'unrepresentative.' "[16] Thus, it was through a British notion of Indianization that British hegemony was maintained during the latter portion of the century. In other words, the British administration of India was initially executed through the compliance of the Indian upper classes, and through an anglicization of the Indians, whereas in the post-Mutiny period, faced with the possibility of losing India as a dominion, the British attempted to reinforce traditional Indian hierarchies to quell dissent and maintain rule. In the early twentieth century it was India's identification of itself as "Indian," and the power of this notion to unify diverse Indians—Hindus, Muslims, Sikhs, Jains, "representative" or not—which enabled the Indians to demand independence as a nation. By the 1920s Indian-led nationalist and independence movements had grown, fueled by peasant and worker rebellions, as well as by many successful actions of noncooperation and civil disobedience practiced under the direction of Mahatma Gandhi. India achieved independence in 1947.

In the set of debates about *A Passage to India* among the Indian critics, one can trace a similar controversy regarding the roles of anglicization and Indianization with regard to the Indian critical project. If it is fair to generalize and say that the very instruments and strategies of British rule (that is, the British project of Indianization following 1850) provided some of the foundational context for the emergence of the Indian independence movement, then one can see analogous tensions reflected in the Indian discussions of Forster's novel. In the debates about Hindu and Islamic influences on Forster's novel, about the novel's political or religious merits, and about the novel's representation of Indians, significant members of the group of Indian critics take positions that might lead to an argument for an Indianization of English literary criticism, and particularly of English literary criticism about Forster. The emergence of an Indian literary critical voice is focused in the discussion of Forster's novel, a novel whose very writing and circumstances of writing (the social and political policies that placed Forster in India at the time, for example) express the conditions of British imperial rule. In other words, without promoting the colonialist assumption that Indian development was set in motion by

[16]Francis Hutchins, *The Illusion of Permanence: British Imperialism in India* (Princeton: Princeton University Press, 1967), pp. 155, 156. See also Michael Edwardes, *British India, 1772–1947: A Survey of the Nature and Effects of Alien Rule* (New York: Taplinger, 1967).

British imperialism, one can still remark that the very history of British rule—including not only the elaborate British educational and administrative occupation of India but also the imposition of the English language itself—contributed to the apparatuses, in paradoxically both a productive and a regulatory sense, through which these Indian intellectuals came to study and write about English literature. The irony remains that the dialogues between English, American, and Indian intellectuals, addressed, in English, the subject of an Englishman's novel; it was only in the 1980s that dialogues between these communities began to take place around Indian literary works in English.[17]

In the discourse of British orientalism, the Anglo-American literary critical response to *A Passage to India* functions in many ways as an analogue for the earlier British position toward Indians. Just as the British narrating subject in literary orientalism had access to language and to the representation of Indians, Anglo-American literary criticism, from the period beginning in the late 1920s through the 1960s, reiterated this exclusion of Indians from the discourse. This exclusion was performed, on the one hand, by critics who either dismissed or studiously overlooked discussion of India or Indians as factors in the literary value of the novel and, on the other hand, by the structure of the literary institution itself, which reflected the scarcity of Indian critics writing about English literature. For although Bhupal Singh's landmark book of criticism, *A Survey of Anglo-Indian Fiction*, which includes a short chapter on *A Passage to India*, appeared in 1934, the greater part of Indian criticism of Forster emerged during the 1950s and 1960s, after independence, and after it became acceptable for a certain number of Indians to enter the British-dominated field.

Curiously, until after Forster's death in 1970, the majority of Anglo-American criticism on *A Passage to India* was written by critics in the United States.[18] Lionel Trilling explained the American attention as

[17]I am referring here to the relatively recent Anglo-American critical attention given to Indian immigrant and diaspora novelists such as Bharati Mukherjee, Salman Rushdie, and Hanif Kureishi, and to the interpretation of Indian literature in the context of colonialism and postcolonialism. See, for example, Timothy Brennan, *Salman Rushdie and the Third World* (New York: St. Martin's, 1989), and *South Atlantic Quarterly* 87, no. 1 (Winter 1988), on Third World literatures.

[18]Other than Rose Macaulay's 1938 book-length study of Forster, the attention given to *A Passage to India* by British critics was primarily editorial (for example, Oliver

being due to "the superiority Americans could feel at the English botch of India."[19] The appreciations of Forster's work in the United States might be characterized as thematic, archetypal, and formalist; they have viewed the novel in terms that strictly separate literary and philosophical criteria from issues such as the history of the British presence in India and its influence on the novel or, equally, the novel's representation of these social and historical circumstances.[20] Most of the American criticism of the 1950s was characterized by this distinct separation of "literary" from historical context: E. K. Brown's study of rhythm (1950), Reuben A. Brower's analysis of irony (1951), and Gertrude White's essay on the dialectical pattern of the novel (1953) exemplify this type of study. In the 1960s, critics such as Frederick Crews (1962), Wilfrid Stone (1966), and George Thomson (1967) continued to discuss the novel in terms of the limits of its humanism, its use of symbols and archetypes, the author's narrative voice, and the tripartite dramatic structure.

Within this formalist approach, the novel was most often accounted for by being seen as the culminating treatment of themes introduced in Forster's previous novels. In considering the novel within a chrono-

---

Stallybrass's Abinger editions of Forster's novels). Most criticism during Forster's lifetime focused on the earlier novels (which seem more easily characterized as Edwardian, as not modernist). After his death, when most of the material revealing Forster's homosexuality emerged and became accessible, a number of British biographies and works of criticism considered Forster in terms of his sexuality. See John Colmer, *E. M. Forster: The Personal Voice* (London: Routledge and Kegan Paul, 1975); Francis King, *E. M. Forster and His World* (London: Thames and Hudson, 1975); and especially P. N. Furbank's authorized biography *E. M. Forster: A Life* (New York: Harcourt Brace Jovanovich, 1977).

My discussion does not specifically concern itself with Forster's homosexuality. What is of interest to me is the role attributed to India and Forster's Indian friends by the post-1970 British biographies of Forster—that is, how the biographers form a narrative that reconciles Forster's two notable "deviant" fascinations, with India and with other men. King's biography, for example, which is very much concerned with Forster's "pederasty" and "onanism," associates Forster's first trip to India with his homosexual interest in Syed Ross Masood and represents Forster's interest in India as homoerotic; there is no mention of any cultural or political interest in India and the Indian people, a view that is, of course, in absolute contrast with the Indian discourse, which never mentions Forster's homosexuality and represents Forster's interest in India as purely cultural and politically sympathetic.

[19]Lionel Trilling, *E. M. Forster* (Norfolk: New Directions, 1943), p. 123.

[20]Greenberger, *The British Image of India*, and Parry, *Delusions and Discoveries*, as well as M. M. Mahood, *The Colonial Encounter* (Totowa, N.J.: Rowman and Littlefield, 1977), are some of the few British and American works for which the context of British colonial rule of India is crucial to the discussion of the novel.

logical development of themes traced through *The Longest Journey* to *A Room With a View* to *Howards End*, as did Peter Burra (1934), Crews, and Thomson, the criticism leveled the different social and political positions of Indians. India is considered a colorful backdrop, a literary device or leitmotif, a new setting in which to treat the same questions. Burra writes about the theme of "the clash of opposites": "The intrusion of the English at Mau is incidental and designed only to reintroduce what is the real theme of the book—the friendship of Fielding and Dr. Aziz. The rocks that rise between them on their last ride together, the horses that swerve apart—they symbolize Indian differences, it is true, but differences that are not more great, only more particular, than the differences that exist between any two men, between Philip and Gino, Ricky and Stephen, Schlegels and Wilcoxes."[21] Later critics such as Barbara Rosecrance (1982) considered *A Passage to India* to be an eccentric break with the previous novels; yet this inverse interpretation serves an identical purpose—that is, avoiding an engagement with the novel's treatment of Indian difference through a logic that constructs it as anomalous, as too different. Rosecrance contrasts the early Forster with the late: "But *A Passage to India* presents a new cosmos. Vanished are Italian landscapes and English countryside. Instead, Forster has given us India, monstrous, extraordinary, chaotic, a context in which humanity can never be easy, a symbol, rather of man's helplessness and alienation."[22] The interpretations that find continuity are not dissimilar to those that find discontinuity; both narratives construct relationships among Forster's novels rather than engaging with the historical circumstances of the British in India, of which the novel is a representation as well as a product.

The 1950s also produced a strain of "philosophical" commentaries on the novel among the American critics. Glen O. Allen (1955) and James McConkey (1957) considered the Indian influences on the novel's structure and symbology. These American interpretations of the novel represented the first attempts to take as a central problem of interpretation the forceful role of Indian culture and symbols. Allen's and McConkey's readings of the novel as a dramatization of Hindu concepts stimulated both interest and controversy among the Indian

[21]Peter Burra, *The Novels of E. M. Forster* (London: Whitefriars Press, 1934), p. 35.
[22]Barbara Rosecrance, *Forster's Narrative Vision* (Ithaca: Cornell University Press, 1982), p. 241.

critics. Indeed, the Indian critics who examine Hindu symbology both address and specifically take issue with Allen and McConkey; M. Sivaramakrishna, among many others, declares that Allen's view of the *margas* is "confused" and "in error."[23] The particulars of this debate are discussed later in this chapter, but what is important to these remarks about the dialogic and mutually constitutive relationship between the Anglo-American and Indian criticisms is that the Indian entrance into the discourse of orientalism is made possible by the address of, and in this case the refutation of, Anglo-American representations of Indians; the representation and appropriation of India as Other offers the opening for the Indian response that follows.

The Indian Debates

When Indian criticism on Forster generally began to emerge during the 1950s and 1960s, Forster, at that time in his mature seventies and eighties, was offering encouragement to his Indian friends as scholars and writers.[24] The major figures in the Indian branch of Forster scholarship include Vasant A. Shahane, Nirad Chaudhuri, G. K. Das, and C. L. Sahni, although a number of other professors, authors, and officials have written influential articles on Forster and *A Passage to India*.[25] The Indian materials naturally contain a variety of approaches

[23]M. Sivaramakrishna, "Marabar Caves Revisited," in Shahane, *Focus on Forster's "A Passage to India*," p. 16.

[24]Forster first visited India in 1912, and finished *A Passage to India* after his second visit (when he served as secretary to the Maharajah of Dewas) in 1922–23. He made a third trip to visit friends in 1945. Some of his Indian friends, including the scholars and writers he encouraged, are the authors and editors of affectionate tributes to the novelist. See especially K. Natwar-Singh, ed., *E. M. Forster: A Tribute* (New York: Harcourt Brace, 1964); H. H. Anniah Gowda, ed., *A Garland for E. M. Forster* (Mysore: Literary Half-Yearly, 1969); Mulk Raj Anand, "Under the Chestnut Tree in Tavistock Square with E. M. Forster and Leonard Woolf," in *Conversations in Bloomsbury* (New Delhi: Arnold-Heinemann, 1981).

[25]Vasant A. Shahane is very widely acclaimed in Forster studies with many publications, including *E. M. Forster: A Reassessment* (New Delhi: Kitab Mihal, 1963); *Perspectives on E. M. Forster's "A Passage to India"* (New York: Barnes and Noble, 1968); *"A Passage to India": A Study* (London: Oxford University Press, 1977).

See also Nirad Chaudhuri's "Passage to and from India," *Encounter* 2, no. 6 (June 1954), 19–24; G. K. Das, *E. M. Forster's India* (Totowa, N.J.: Rowman and Littlefield, 1977); Chaman L. Sahni, *Forster's "A Passage to India": The Religious Dimension* (Atlantic Highlands, N.J.: Humanities Press, 1981).

and rhetorics, but there are several debates that recur, expressing in the terms of their opposing arguments particular Indian concerns and specific methods for identifying "Indianness."

Whether they address Hindu or Muslim influences on the structure of the novel, commend or criticize the portraits of India and Indians, or argue for or against the historical realism of the novel, what is common to the Indian criticism is the articulated attention given to the writing position from which India and Indians are represented. The arguments critical to the debates mark the differences between the representation of India by the non-Indian and the Indian representation of Indian culture. For even though many Indian critics hail *A Passage to India* as an emblem of British understanding of the Indian, and the first "successful" representation of Indian life, the very fact of writing by the Indian critic is a crucial disruption of the model in which British subjects write about Indian objects. Indianness is established not merely as the explanations of India that are in contradistinction to occidental misinterpretations, but as the establishment of writing positions that alter and revise the relationship between the binary poles of British writing subject and Indian object, that diversify and transform the scope, language, and criteria of the field of English literature.

In light of the Indian concern with establishing and distinguishing Indianness, it is not surprising that the Indian critics tend to analyze the novel in terms of Indian cultural influences, both Hindu and Muslim. Book-length studies by C. L. Sahni and V. A. Shahane consider the Hindu and Muslim religious and philosophical influences on the narrative structure, the resolution of dramatic conflict, and the portrayal of characters in the novel. The writers who wish to argue that the novel privileges Hinduism and utilizes Hindu symbology tend to concentrate on the novel's ending section, "Temple," whereas those who understand the novel in terms of Islamic influence tend to discuss the strength of the central protagonist, Aziz, a Muslim doctor. Other analyses also center on the question of Indian influences: essays by H. H. Anniah Gowda, M. Sivaramakrishna, and G. Nageswara Rao consider primarily Indian influences on the novel; K. Natwar-Singh, Mulk Raj Anand, Shahane, and Raja Rao establish the Indian influences on Forster the man and author. There is also considerable debate about the merits of the book as a political allegory or a religious novel, and, in addition, as to whether Forster himself was a political or a religious man. Sahni and Shahane expressly choose not to treat *A Passage to India* as a political novel, preferring to consider it as a work whose ending symbolizes Hindu notions of reconciliation and unity. Forster's own claim that "in writing it . . . my main purpose was not political, was not even sociological" is often cited by critics—British, American, and Indian alike—who wish to distinguish the novel as a literary object separate from the social and political conditions of which it is a product. It is worth noting that a majority of the Indian criticism that concentrates on Indian influence does not treat the novel as a political allegory of British imperialism; rather, the critics concerned with Indianness limit their discussions to questions of Indian culture and religion and do not mention either the political allegory in the novel or the political circumstances of its writing.

Some Indian critics, such as G. K. Das, do evaluate the novel primarily in terms of its political references and meanings. Das's study *E. M. Forster's India* (1977) examines the ways in which the Islamic conflicts with Britain during the period before the First World War enabled Forster to express at one time his sympathies toward Muslim Indians and their desires for Islamic unity, as well as his Liberal disenchantment with British imperialism. Das's book argues that it is this sympathy for Muslims which is expressed in the dimension of political allegory in *A Passage to India*. Referring to instances in Forster's essays that criticize British imperial policy, Das asserts that although Forster did not explicitly declare a pro-Indian position, the criticism of British policy implies a pro-Indian stance. Das argues that the novel renders with sympathy both the plight of Indian subjection during the period of British rule and the necessity for Indian independence; for these reasons Das considers the novel strongly political.

In distinct contrast, Nirad Chaudhuri (1954) and M. K. Naik (in Shahane 1975) assess the weaknesses of the novel as political allegory. It is the interventions of these two critics, I would suggest, that accomplish the greatest displacement of Anglo-American literary criticism. Because they neither limit their discussion of the novel to terms of literary and aesthetic evaluation nor reiterate praise for the novel as an emblem of the British-Indian relationship, Chaudhuri and Naik problematize the Anglo-American terms of the debate. Unlike the many Indian critics who laud the accuracy and justness of the novel's portrait of the Indian situation, Chaudhuri and Naik, each in differently emphasized arguments, consider the novel both an inadequate representation of Hindus and Muslims and an oversimplification, and therefore an obfuscation, of the political dimensions of Indo-British relations. Chaudhuri strongly criticizes the reduction of the "cultural apartheid" of Indo-British politics into the personalized relationship between two men, Aziz and Fielding: "At the root of all this lies the book's tacit but confident assumption that Indo-British relations presented a problem of personal behavior and could be tackled on a personal plane. They did not and could not." He further objects to the implication that India is primarily Muslim, because the Indian protagonist of the novel is the Muslim doctor Aziz; he points out that India is not only more diverse that this but also not predominantly Muslim but Hindu. In addition, Chaudhuri expresses disdain for the representation of Aziz as servile, simple, and hotheaded, arguing that many Muslims were fiercely anti-British and would not have accepted a subservient role. Naik is also critical of the novel as a portrait of race relations in the India of the 1920s: "First, considered as a historical document or a picture of race-relations, the novel is patently inadequate in conception and lop-sided in the presentation of its material." Like K. Natwar-Singh (in Shahane 1975), Naik points out that the novel collapses a notion of Indo-British relations as they existed in prewar India into that of India during the 1920s, and that this conflation renders invisible the noncooperation and civil disobedience movements of Mahatma Gandhi, as well as other organized efforts toward Indian independence which had begun by 1920. Naik argues further that the nostalgic Aziz "does not represent the average educated Nationalist Indian youth of the period. . . . Aziz, with his face turned back towards Babar and the medieval imperial glory of the Muslims, is totally unrepresentative of the mind of India during the 1920s." The novel, he adds, offers very inadequate portraits of both Islamic and Hindu beliefs: Godbole and the Hindu doctor Panna Lal are drawn from stereotypes, and the description of the Gokul Ashtami ceremony in the "Temple" section is a comic parody.[26]

Despite the interventions by Chaudhuri and Naik, however, there are evident limits to the degree to which the Indian scholars' articula-

[26]Chaudhuri, "Passage to and from India," p. 119; M. K. Naik, "A Passage to Less than India," in Shahane, *Focus on Forster's "A Passage to India,"* p. 63.

tions as a whole shift the discourse. I will discuss some of these in greater detail in the next section. For the moment it is enough to remark that because certain criteria remain unchallenged—the use of English as the language in which the intervention must be made, and Forster's English novel as object of study—neither the critical discussions about the political merits of the novel nor the debates about the religious dimension of Indian influences ever represents an exclusively Indian dialogue: that is, Indian critics addressing interpretations by other Indians. Rather, it must be emphasized that the Indian debates are always inscribed in a context already marked by the English literary critics. For example, the Indian critics who examine Hindu symbology address and specifically disagree with the Anglo-American—and not the Indian—critics who attempt to draw parallels between the novel and Hinduism. Glen O. Allen's "Structure, Symbol, and Theme in E. M. Forster's *A Passage to India*" (1955) interprets the structure and resolution of the novel in terms of a Hindu theme, identifying the three sections of the novel, "Mosques," "Caves," and "Temple," with the "trichotomous division" of the Hindu attitude toward life and the doctrine of salvation: *Karma Marga* (path of action), *Jnana Marga* (path of knowledge), and *Bhakti Marga* (path of devotion). Allen's interpretation is refuted by *all* of the Indian scholars who address the issue of Hindu influences and symbolism. C. L. Sahni dismisses Allen and other American critics for not shedding any light on the problem of Forster's knowledge of fundamental concepts of Indian thought and the sources of that knowledge. M. Sivaramakrishna targets Allen's "astonishing statement" that the mysticism underlying devotion to Shri Krishna amounts to an "utter renunciation of the intellect, the disintegration of the categories which make distinction, and therefore thought, possible" (p. 16). T. G. Vaidyanathan argues that the American critics have mistakenly placed undue emphasis on one branch of Hinduism, *Advaita Vedanta*, exaggerating it while ignoring the implications of the other branches. Thus, the Allen interpretation focuses a number of Indian concerns; as the center of certain Indian objections, the controversy foregrounds the history and context of the Indian criticism: an American elucidating Hindu concepts in Forster's novel is entirely different from an Indian, even a Muslim Indian, proposing the same.[27] At issue is the position from

[27]Athough Das, *E. M. Forster's India*, treats primarily the Islamic influences on the novel, Das also criticizes Allen: "According to Allen, Forster portrays the three Hindu

which a culture is characterized; the refutation of Allen by the Indians calls attention to the different social texts within which American and Indian criticisms are situated. In *E. M. Forster: A Reassessment*, Shahane, who also addresses Allen's thesis, states this premise ever so politely: "It is odd that no Indian has contributed anything significant towards interpreting *A Passage to India*. It may be conceded that such a critic, in a limited way, enjoys advantages denied to an Englishman or American. Trilling, says F. R. Leavis, could see 'England and the particular milieu to which Forster as a writer belongs, well from the outside.' An Indian critic is perhaps even better placed than an American in relation to *A Passage to India*."[28] One essential component, then, of the Indianness named by Shahane is the marking of difference between the representation of India by the non-Indian and the representation by Indians of their own culture. Indianness is established, in these debates, as an explanation of India from a different social and historical writing position in contradistinction to occidental representation of Indians as Other.

Critical Legacies of Orientalism

I have suggested that within the discourse of orientalism there exists at all moments a variety of conflicting and converging discursive positions and formations. Any orthodoxy or hegemony within the discourse must always be founded on heterodoxy, a condition of difference; the simultaneous inscription of the orthodox and the heterodox is the necessary condition of any moment of the discourse. To illustrate this scene of heterodoxy, I have explored a series of heterogeneous sites of contestation: the critical role of Forster with regard to the previous tradition of British writing about India, the different discursive positions of the Anglo-American literary establishment and the Indian literary critics, and the rhetorical and interpretive diversity among the Indian critics' assessments of Forster and his work. By complicating the notion of discourse in this way, however, I do not

---

ways in the three parts of the novel in order to advocate that a wholesome way ought to be a combination of all three 'in proportion.' But in Hindu philosophy it is in fact thought that a life lived according to any one of the three ways actually partakes of elements of the other two, and may lead to perfection of the entire self" (pp. 141–42).

[28]Shahane, *E. M. Forster: A Reassessment*, p. 21.

mean to underestimate the existence of powerful regulating formations within the discourse. What I address in this section is the role
and power of orthodoxy in orientalist discourse. Participation in the
discourse can require accommodation to its orthodox components,
and despite changes in the modes of participation, the discourse may
overdetermine and restrict the spectrum of differences. In this sense a
discussion of how the structures of argument used in Indian criticism
of *A Passage to India* bear traces of logic inherited from British discussions is one means of elucidating the dynamic of orthodoxy within
heterodox conditions.

I have already mentioned that in the 1950s and 1960s Anglo-American criticism of Forster's novel very rarely mentioned the history of the
British in India as a formative condition for the writing of the text.
What is equally striking is that the analyses of the Indian critics for the
most part also steered away from explicit discussion of the cultural and
political imperialism through which the British occupied and managed
India for nearly 150 years. In the examination of formal features of the
novel—such as symbols, archetypes, and characterization—there was
a tendency on the part of the literary critical establishment, both
Anglo-American and Indian alike, to separate the literary and textual
from the social or historical, and by implication nonliterary. In stating
that the Anglo-American literary criticism about *A Passage to India* was
an extension of the tradition of British orientalism which constituted
itself as a central and coherent power through the objectification of the
Indian people as peripheral and Other, I have already implied that the
English and American critics had a vested interest in the separation of
literary and historical domains.[29] For in omitting, or obfuscating, the
relationships between the historical conditions of social and literary
production and the structure, rhetoric, and language of the texts produced, it was possible to limit the referentiality of the text—that is, the
degree to which it could be a political allegory about the decline of
British influence in India, as well as a condemnation of British presence in India during the 1920s. Likewise, the Anglo-American separa-

[29]My discussion treats British and North American literary criticism as connected and
complementary traditions, which is not to ignore the differences among critics in England and in the United States but to appreciate the profound ties between, on the one
hand, the two academic communities and, on the other hand, the history of political
alliances and diplomatic sympathies uniting Britain and the United States during the
twentieth century.

tion of the literary from the historical narrowed the recognized scope of literary language and concerns, and produced a literary exclusivity that tended to delimit the novel as a discretely English object, inasmuch as this delimiting served to erect obstacles to Indian participation in this exclusive literary discussion.

One might suppose that with the beginning of Indian criticism of the novel, a wider discussion of the relationship between the literary and the historical would have taken place. Although this did occur to some extent, it is interesting to note the degree to which many of the Indian discussions perpetuated distinctions between the literary and the historical practiced by the Anglo-American critics, continuing, for example, a muting of the ties between Forster's text and the conditions of British rule which were the occasion for his writing the novel. Just as the occasion for the entry of the Indian critics into the discussion of English literature necessarily had to be the work of an English author, it seems equally clear that participation in the dialogue was restricted and disciplined in other ways—not only in terms of the objects of discussion but also in terms of the critical framework and possible methods used to interpret these objects.

As a result, as in the Anglo-American discussions, the situation of the novel as an expression and consequence of British rule in India is not always explicit in the Indian studies, and when it is addressed, the British presence in India is invoked as a preliminary to the praise of Forster and his work as exceptions to a long history of British misunderstanding of the Indians. Among thirty essays by Indian scholars, only two (those by Chaudhuri and Naik) are overtly critical of British representations of Indians in Forster's novel as a symptom of the British imperial tradition ruling, and misunderstanding, the Indians. Among the book-length Indian studies of *A Passage to India*, the relationship between British rule and the writing of the novel is a central concern only in G. K. Das's *E. M. Forster's India*. Only here does the notion of history as a context for the writing of literature emerge as an explicit focus of the discussion. The general problem of the representation of Indians by British writers is not widely discussed in the larger body of Indian criticism, and other than the two essays by Chaudhuri and Naik, all the studies hail Forster as the first British novelist to represent Indian character and culture accurately and sympathetically. Many of the essays and tributes to Forster express similar praise and base their eulogies on examples of either Forster's understanding or the novel's successfully "realistic" representation of social and historical situations in India.

But the standard of realism as a predominant means by which the value of Forster's work is assessed by the Indian critics is not a neutral methodology or criterion. The model of realistic representation, based on a faith in the project of mimesis as well as an acceptance of an unproblematic relationship between representation and the historical fact represented, is strongly present in the tradition of European historical narrative. The long tradition of European historical realism relies on an accepted separation of the discourses and methodologies of science and art, between, on the one hand, a positivist paradigm which assumes the possibility of apprehending historical knowledge through the mimetic representation of events in narrative and, on the other, linguistic and literary modes of representation (the poetic and tropological); the "realist" historical project has been traditionally associated with the scientific paradigm.[30] My aim here is not to discuss the validity of the notion of realistic representation, although the mimetic project is certainly a troubled and inexact one, particularly if we understand that in the act of representing, the very mark and act of representation necessarily attests to the absence (or "difference") of the object or concept for which the mark stands, for the incommensurability of the signifier and signified. Rather, more significant to this discussion is, first, that an epistemological legacy separating the historical from the literary is accepted for the most part by the Indian critics. And second, in the few studies in which the boundaries between the historical and the literary are explored, the nineteenth-century European notion of history as representable fact, rather than something narrativized and literary, is accepted and employed.

Thus, when the relationship between the novel and the history of British rule in India is addressed, it is evaluated in terms of its "realistic" representation of British-Indian relations. Das, for example, draws parallels between the Amritsar massacre in 1919 and the riots sur-

---

[30]The criticism of the distinction between science and art has been the subject of many studies. For example, a discussion of the poetic and tropological aspects of European historical writing is the focus of Hayden White's *Metahistory: The Historical Imagination in Nineteenth-Century Europe* (Baltimore: Johns Hopkins University Press, 1973). See also Dominick LaCapra, "Rhetoric and History," in *History and Criticism* (Ithaca: Cornell University Press, 1985).

rounding the trial of Aziz; he further notes that the events at Amritsar included an incident involving an Englishwoman, Miss F. Marcella Sherwood, who had been "brutally assaulted by a group of Indians," after which fifty Indians were made to crawl across a public square while others were subjected to public floggings. The portrait of Anglo-Indian hysteria following Adela Quested's accusation of Aziz, Das suggests, alludes to these historical events, thus demonstrating Forster's sympathies for the Indians and his criticism of British imperialism. Throughout *E. M. Forster's India*, using the standard of realism to praise Forster, Das is concerned with recuperating Forster as a true advocate of Indian nationalism, even though Forster was not "pro-Indian"; he "looked at the issue between India and British Imperialism dispassionately, and although ideologically he disliked an empire, he was not carried away by his ideological differences to condemn the British Empire outright." In discussing the growing Muslim discontent as Britain and Turkey became enemies in the First World War, Das asserts that Forster defended Islamic unity through his writings, including the portrait of Aziz in *A Passage to India*: "Although [Forster] did not wish to support the Khilafat as an institution, he was strongly opposed to Britain's continued conflicts with Turkey after the First World War." At certain moments Das's book even verges on being an apology for the ambiguity of Forster's novel, a politicizing interpretation of Forster's apolitical stance. Although Das's book provides the most thorough argument for the political content of Forster's literary work, this sentiment that Forster was a "true friend" to Indians is repeated by almost all of the other Indian critics. Narayana Menon writes of the novel: "Today it has become synonymous with any bridge of sympathy and understanding that exists between two countries and civilizations. The intimacy with which Forster enters into the mind of Indians is astonishing, almost incredible." "To speak of Forster is, in a way, to speak of a saint," writes Raja Rao.[31] One cannot but be struck by the intense desire, on Das's part and among many of the Indian critics, to find in Forster an Englishman who truly sympathizes with the Indian, and in his work a profound object of unity between Britons and Indians.

---

[31]Das, *E. M. Forster's India*, pp. 23–24, 55–56. Narayana Menon, "Recollection of E. M. Forster," p. 11, and Raja Rao, "Recollection of E. M. Forster," p. 15, both in Natwar-Singh, *E. M. Forster: A Tribute*.

The standard of realism is also used for quite a different purpose in some of the critical Indian essays. Natwar-Singh and Naik both argue that the representation of India in the novel is *not* realistic. Natwar-Singh points out that "it depicts a pre-1914 India, and by the time it was published in 1924 events had overtaken it. It appears to be an almost anti-national book since it makes no mention of the political ferment that was going on in India in the early twenties." But although Natwar-Singh defends Forster on this account, Naik does not. Naik charges that the leveling of the pre- and postwar Indias into one produces a "serious lacuna"; the representation of India in the 1920s as one that contained elements dating from before 1914 levels and mutes the conflicts between Indian nationalists and the British in the years following the First World War. "There is not a single—not even a passing—reference in the novel to Mahatma Gandhi and the Civil Disobedience movement of 1920." Naik's observation about the novel is that it is neither realistic nor historical enough, that it obscures the history of British rule and, more important, the history of Indian opposition. In other words, the standard of realism continues to be one of the dominant discursive formations. Naik, however, employs the "realist" conclusion—that "considered as a historical document or a picture of race-relations, the novel is patently inadequate in conception and lop-sided in the presentation of its material"—to challenge the object and methods of the English tradition.[32]

The realist argument is most often supported by biographical forms of evidence. For example, Shahane in "Life's Walking Shadows" (Das and Beer 1979) identifies friends of Forster's who may have been the models for Aziz and Godbole; and many essays in *E. M. Forster: A Tribute* rely heavily on Forster's often-quoted declaration in "What I Believe" that "if I had to choose between betraying my country and betraying my friend, I hope I should have the guts to betray my country," as well as his tribute to his friend Syed Ross Masood, as

---

[32]K. Natwar-Singh, " 'Only Connect . . .': E. M. Forster and India," in Shahane, *Focus on Forster's "A Passage to India,"* p. 3; M. Naik, "A Passage to Less than India," pp. 67, 63.

Other more common uses of realism as a standard of evaluation consist of demonstrating that Aziz is a credible Muslim or Godbole a convincing Hindu; these arguments are advanced by Shahane more than once in a number of different texts, as well as by Das, Anand, and others. There are those who disagree, however, such as Chaudhuri, who states, "Aziz would not have been allowed to cross my threshold," and "Godbole is not an exponent of Hinduism, he is a clown." Chaudhuri, "Passage to and from India," p. 117.

evidence that Forster truly understood and sympathized with Indians and had therefore written a realistic novel about Indo-British relations. Of Masood, Forster wrote:

> He woke me up out of my suburban and academic life, showed me new horizons and a new civilisation and helped me towards the understanding of a continent. Until I met him, India was a vague jumble of rajahs, sahibs, babus, and elephants, and I was not interested in such a jumble: who could be? He made everything real and exciting as soon as he began to talk, and seventeen years later when I wrote *A Passage to India* I dedicated it to him out of gratitude as well as out of love, for it would never have been written without him.[33]

There seems to be no doubt, for any of the critics writing in *E. M. Forster: A Tribute*, that the intention of the author had found its way, unmediated and unproblematized, into the form, character, and language of the novel.

The variety of arguments illustrates the diverse uses of realism as an emblem of authority; the standard by which textual representations should correspond to historical referents is employed in both the valorization and the criticism of the novel. To the extent that the invocation of the realist model is the means used by the Indians to assess and discuss the value of Forster's novel, these are examples of how "difference" gets structured by orthodox or similar models, how participation in the discourse is prefigured by the conditions of discourse. It is also an illustration of how heterodoxy—the articulation of distinctly differing ideological positions—is limited by the orthodoxy of discussions managed by the criteria of realism.

I have suggested that the entry of Indian writers into the field of Anglo-American Forster criticism emerges as one site within a series of heterogeneous and conflicted discursive moments. Not only is the British representation of the ruling British and the ruled Indians contested by novels such as those written by Candler, Thompson, and Forster, but also, as my discussion of Endrikar and Maconochie implies, even the narratives defining the centrality of British power in India prefigure a critique of that centrality. It is in the context of an already divided and heterogeneous discourse that the Indian critics' commentaries on Forster's novel intervene in the Anglo-American

[33]E. M. Forster, *Two Cheers for Democracy* (London: Edward Arnold, 1951), p. 292.

critical tradition. Finally, the Indian criticism is itself divided in its assessment of *A Passage to India*: the praise of Forster and his work by Shahane and Das is refuted by Chaudhuri and Naik, who analyze the inadequacies of the narrative representation of the history of race relations in India. A review of this series suggests that within each conflicted discursive site, each challenging articulation shifts the existing orthodoxy, transforming the criteria that regulate which discursive objects and methods are acceptable. In addition, not only does every orthodoxy articulate itself within the context of heterodox challenges, but every specific hegemonic formation is itself contradictory: for example, the repeated topos of the Indian's scrutinizing gaze suggests the fundamental instability of British hegemony even during the period of British rule.

I close by arguing for a greater consideration of the multivalence of the oppositional classification of cultural difference, in this case Indianness, for Indianness has a different function in each of the discursive sites considered here: the signifier *Indianness* is used by British narratives in the colonial period as a means of excluding and subordinating colonial subjects, whereas in the early postcolonial period Indian scholars utilized the idea to pose a countertradition within the field of English literary criticism. The Indian scholars' entrance into the discussions of Forster's novel under the signifier of "the Indianness of the native point of view" illustrates how difference can be appropriated from dominant formations and rearticulated from a different position on the discursive terrain. If one continued to map the further trajectory of sites where discussions of Indianness as difference constitute a topos, one could interpret certain postcolonial Indian intellectuals writing in the 1980s and 1990s—Homi Bhabha, Gayatri Spivak, Lata Mani, and Radha Radhakrishnan, for example—as constituting yet another, third moment of this dialogue about cultural difference.[34] The articulations of these critics, heterogeneous them-

[34] I mention these theorists together because they share a postcolonial theoretical perspective that tends to be critical of essentializing categories such as "the Third World," or "Indianness." But it must be emphasized that among this group, too, is represented quite a heterogeneous variety of critical methods, objects, and political projects. Although both theorists make use of post-structuralist and psychoanalytic methods, the essays concerning the intersection of feminism and anticolonialism in Gayatri Spivak's *In Other Worlds* (London: Routledge, 1988) have a distinctly different focus from Homi K. Bhabha's discussion of the ambivalence of nationalism in *Nation and*

selves, deconstruct and displace the uniformity of a notion of Indianness, posing critiques that specifically target the dangers of narrating
Indian subalternity as an essence. Although this third moment—post-
structuralist and postcolonial, as we might name it—falls outside the
scope of this chapter, I gesture toward it not merely to suggest that
there are other discursive loci that provide further challenges to the
dominant formation of British colonialism beyond the sites discussed
here, but also to signal that what I have framed is only one moment in
a dynamic and ongoing series of dialogues between heterogeneous
discursive sites.[35]

Narration (London: Routledge, 1990). Radha Radhakrishnan's discussion of Foucault
and Gramsci and the role of the intellectual in local and global political practice and
analysis in "Toward an Effective Intellectual," although compatible with the observations made by Lata Mani in "Multiple Mediations: Feminist Scholarship in the Age of
Multinational Reception" *Inscriptions* 5 (1989): 1–23, does not share Mani's attention to
feminist subjects and feminist politics, vividly illustrated by her focus on the construction of *sati*.

[35]In limiting my discussion to the discursive site of Forster criticism, I do not intend to
generalize its patterns as being exemplary of all British and Indian dialogues, nor, most
important, do I mean to limit the possible sites of resistance and intervention to the ones
discussed here. For example, a juxtaposition of British colonial accounts with Indian
peasant and worker narratives (such as those reconstructed by the Subaltern Studies
Group) or, conversely, a focus on exclusively Indian dialogues about Indian controversies would provide very different discursive (and perhaps more radical) examples from
the one examined here. Rather, I have chosen Forster criticism because it seems to me to
provide one illustrative "anatomy" of intervention and accommodation in orientalist
discourse; it offers one site in which to trace some of the transformations, as well as the
legacies, of early orientalist arguments and rhetorics.

5

The Desires of Postcolonial Orientalism: Chinese Utopias of Kristeva, Barthes, and *Tel quel*

> On comprend donc comment . . . la révolution culturelle pro-
> létarienne chinoise, plus grand événement historique de notre
> époque, dérange le calcul révisionniste et qu'il fera tout pour la
> falsifier. Eh bien, nous, nous ferons tout pour l'éclairer, l'ana-
> lyser et la soutenir.
>
> [We understand how, then . . . the Chinese Cultural Proletarian
> Revolution, the greatest historical event of our epoch, so dis-
> turbs the revisionist reasoning that they will do everything to
> falsify it. And so, for our part, we will do everything to illumi-
> nate it, to analyze it, and to support it.]
>
> *Tel quel* (1971)

The discourse of orientalism is never independent of the contiguous discourses that figure otherness. Discourses operate in conflict, and each discourse is actively bound to other discourses which may reiterate, contradict, and criticize its ruling figurations. The notion of woman as Other, for example, takes shape in a field defined, on the one hand, by scientific, psychoanalytic, and literary representations of "woman" and, on the other, by feminist critiques of these representations. Likewise, we saw in the last chapter that Indianness as difference forms a multivalent hinge between the British colonialist discourse, which excluded Indians, and the Indian articulations of identity that criticize that discourse. It has been my argument throughout that constructions of difference are multivalent signifiers, and are produced by the active engagement of a plurality of discourses at different moments. Orientalism must be understood as but one discourse in this complex intersection.

In this chapter my object of study is again literary criticism, as I consider a more recent orientalism, the figuration of the Chinese Cultural Revolution and the People's Republic of China by French intellectuals during the early 1970s in Julia Kristeva's *Des chinoises* (1974), Roland Barthes's *Alors la Chine?* (1975), and the avant-garde theoretical journal *Tel quel* (1968–1974). An assortment of discourses invents and circulates the multivalent signifier "China" in these three examples; although each representation of China arises from the social circumstances of Paris in the 1960s and 1970s, each is figured differently, answering differently urgent quests emerging from the social circumstances and discursive formations of that period. Kristeva represents China as a culture descending from a pre-oedipal matriarchal heritage; her figuration of Chinese otherness is part of a strategy to subvert western ideology by positing a feminine, maternal realm outside its patriarchal system. Kristeva's China expresses a confluence of the discourses of feminist theory, psychoanalysis, and semiotics, as well as orientalism. Barthes's China—which he constitutes as a poetic site outside western signification, a pre-Symbolic space also coded as maternal—marks another intersection of these same semiotic, psychoanalytic, and orientalist discourses. Finally, the embrace of Maoism by the theorists of the journal *Tel quel* in 1971, in which communist China is figured as the revolutionary Other of western society and western Marxist theory, occurs at the nexus of orientalism and the discourses of the French Left after 1968.

Within the context of my discussion of earlier orientalisms, one can see that these expressions of postcolonial French relations to the Orient are at once both strikingly different from the earlier French colonial orientalism and disturbingly reminiscent of its postures and rhetorics. The main manner in which the China of Kristeva, Barthes, and *Tel quel* differed from the orientalist texts produced during the earlier periods was that their various deployments of the orientalist trope were meant to represent a break with colonialist ideology; Kristeva, Barthes, and *Tel quel* were openly antagonistic toward the ideologies of national homogeneity, centralized state power, and the French subordination of North Africa and Indochina. Indeed, the French construction of

China in the 1970s was central to a counterideological politics; China was constructed as an object of desire within particular veins of the counterideological discourses of feminism, psychoanalysis, and French Maoism, whose project was the criticism of French culture and whose key theoretical strategies depended on an assertion not of national homogeneity but of difference and the self-determination of a variety of peoples. In this sense the postcolonial discourse about China appropriated certain orientalist tropes in order to criticize the state apparatus of which the earlier colonialist orientalism was a product. Opposed to, yet in a dialogic relation with, traditional orientalism, this postcolonial form of orientalism departed from, yet was determined by, the discursive conditions of the previous orientalisms. Although Kristeva's, Barthes's, and *Tel quel*'s representations of China served as critiques of the nationalist ideologies supported by earlier orientalisms, their figurations of the Orient utilized some of the very same terms, postures, and rhetorics employed in the earlier texts.

Before the pieces about China, both Barthes and Kristeva were known for their significant works in semiological theory, Barthes's *Eléments de sémiologie* (1965) and Kristeva's *Révolution du langage poétique* (1974). Both theorists wrote their pieces on China at a moment in theoretical debates when the binary oppositions upheld by structuralist analysis—self and Other, male and female, culture and nature— were being targeted by theories of language, psychoanalysis, and anthropology as reductive logics to be revised and superseded. It is in this context that Kristeva and Barthes constituted China as an irreducibly different Other outside western signification and the coupling of signifier and signified. Yet the desires shaping their texts were inscribed by the very terms they wished to escape; for the wish to exceed western binary systems is a desire that is itself structured by the opposition between the location of one's writing—within structure— and the place of the transcendent Other—beyond structure.

The reassertion of the oppositions that Barthes and Kristeva sought to escape in their writings on China can be most clearly traced, interestingly enough, in the way in which their texts ultimately privilege psychoanalysis, a paradigm that stubbornly returns to the binarism of male and female. Invoking French debates on feminism and psychoanalysis during the 1970s, both writers coded China as feminine or maternal, in contradistinction to the paternal order of French society.

Kristeva's *Des chinoises* (1974) invokes the matriarch of pre-Confucian China as a means of naming and projecting a figure that occupies a space beyond the structured and determined sexuality of western Europe. She associates the period of matriarchy and matrilineality in China with the "phase pré-oedipienne," a reconstituted period in which the child is intensely allied with the mother before its entry into the Symbolic order of socialization and language. In this sense, *Des chinoises* is a text that embodies several desires: a theoretical desire to locate a position outside French structuralism and psychoanalysis from which these paradigms may be criticized; a feminist desire to discover and praise a figure of absolute feminine power and to locate a matriarchal society in which this power is effected; and finally a desire, inherited from the discourse of orientalism, to find in the history of the Orient the opposite of the Occident, to find there all that is absent from and beyond the West.

Barthes's *Alors la Chine?* (1975) also juxtaposes China—in cultural, semiotic, and psychoanalytic terms—to the overstructured, signifying West. Like Kristeva, Barthes constitutes China as a feminine, maternal space that disrupts the "phallocentric" occidental social system. By associating China with the maternal, Barthes suggests that the Orient is opposed to the representational Symbolic system of the West; for Barthes, China opens up the possibility of a preverbal Imaginary space, before "castration," socialization, and the intervention of the Father. In the sense that China is conflated with the significance of the maternal in Barthes's critical project, orientalism becomes a means of figuring this critical poetics of escape, a topos through which one writes oneself outside western ideology.

Kristeva's and Barthes's interests in the People's Republic of China were shared by other intellectuals and critics who were their contemporaries. At the same time that *Des chinoises* and *Alors la Chine?* were written, the editorial committee at the journal *Tel quel* (which included Kristeva, as well as Philippe Sollers, Jean-Louis Baudry, Marcelin Pleynet, and others) had become ardent followers of the Chinese Cultural Revolution. After 1968 these critics and intellectuals, who judged the promising yet ultimately suppressed May revolts in France a failed revolution, turned to the Cultural Revolution as an alternative example of revolutionary theory and practice. These intellectuals adopted "Maoism" and defined it as a more radical critique of society, one that took its theoretical inspiration from a source outside western Marxism. In 1971 *Tel quel* issued a "Déclaration" of its embrace of "la pensée maotsétoung." In this document, "la pensée maotsétoung" was the sign for French communism's Other, a manner of signifying a more revolutionary practice, whose very political and geographic distance from the West rendered it more powerful because it could not be subsumed by western social systems or explanations. Although the China constituted by *Tel quel* as the political Other of western Marxist theory and practice was inflected differently from Kristeva's or Barthes's, the three representations resembled one another to the degree that they constituted China as a utopian antithesis to French society and culture.

The fascination with this China in the works of Kristeva and Barthes and in *Tel quel* expressed the dilemmas of a particular historical context and a specific set of issues and controversies: these invocations of China were written within theoretical, and political debates particular to Paris in the early 1970s—feminist, psychoanalytic, and French Maoist. Most important, they were also written following the student revolts and workers' strikes of May 1968, which demanded radical changes in the authoritarian structures of the university, the factory, and in society at large. In the aftermath of 1968, when the revolts had been suppressed and Gaullist power restored, leftist intellectuals struggled to explain what had happened, what might have happened, and what remained to be done. In this sense all three figurations of China—as feminist, psychoanalytic, and leftist utopias—were indirect responses to the events of 1968; they attempted to continue the project of cultural politics begun in 1968, but in choosing to constitute as utopian a revolutionary experience outside Europe, they betrayed their disillusionment at the suppression of the French revolts.

Des Chinoises: Orientalism, Psychoanalysis, and Feminine Writing

Des chinoises was written in the context of both the western Continental feminist debates of the early 1970s and the structuralist and psychoanalytic theoretical debates of the same period; in this sense writing about "la chinoise" was an occasion for Kristeva to critique the lack of psychoanalytic sophistication in the French and North American women's movements, as well as a means of providing a feminist critique of the Freudian and Lacanian paradigms of sexual difference.[1] *Des chinoises* invokes the powerful figure of an ancient Chinese matriarch as the disrupting exception to western patriarchy and psychoanalysis, and the People's Republic of China is praised as a political antithesis to contemporary France. In both senses the examples of China and Chinese women are cited only in terms of western debates, are invented as solutions to western political and theoretical problems.

A hierarchical opposition of occidental and oriental is stated in the formal divisions themselves which frame and structure the entire text: a first section, "De ce côté-ci," (From this side), and a second section titled "Femmes de Chine" (Chinese women). "De ce côté-ci" contains five chapters describing the oppression of women in the western traditions of sexual differentiation and definition: first, the patrilinear monotheistic tradition exemplified by the Old Testament separating men and women into two races and subjugating "la femme" to the privileged identity of "l'Homme"; and second, the Freudian and Lacanian psychoanalytic explanation of sexual difference. Subsequently, in the section "Femmes de Chine," this bipartite narrative about

---

[1]The Mouvement de libération des femmes (MLF), very active after May 1968, was, in 1974, discussing issues of psychoanalysis, socialism, Marxism, Maoism, and the bearing of these systems of thought and social analysis on the question of women's liberation. By 1977 the MLF had split into at least two factions: those who allied themselves with "psychanalyse et politique" and those who allied themselves with "questions féministes." The "psychanalyse et politique" group, with which Kristeva was associated, concerned itself with women's psycholinguistic position, and explored psychoanalysis as an emancipatory theory of sexual difference. The supporters of "questions féministes," coming out of Simone de Beauvoir's existential feminism, were more concerned with the material conditions of women as a subordinated class. The concerns of Christine Delphy, who, along with Beauvoir, was one of the founding members of the journal *Questions féministes*, may be considered to have much more in common with the Marxist feminism practiced in the United States. For other discussions of the recent history of French feminism, see Elaine Marks and Isabelle De Courtivron, eds., *New French Feminisms* (Amherst: University of Massachusetts Press, 1980); Ann Rosalind Jones, "Writing the Body: Toward an Understanding of L'Écriture Féminine," *Feminist Studies* 7, no. 2 (Summer 1981): 247–63; and Toril Moi, *Sexual/Textual Politics: Feminist Literary Theory* (London: Methuen, 1985). See also the special issues of the journals *Signs* 7, no. 1 (Autumn 1981); *Feminist Studies* 7, no. 2 (Summer 1981); and *Yale French Studies* 62 (1981), each addressing the question of French and Anglo-American feminism. In particular, see Gayatri Spivak's "French Feminism in an International Frame," in *In Other Worlds* (London: Routledge, 1988), first published in *YFS* 62 (1981): 154–84, for both its instructive discussion of *Des chinoises* and its equally relevant critique of French feminism.

women in western history is posed against a bipartite narrative about China; with the parallelism of the two cleft narrative reconstructions of Occident and Orient, Kristeva argues that the ancient matriarchal origins of China contrast with the patrilinear monotheism of the Judeo-Christian biblical tradition, whereas the long Confucian period of Chinese history resembles that of the western psychoanalytic repression of femininity.

In chapter 2 of part 1, "La guerre des sexes," Kristeva discusses western religious and legal discourse; man is genealogically linked to the one God, she argues, whereas woman is excluded from this genealogy.[2] The woman qualifies as human subject only in her relation as "épouse," and in her contractual agreement to bear man's children. Within these traditions, man possesses social subjectivity, access to language, and legal and historical presence; woman, Kristeva argues, is constituted by the tradition as the Other, who is mute, powerless, outlawed, ahistorical, and absent. Kristeva's analysis of the Old Testament tradition is a structuralist one, which relies on binary systems of classification (presence and absence, speeched and speechless, man and woman, and so on). In a sense, her interpretation foregrounds the inherent limitations of structuralism as a method of criticism for articulating a feminist project: the fixed nature of the paradigm, and the extent to which structuralism posits and assumes the binary complementarity of the dyad man/woman without providing the tools for an adequate critique of the production of this binary logic. In effect, the structuralist method utilized here constitutes the binary oppositions it ostensibly identifies.[3] In order to find a critical methodology less static

[2]Kristeva observes: "Coupée de l'homme, faite dans cela même qui lui manque, la femme biblique sera épouse, fille ou soeur. . . . Sa fonction est d'assurer la procréation . . . elle n'a pas de rapport direct: Dieu ne parle généralement qu'à l'homme" (Cut from man, made from that which he lacks, the biblical woman will be wife, daughter or sister. . . . Her function is to insure procreation . . . she has no direct relationship: God speaks only to man; p. 21).

[3]For example, structural anthropology assumed that the cultural order was founded on the division of society into two sexes: men, who were the social and cultural actors, and women, who were the objects of exchange among men. In Claude Lévi-Strauss's "Language and the Analysis of Social Laws," in *Structural Anthropology* (New York: Basic Books, 1963), the observation that women serve as objects of exchange in culture is offered as "proof" that women are the signifiers of men's roles as producers of culture. The structural paradigm is essentially a description—as opposed to a historical, hermeneutical, or dynamic explanation—that presumes sexual difference as a given binary relationship.

than structuralist description, "De ce côté-ci" then turns to psycho-analysis as a method that attempts to account for the formation of the subject in language and culture. Yet whereas the theoretical limitations of psychoanalysis are different from the problems of binary reduction-ism inherent in structuralism, Kristeva's particular use of psycho-analysis in *Des chinoises* implicates its arguments about sexual differ-ence in another set of determined relations.

Psychoanalysis presumes that sexuality is at the center of a subject's identity within family, language, and social arrangements; because the issue of sexuality is central to so many feminist theorists, the attraction to psychoanalysis among feminists is understandable.[4] But the ulti-mate psychoanalytic revelation that gendered subjectivity is deter-mined by the presence or lack of a penis (in the case of Freud) or the phallus (in the case of Lacan) insistently frustrates the feminist project, to the extent that psychoanalytic explanation of gender tends to rely on an arbitrary assignment of a masculine mark to describe a differ-ence that needs also to be explained by other, more varied methods of analysis and explanation, such as sociology and the construction of sexual difference, economics and the relationship of class and gender, or social history and the production of race and gender.[5] In *Des chi-noises*, Kristeva's critique of psychoanalysis consists in revalorizing Freud's formulation of a pre-oedipal phase by imputing to it certain characteristics extrapolated from Lacan's notion of the Imaginary.[6] In

[4]As this chapter implies, Freud and Lacan were prominent influences in the formation of French feminist theories, particularly on the work of Luce Irigaray, Hélène Cixous, Claudine Hermann, and Xavière Gauthier. Feminists in the United States, on the contrary, have been more critical of psychoanalytic theories (unlike English feminists; see, for example, Juliet Mitchell's *Psychoanalysis and Feminism* [New York: Viking, 1974]). In the years since the mid-1970s, however, more American feminists have written about the question of sexual difference from psychoanalytic standpoints; see, for example, Jane Gallop, *The Daughter's Seduction* (Ithaca: Cornell University Press, 1982).

[5]Some of these other methods of explication are represented in the works of Rosalind Pechesky (1981) on reproductive rights; Catharine MacKinnon (1987) on the position of women in legal discourse; Nancy Chodorow (1978) on the role of mothering in the social construction of gender; bell hooks (1981) on black women and feminism; and Donna Haraway (1985) on science, technology, and socialist feminism.

[6]Although it was Freud who originally described the "pre-Oedipus period" in the lecture "Femininity," in *New Introductory Lectures on Psychoanalysis*, trans. James Strachey (New York: Norton, 1964), as the period of preinfantile sexual attachment of the daugh-ter to her mother before she discovers that she and her mother are "castrated," Freud's references to the pre-oedipal stage are associated with an interest in describing how female "regressions" into the "prehistory" of the bond between mother and infant affect

chapter 3 of part 1, "Vierge du verbe," Kristeva expands Freud's notion of the pre-oedipal stage—a period anterior to the legendary castration, before the child acquires speech and enters into social relations—by stressing the importance of rediscovering the powerful sexuality of the mother. Following Freud and Lacan, Kristeva adopts the pre-oedipal as a "prehistory" to oedipalization, but in contradistinction to Freud and Lacan, for whom the overwhelming significance lies in the process of oedipalization, Kristeva inflects the "regressions" toward pre-oedipal eroticism for the mother with a positive value.

[Il y a] deux processus d'ordre psychanalytique, l'un relatif au rôle de la mère, l'autre au fonctionnement du langage.

Le premier consiste à lever le refoulement sur le fait que la mère est *autre*, n'a pas de pénis, mais jouit et enfante. De lever le refoulement jusqu'au préconscient seulement : tout juste pour imaginer qu'elle enfante, mais en censurant le fait qu'elle a joui dans un coït, donc qu'il y a eu la "scène primitive." Une fois de plus, le vagin et la jouissance de la mère sont méconnus et immédiatement remplacés par ce qui place la mère du côté de la communauté socio-symbolique : l'enfantement, la filiation au nom du père. Cette opération de fausse reconnaissance—de méconnaissance—de la jouissance maternelle s'accomplit grâce à un processus dont Ernest Jones a le premier entendu la source.[7]

[There are two processes in psychoanalysis, one pertaining to the role of the mother, the other as a result of language.

The first one consists in lifting the repression of the fact that the mother is *other*, has no penis, but enjoys pleasure and brings forth children. To lift the repression only to the preconscious, just to imagine that she is procreative, but censoring the fact that she has had sexual pleasure in intercourse, in which there was a "primal scene." Further, the mother's vagina and pleasure are misrecognized and immediately replaced by the circumstances which situate the mother on the side of the socio-symbolic community: childbirth, the relationship to the name of the father. This operation of false recognition—of misrecognition—of maternal pleasure is realized according to a process of which Ernest Jones was the first to understand the source.]

---

the development of femininity; see, for example, his theories that jealous paranoia and female homosexuality are conditions "which went back to a fixation in the pre-Oedipus stage" (p. 115). Indeed, Freud suggests in this lecture that the claims of women patients that they had been seduced by their father were "hysterical symptoms," but that the fantasy of seduction by the mother "touches the ground of reality, for it was really the mother who by her activities over the child's bodily hygiene inevitably stimulated, and perhaps even roused for the first time, pleasurable sensations in her genitals" (p. 106).

[7]Kristeva, *Des chinoises*, p. 30.

This passage refers to the premises of castration and the repression of the knowledge of women as both generative and sexual to explain, on the one hand, the Symbolic appropriation of the woman's body and sexual pleasures, and, on the other hand, the exclusion of women from a masculine model of socialization and subjectivity. Kristeva asserts that the multiple and nonexclusive sexual pleasures of the mother— "le vagin *et* la jouissance" (emphasis added)—are misrecognized, or repressed, and that psychoanalysis accounts for this misrecognition as necessary for the preservation of a male order. The implicit reference to castration is significant, for it is through the drama of castration as the repression of the child's vision of the mother's sexuality that psycho-analysis explains the formation of masculine identity. Kristeva argues that it is the child's belief in castration that represses a knowledge of the mother—as sexual, fertile, *and* vaginal—and in this belief that the denial and appropriation of women's sexual pleasure, or "jouissance," takes place.

Kristeva's refiguration of the pre-oedipal phase draws somewhat upon the Lacanian notion of the Imaginary—a hypothetical, specular, preverbal topos reconstructed from the standpoint of the Symbolic. Lacan's definition of the Imaginary includes a "mirror stage," a hypo-thetical phase in which the preverbal child identifies with a specular reflection (or misidentifies, in that it is through identification with images that the subject misrecognizes itself, and constructs the alien-ated self, which Lacan calls the *ego* or *moi*). It is termed the Imaginary, because for Lacan the supposition of a period of narcissistic identifica-tion and fullness is a mythical stage; it exists only as a recapitulation of an "imaginary" pre-Symbolic state from the standpoint of the subject who is always already within language, the paternal order, social hierarchy, and law. Lacan discusses oedipalization, therefore, not as Freud's scene in which the child fears castration and identifies with the father's masculinity, but rather as a metaphor for the accession of the subject to the socialized sphere of Symbolic relations. The Lacanian Oedipal phenomenon consists of this initiation into the Symbolic, emblematized by the naming/castration of the subject in language, the receipt of the *nom* and the *non* of the father. With the entry of the named subject into language and the social order, the unnamed, re-pressed desires of the subject are driven underground. This division of the subject in language is crucial to the functions of desire and symbolization, for it is in the Symbolic relations of language that the subject attempts to reconstruct the identities and equivalences of the Imaginary. In rewriting the Lacanian notion of the Imaginary as a female pre-oedipal phase, Kristeva privileges the infant's identification with the mother rather than the specular identification stressed by Lacan: "L'Enfant est lié au corps de la mère sans que celui-ci soit encore un 'objet-en-face,' mais jouant, avec le corps enfantin lui-même, comme un continuum socio-naturel" (The child is bound to the mother's body without that body being, as yet, 'other'; rather, her body 'pleasures' with the child's body itself, in a kind of natural/social continuum; p. 32). Thus, Kristeva expands the notion of the pre-oedipal/Imaginary in opposition to castration, oedipalization, and the Lacanian Symbolic; the formulation of the pre-oedipal represents an attempt to locate a space outside the phallic-dominated Symbolic for a maternal, feminine-dominated phase of psychosexual development.[8]

Kristeva's revalorization of the pre-oedipal as an absolute state of otherness with regard to the paternalistic Symbolic and its systems of signification is figured in an idealized Other—the Mother—located outside the hierarchical, oedipalized overdetermination of western psychoanalysis. But Kristeva does more than idealize this Mother; she "orientalizes" her. In the book's second section, "Femmes de Chine," Kristeva constitutes an ancient matrilinear-matrilocal society as the historical analogue to the female-dominated pre-oedipal topos, conflating the matriarch of pre-Confucian China with the mother in pre-

---

[8]Kristeva adopts, yet revalorizes, Freud's notion of the pre-oedipal phase. For Freud, children discover the difference between the father and mother when they observe the father has a penis; assuming that the mother's penis has been cut off, they identify with the father, refusing bonds with the mother, owing to the imagined threat of castration. According to Freud, the imagined castration is all the more important to the male child, for the successful repression of his desire for his mother, through the fear of castration, allows him to adjust to the conditions of adult society, to become socialized as a man. Kristeva suggests that the oedipal repression must be lifted and the mother rediscovered as the child's object of desire and union.

The construction of the ego in the mirror stage, as well as the relationship between the Imaginary and the Symbolic realms, is developed in Jacques Lacan's essay "The Mirror Stage as Formative Function of the I as Revealed in Psychoanalytic Experience," in *Ecrits*. The Symbolic, the oedipal phenomenon, and the naming and splitting of the subject are discussed in "The Agency of the Letter in the Unconscious or Reason since Freud," also in *Ecrits*. Useful exegeses of Lacan's work include Coward and Ellis 1977; Jameson 1977; Lemaire 1977; Wilden 1968; and Mitchell and Rose's preface to Lacan, *Feminine Sexuality* 1983.

oedipal discourse. Both projects place the Mother at the center of their respective paradigms: as the primary figure in child development and gender acquisition, and as the origin of social and economic organization. Both efforts depend on the retrospective invention of a prehistorical moment, an idealized state outside society and history, created from a point located within social arrangements. In the argument that Chinese matriarchy is the antecedent of a twentieth-century revolutionary society, the generalizing narrative, undaunted by the large scope of its project, leaps quickly and simply across two thousand years of Chinese history to propose that, because of China's matriarchal heritage, the communist politics of the People's Republic hold powerful lessons for the French Left in the 1970s. Throughout *Des chinoises* a historical extravagance, which so easily establishes a correspondence between an ancient modality and a contemporary one, lacks an adequately complex appreciation of the heterogeneous and contradictory forces of history; despite an ostensible allegiance to Marxism, Kristeva finds no apparent difficulties in generalizing Chinese history in so undialectical a fashion.

Kristeva first evokes the mother-centered society of pre-Confucian China in chapter 1 of part 2, "La mère au centre," in a fantasy-description of matrilinear kinship and matrilocal systems of exchange in ancient China. She suggests that genealogy issued from mother to daughter, and that the family groups within each region were organized along maternal lines; that is, the son-in-law moved to the wife's mother's district. In addition, males and females had equal power in the social and political spheres of activity; this is symbolized, she claims, by symmetrically binomial names that include the name of the mother (also the name of the region) as well as the paternal family name. Kristeva employs conditional verb tenses to evoke this ancient system, calling attention to its hypothetical and fictive qualities: "Une certaine prépondérance des femmes *pourrait* pourtant être logiquement nécessaire à une époque archaïque et *expliquerait* une filiation matrilinéaire et matrilocale" (A certain preponderance of women *would be* however logically necessary in this period, and *would explain* a lineage both matrilinear and matrilocal; p. 51, emphasis added). Indeed, Kristeva candidly comments on the quality of invention, and of phantasm in her history of the woman-dominated Chinese society— "hypothétique (utopique? fantasmatique?)" (p. 48)—and the fact that she selectively chooses this image of matrilinear-matrilocal society from particular, and few, western sinologists' texts. As with the embellishment of the pre-oedipal phase in the first section of *Des Chinoises*, in this second section the invented matrilinear-matrilocal society is likewise exploited for its quality of utopia and phantasm; as an Imaginary, and therefore untextualized, Other, the Chinese matriarchy offers the writer of "écriture féminine" a powerful topos with which to subvert the narratives of western patrilineality.

Kristeva also justifies the mother-centered theories of the pre-oedipal phase and the pre-Confucian matriarchy in an "analysis" of Chinese language. She argues that the independence of two linguistic systems—of tonal speech and of written ideogrammatic symbols—is particular to the Chinese language, and that the independent system of tonal speech is a preserved remnant of the matrilinear-matrilocal society, in which the mother and her bodily preverbal tones and rhythms were dominant. Earlier, Kristeva had characterized the pre-oedipal relationship of infant and mother as one of preverbal "echolalia": "La phase pré-oedipienne corresponde à des écholalies intenses, à des rythmes d'abord et à des intonations ensuite, avant que ne s'installe la structure phonologico-syntaxique de la phrase" (The pre-oedipal phase corresponds to an intense echolalia, first in rhythm and then in intonation, before the phonologico-syntactic structure is imposed on the sentence; p. 34). In this discussion of the relationship between written and spoken Chinese, Kristeva suggests that the written language embodies the oedipal-Confucian suppression of the pre-oedipal echolalia present in the intoned spoken language.

> La logique de l'écrit . . . laisse présupposer, à la base, un sujet parlant-écrivant pour lequel ce qui nous apparaît aujourd'hui comme une phase pré-oedipienne, dépendance du continuum maternel et socio-naturel, absence de coupure nette entre ordre des choses et ordre des symboles, prédominance des pulsions inconscientes,—aurait eu une importance majeure. L'écriture idéographique ou idéogrammatique s'en sert pour les buts du pouvoir étatique, politique et symbolique, mais sans les censurer. Un pouvoir despotique qui n'a pas oublié ce qu'il doit à la mère et à la famille matrilinéaire qui l'a sans doute précédé mais de pas très loin. Hypothèse? Fantasme?   (p. 61)

> [The logic of (Chinese) writing . . . presupposes, at its base, a speaking, writing individual for whom what seems to us today a pre-oedipal phase—dependency on the maternal, socio-natural continuum, ab-

sence of clear-cut divisions between the order of things and the order of symbols, predominance of the unconscious impulses—must have been extremely important. Ideogrammatic or ideographic writing makes use of this (pre-oedipal phase) for the ends of state, political, and symbolic power, but without censuring them. A despotic power that has not forgotten what it owes to the mother and the matrilinear family that has certainly preceded it, though not by long. Hypothesis? Fantasy?]

In equating the intoned rhythms associated with the pre-oedipal phase of mother-child union with the ancient, prepatriarchal phase of Chinese history, Kristeva creates a deliberate confusion and conflation of the paradigms of individual psychology and language acquisition, the history of language and civilization. Furthermore, the argument that the intoned quality of Chinese language is evidence that the mother-child union was valued in ancient China is, to say the least, deluded exaggeration; indeed, a great number of contemporary spoken languages are intoned. Although the paradox of an intoned spoken language and a highly coded written language is noteworthy, Kristeva makes extremely speculative use of this paradox in suggesting that the independent system of written ideograms represents a later attempt to repress the ancient maternal tones. Finally, by romanticizing the Chinese language as a system of codes within which one can read about an earlier, tonal, pre-oedipal society which has survived the later symbolic ordering of written language, Kristeva casts the Chinese linguistic example as the *semiosis* she elsewhere suggests occurs in western poetics, in which the feminine pre-oedipal is brought into paternal language.[9] The example of Chinese language, as it is constituted in *Des chinoises*, conveniently serves Kristeva's theory of the semiotic *chora* elaborated at length in *La révolution du langage poétique*. She subjects

[9]In *Révolution du langage poétique*, Kristeva discusses the breaking of the Symbolic with the enunciation of "echolalic" or presymbolic tones, associating this phenomenon in avant-garde European poetry with the Chinese system of language. Poetry is described as a process of reinvestment in a maternal, semiotic *chora* that transgresses the symbolic order, or a *genotext* of semiotic processes which interrupts the communicative *phenotext*. Kristeva cites Mallarmé and Joyce as writers who are able to "reach the semiotic *chora*." *The Revolution in Poetic Language*, trans. Margaret Waller (New York: Columbia University Press, 1984); see sections 9–12 in "The Semiotic and the Symbolic," pp. 62–89.

"Women's Time," *Signs* 7, no. 1 (Autumn 1981): 13–35, represents a later statement of Kristeva's feminism which is also concerned with a radically different female location outside the masculine linear time of history and politics, and which emphasizes the sociosymbolic materiality of language and writing as well.

Chinese language, like Chinese history and culture, to French linguistic and psychoanalytic paradigms; China is constituted as a utopian text ("Hypothèse? Fantasme?") which illustrates the answers to some pressing theoretical problems for the western semiotician.

Chapter 2, "Confucius—un 'mangeur des femmes,'" discusses the Confucian era, generalized and homogenized into a period ranging from 1000 B.C. to the twentieth century (the text does not become less imperializing). In Confucian society, the text argues, an oppressive backlash extensively excluded women by law and social hierarchy. This is compared to the western biblical and psychoanalytic oppression of western women, described in the first five chapters of part 1. Absolute language is used to express the oppression of women under Confucianism: "elles subissent l'autorité," "elles se soumettent à la nouvelle autorité des beaux-parents et des maris," "elles doivent une obéissance filiale absolue" (They are subject to authority, they submit themselves to the new authority of parents-in-law and husbands, they owe absolute filial piety and obedience; p. 82). The "pied bandé" (bound foot) is invoked as an ornate symbol of their profound capacity to obey. The absolute language of persecution calls attention to the polar opposition the text draws between the powerful position of women in the legendary ancient matriarchy and the extreme oppression of women under Confucianism. The developmental opposition between pre-Confucian and Confucian times puts forth a thesis about the history of Chinese woman which is analogous to the paradigmatic splits characterized by the notions of pre-oedipal and oedipal phases of human development. If Chinese women formerly had power and coequal status during the ancient period of Chinese civilization, the backlash against Chinese woman under Confucianism constitutes a "refoulement" like the psychoanalytic repression of the mother's "jouissance." Because Chinese women have a point of origin in which they were powerful and dominant, the repressed woman is described as both subject to authoritarian structures of obedience and simultaneously undetermined and outside those structures. Kristeva argues that the Chinese woman is at once within familial and social relations and yet beyond those relations, and that her hysterias, suicides, and pregnancies are statements of her power, and examples of the ways in which the Chinese woman under Confucianism protests her subjection and subverts paternal authority.

Finally, chapters 3–6 discuss the conditions of women in the People's Republic of China. Kristeva concludes that contemporary women in China have liberated themselves and reemerged as fully autonomous political subjects in a restoration of the coequal status and power they had possessed in the original matrilinear and matrilocal society. Because of its matriarchal roots, the Chinese Revolution of 1949, the text asserts, was an antipatriarchal revolution; the socialist revolution in China, Kristeva argues, brought a fundamental revolution in the patriarchal family and in the roles of women. The essential premise is that throughout the history of Chinese women, "her" experience has been completely *other* than the experience of western women under patriarchy. Confucianism and feudalism are juxtaposed with monotheism and capitalism; western saints are contrasted with Chinese concubines. For if the Chinese woman is constructed as impenetrably and incomprehensibly different, then it is possible to constitute her as "outside" western socialization, not reducible to western binary and hierarchical classifications. Kristeva rhetorically juxtaposes European and Chinese women, as if in the act of writing an encomium to Chinese women as an exemplary exception to western oppressions of women her text posits a radical maternal "semiotic" otherness that surges up through the Symbolic order. The implicit recommendation of the text is that "feminine writing" ought to regard, praise, and write about Chinese women, for the identification with a position eccentric to western ideology constitutes a "revolutionary" political strategy for objecting to that structure.

> Le rôle de La Révolutionnaire (ou Le Révolutionnaire): refuser tout rôle, pour au contraire, rappeler cette 'vérité' hors temps, ni vraie ni fausse, inencastrable dans l'ordre de la parole et du symbolisme social, écho de nos jouissances, de nos paroles en vertiges, de nos grossesses. Les rappeler comment?—En écoutant, en remarquant le non-dit du discours . . . enrelevant ce qui, à chaque instance, reste insatisfait, réprimé, neuf, excentrique, incompréhensible, dérangeant l'entente des installés. (p. 43)

> [The role of the revolutionary (female or male): to refuse all roles, in order, on the contrary, to summon this timeless "truth"—formless, neither true nor false, echoes of our *jouissance*, of our words spoken in delirium, of our pregnancies—into the order of speech and social symbolism. But how do we call it into being? By listening, by recognizing the unspoken in discourse . . . by calling attention at all times to whatever

remains unsatisfied, repressed, new, eccentric, incomprehensible, disturbing to the status quo.]

The identification and alliance with the eccentric, the Other, the Imaginary, is valorized as a political strategy that challenges the structures of domination in the western social order. Furthermore, language is considered the material medium of the ideological apparatus, and therefore a material site of political practice and change; writing from a position within western ideology about a phenomenon outside western history and ideology is essentialized as a means of displacing that ideology. But in inventing and appropriating the place of "Chinese woman," *Des chinoises* erases the situations of women in contemporary China, the complex interrelation of certain qualified freedoms with remnants of centuries of sexual discrimination and oppression in family, professional, and political life. The Chinese woman is fetishized and constructed as the Other of western psychoanalytic feminism, a transcendental exception to the overstructured bind of women in western Europe. *Des chinoises* curiously reproduces the postures of desire of two narratives it ostensibly seeks to subvert: the narratives of orientalism and romantic courtship, whose objects are the "oriental" and the "woman."

A Poetics of Escape: Roland Barthes

As early as *Mythologies* (1957), French exoticism—and the fascination with the oriental world—is both object and topos in Barthes's work. In *Mythologies* French cultural texts and practices that constitute the oriental as exotic and Other are objects of semiological and mythological criticism (as in "Continent perdu"); in the same volume, however, rhetorical postures that exoticize the East are practiced by the mythologist as parts of a critical project or methodology (as in "Le monde où l'on catche"). It is the latter practice that is developed and elaborated in Barthes's work of the 1970s. His later elaboration of exoticism occurs in two forms: initially as a critical appeal to a text outside western signification—as in the references to Japanese judo in "Le monde où l'on catche" (1957), or the midcareer text valorizing Japanese cultural texts as antitheses of occidental culture, *L'empire des signes* (1970). The second form of the ironic use of exoticism as a critical strategy is exemplified by *Alors la Chine?* (1975), in which Barthes invents a writing posture that dramatizes the critic's subjective encounter with an oriental system that refuses western paradigms and ideologies. Paradoxically, Barthes's corpus commences with a politicized criticism of exoticism, yet ends with a greatly elaborated practice of this very posture.

The shift in Barthes's writing—from the targeting of orientalism as an object of criticism in the late 1950s to the dramatic practice of orientalism as a writing strategy in the mid-1970s—marks the changes of emphasis in his larger critical project during this period. The semiological critique of orientalism as an ideological text and the practice of exoticism and/or utopianism as a post-structuralist method of subverting western ideology represent twin, although paradoxical, impulses in Barthes's work. The semiological critique of western institutions and signifying practices (one of the practices being orientalism and its relationship to the colonizing of Asians and North Africans) is very clear in his early writing. In the middle and late periods, however, Barthes comes to consider semiology itself central to western constructions of meaning; semiology has become an orthodoxy in its own right, an apparatus that produces more meaning. The theoretical and political problem for Barthes during the early 1970s is the dilemma of how to write in a way that will further a critique of western institutions and yet speak from a position which does not dominate or master (as a critical discourse such as semiology does), and which eludes appropriation by the logics of western signification and epistemology. Barthes attempts several writing practices for the purpose of opening up different utopian spaces in order to challenge the structural binarisms of the early semiology. His forays into noncritical discourse include a representation of a pre-Symbolic Imaginary space in the unstructured image repertoire of the autobiography *Roland Barthes par Roland Barthes* (1975) and the collected utterances of the lover's discourse in *Fragments d'un discours amoureux* (1977), as well as the book on Japan and the essay on China.[10] In *L'empire des signes* Barthes dramatizes the western

---

[10]Steven Ungar's book *Roland Barthes: The Professor of Desire* (Lincoln: University of Nebraska Press, 1983) offers an interesting discussion of *Barthes by Barthes* and *A Lover's Discourse*. Other notable studies and assessments of Barthes include Stephen Heath, *Le vertige du déplacement* (Paris: Fayard, 1974); Annette Lavers, *Roland Barthes: Structuralism and After* (Cambridge, Mass.: Harvard University Press, 1982); Réda Bensmaïa, *The Barthes Effect* (Minneapolis: University of Minnesota Press, 1987); Paul Smith, *Discerning the Subject* (Minneapolis: University of Minnesota Press, 1988).

traveler's desire for interpreted meaning when confronted with Japanese cultural texts—foods, literature, etiquette, urban design—that refuse to signify for the western reader. *Alors la Chine?* in a like manner conjures China as a space absolutely apart from western institutions and signifying logics. All four of these texts posit a space outside the symbolic semiological system; in *Barthes* and *Fragments* the space is designated as "maternal" and outside symbolic relationships determined by the Father. In *L'empire* and *Alors*, although no less maternal, this space is figured as an "oriental" space. Ironically, Barthes's attempt to resolve the dilemma of criticizing western ideology while escaping the tyranny of binary logic takes a form not unlike that of traditional orientalism: through an invocation of the Orient as a utopian space, Barthes constitutes an imaginary third position. The imagined Orient—as critique of the Occident—becomes an emblem of his "poetics of escape," a desire to transcend semiology and the ideology of signifier and signified, to invent a place that exceeds binary structure itself.

Having offered this sketch of the importance of the Orient as signifier for Barthes's, I turn now to a more detailed discussion of a few of the precise figurations of this poetics of escape. The early semiological Barthes—of *Mythologies* (1957) and *Éléments de sémiologie* (1965)—is concerned with the processes through which the literal meanings of common objects and practices are appropriated and encoded, through social function and usage, with mythic significations: for example, the practice of drinking wine has the literal function of refreshment—its "first-order" meaning—but the social usage of wine invests the practice with a "second-order" myth of symbolic participation in French nationalism ("Le vin et le lait"). Like the other demystifications of social symbols and practices, the piece "Continent perdu" criticizes the ethnographic expedition as object and site of the myth of exoticism, as well as the appropriation of the Orient-as-a-sign by the ideology of French nationalism.

In "Continent perdu" Barthes argues that the filmic representation of an ethnographic expedition to the Orient has the literal meaning of documenting European interest in the oriental world, with a second-order level of signification as "exoticism," a cultural form for acknowledging and rendering acceptable colonialist ventures. Barthes suggests that exoticism works through the assimilation of the oriental world to French conventions. In the film the Orient visited by the anthropologists is represented as being superficially different, yet with an essence absolutely similar to that of the Occident; Buddhism is portrayed as sharing the formal features of a ubiquitous Catholicism, including nuns with shaved heads and rites in which monks kneel and confess to their superior. The final result of the expedition, which employs an occidental palette to "color" the Orient—"colorier le monde, c'est toujours un moyen de le nier" ("to *color* the world is always a manner of annihilating it")—is an erasure of the history and the specificity of the "native" culture: "En somme, l'exotisme révèle bien ici sa justification profonde, qui est de nier toute situation de l'Histoire" ("All told, exoticism here shows well its fundamental justification, which is to deny any contextualization by History").[11] Thus, in "Continent perdu" the mythologist criticizes the manner in which the film of an anthropological expedition represents the Orient as pure reflection of the Occident, how the cultural object of the voyage is mythically appropriated by the ideology of colonialism.

Even the early Barthes of *Mythologies*, however, appeals to the Orient as a "different text" which contrasts a western semiotic model of signification. In the piece "Le monde où l'on catche" Barthes analyzes the wrestling match as a text that stages, through a drama of adversaries, well-worn cultural themes: "Ce qui est ainsi livré au public, c'est le grand spectacle de la Douleur, de la Défaite, et de la Justice" ("What is thus displayed for the public is the great spectacle of Suffering, Defeat, and Justice").[12] The Japanese art of judo is posed in this piece as an opposite genre to wrestling: whereas the wrestling match is a display of excess, a choreography of roles and gestures, judo is described as an economy of moves used not to signify but to win; whereas defeat in wrestling must be apprehended as a long enactment of suffering, the loser in judo disappears immediately. This contrast is a praise of Japanese culture as much as it is a critique of wrestling as a French cultural text. Paradoxically, the formulation of praise is also exoticizing: the "coloring" of the oriental world Barthes criticizes in

[11]Roland Barthes, "Continent perdu," in *Mythologies* (Paris: Seuil, 1957), pp. 163, 165; translations from *Mythologies*, trans. Annette Lavers (New York: Farrar, Straus and Giroux, 1972), pp. 94, 96. All translations are from this edition.

[12]Roland Barthes, "Le monde où l'on catche," in *Mythologies*, p. 17; trans. Lavers, *Mythologies*, p. 19.

"Continent perdu" is accomplished in this gesture toward judo. Although *Mythologies* expresses a position that is critical of orientalism as a cultural practice, the allusion to the Japanese social text of judo reveals the early coexistence of an orientalist interest in the East as an antidote to western signification.

The middle-period Barthes is represented by the book on Japan *L'empire des signes* (1970) and by *Le plaisir du texte* (1973) as well as essays from the period 1968–1971.[13] During this period Barthes addresses doubts that semiology adequately describes how meaning and representation occur in language and culture. One of the central themes of these middle essays is that analytical or critical modes of writing of the sort practiced in *Mythologies* and *Éléments* are capable for the moment of demystifying the workings of ideology and commenting on the means by which ruling ideas are accepted as natural and proliferated as popular opinion, but that eventually critical modes of writing are appropriated by the very ideology or set of ruling ideas originally criticized. Barthes discusses this matter in structural terms of the critical discourse itself becoming another level of myth, a "third-order" meaning. In this sense Barthes revises his previous position on the concept of metalanguage. Metalanguage is not possible, he now declares, as one is always contained in language, its social circulation, and its production of meanings. Barthes argues that semiology, as a critical discourse analyzing the distinction between signifier and signified, has become in itself a myth, a reification, another ideology: "In other words, a mythological doxa has been created: denunciation, demystification (or demythification), has itself become discourse, stock of phrases, catechistic declaration . . . it is no longer the myths which need to be unmasked (the doxa now takes care of that), it is the sign itself which must be shaken."[14] He declares that new tasks, "a science of the signifier," (p. 166), will replace semiology. Thus, the object of study for the middle Barthes is no longer the cultural symbol; rather, he concentrates on *reading* as the production of multiple meanings (*Le plaisir du texte* of 1973 is the strongest representation of this emphasis), celebrating the moments and occasions when the institution of single meaning fails, when the overdetermination of the signi-

---

[13]The essays from 1968–1971 are collected in a volume translated into English by Stephen Heath, titled *Image Music Text* (New York: Farrar, Straus and Giroux, 1977).

[14]Roland Barthes, "Change the Object Itself," in *Image Music Text*, p. 167.

fier-signified relationship is disrupted. Whereas the early Barthes is interested in *parole,* or in decoding mythical speech, the middle Barthes is interested in *langue,* the social space of language in process, the unlimited, plural deferral of meaning. Hence, in "From Work to Text" in *Image Music Text),* Barthes opposes the "work" (as static, canonized literary meaning) to the notion of the "Text" (as an irreducible, unending, "stereographic" weave of signifiers) for the purpose of furthering the notion of reading as the infinite production of meaning. The distinction between "l'oeuvre" and "le Texte" is a polemical one; they do not represent two different physical objects but rather two different notions of reading, one limited to a singular intended meaning, the other asserting an infinite polysemous simultaneity of meanings.

In the "autobiography" *Barthes par Barthes,* the crisis of the middle work is posed most succinctly: when semiology as a "counterideology" itself becomes part of a *doxa,* or ideology, then ideology and counterideology are seen to be mutually constitutive "reactive formations":

> Formations réactives: une *doxa* (une opinion courante) est posée, insupportable; pour m'en dégager, je postule un paradoxe; puis ce paradoxe s'empoisse, devient lui-même concrétion nouvelle, nouvelle *doxa,* et il me faut aller plus loin vers un nouveau paradoxe. . . . Il faut donc s'en couper, introduire, dans cet imaginaire raisonnable, le grain du désir, la revendication du corps: c'est alors le Texte, la théorie du Texte. Mais de nouveau le Texte risque de se figer: il se répète, se monnaye en textes mats, témoins d'une demande de lecture, non d'un désir de plaire: le Texte tend à dégénérer en Babil. Où aller? J'en suis là.

> [Reactive formations: a *Doxa* (a popular opinion) is posited, intolerable; to free myself of it, I postulate a paradox; then this paradox turns bad, becomes a new concretion, itself becomes a new *Doxa,* and I must seek further for a new paradox. . . . One must then sever oneself from that, must introduce into this rational image-repertoire the texture of desire, the claims of the body: this, then, is the Text, the theory of the Text. But again the Text risks paralysis: it repeats itself, counterfeits itself in lusterless texts, testimonies to a demand for readers, not for a desire to please: the Text tends to degenerate into Babel. Where to go next? That is where I am now.][15]

[15]Roland Barthes, *Roland Barthes par lui-même* (Paris: Seuil, 1975), p. 75; translated from *Roland Barthes by Roland Barthes,* trans. Richard Howard (New York: Farrar, Straus and Giroux, 1977) p. 71. All translations are from this edition.

Barthes poses the theory of the Text as an antidote to the "concretion" of semiology; a notion of a plurality of meaning challenges the tyranny of singular meaning. But, as this passage confesses, this "theory of the Text" also "risks paralysis"; it is in jeopardy of being fixed, deadened, co-opted. It is within the context of this dilemma that Barthes devises different writing practices to escape the collapse into *doxa*. After the theory of the plural Text, Barthes then attempts to imagine a site beyond opposites, beyond *doxa* and *paradoxa*. In *Barthes par Barthes* one of the designations for this space is *atopia*: "L'atopie est supérieur à l'utopie (l'utopie est réactive, tactique, littéraire, elle procède du sens et le fait marcher)" (p. 53) ("Atopia is superior to utopia [utopia is reactive, tactical, literary, it proceeds from meaning and governs it]"; p. 49). The book on Japan and the piece on China both represent this desire to invent "atopia," to devise new writing practices in order to escape the reactive formation of ideology and counterideology.

In keeping with the desire to imagine an "atopia," Barthes invents a mythical place named "Japan" in *L'empire des signes*: "Si je veux imaginer un peuple fictif, je puis lui donner un nom inventé, le traiter déclarativement comme un objet romanesque . . . de façon à ne compromettre aucun pays réel dans ma fantaisie . . . que j'appellerai: le Japon" ("If I want to imagine a fictional people, I could give it an invented name, treat it openly like a novelistic object . . . so as to compromise no real country by my fantasy . . . which I shall call: Japan").[16] In this imagined country, not only do the particular social arrangements, language, and cultural practices represent a deviation from western forms of meaning, but also the western binarisms themselves—signifier and signified, inside and outside, self and Other— are thematized and undone by Japanese texts; these relationships essential to western meaning are thwarted and rendered unintelligible by the Japanese system. The experience of this Japan is described as being like a "dream" of learning another language in which occidental logic fails to signify:

> Le rêve: connaître une langue étrangère (étrange) et cependant ne pas la
> comprendre: percevoir en elle la différence sans que cette différence soit

[16]Roland Barthes, *L'empire des signes* (Geneva: Skira, 1970), p. 13; translation from *Empire of Signs*, trans. Richard Howard (New York: Farrar, Straus and Giroux, 1982), p. 3. All translations are from this edition.

jamais récupérée par la socialité superficielle du langage . . . défaire
notre "réel" sous l'effet d'autres découpages, d'autres syntaxes . . . en
un mot, descendre dans l'intraduisible . . . jusqu'à ce qu'en nous tout
l'Occident s'ébranle et que vacillent les droits de la langue paternelle,
celle qui nous vient de nos pères et qui nous fait à notre tour, pères et
propriétaires.   (p.13)

[The dream: to know a foreign (alien) language and yet not to understand it: to perceive the difference in it without that difference ever being
recuperated by the superficial sociality of discourse . . . to undo our own
"reality" under the effect of other formulations, other syntaxes . . . in a
word, to descend into the untranslatable . . . until everything Occidental
in us totters and the rights of the "father tongue" vacillate—that tongue
which comes to us from our fathers and which makes us, in our turn,
fathers and proprietors.]   (p. 6)

Barthes evokes Japan as an imaginary topos of "untranslatable" difference (just as the "Text" is earlier imagined as "irreducible" plurality).
The imagination of Japan is an occasion to wish, as in a dream, the
toppling of the West: the undoing of its systems of language and
discourse, its institutions of meanings, its symbolic paternal order. In
the dream-text of Japan, Barthes reads *sukiyaki* as "une nourriture
décentrée," the Japanese face as "un signe vide," and celebrates the
"nullité du sens" of Japanese Zen Buddhism. By creating the fictive
text of Japan, Barthes ventures a possible resolution to the question
battled in midlife: Where do critics go where they will not be determined by the very theories, the very texts, they have authored?

As antitext to the West, however, Japan is ultimately not an "atopia"
but a "utopia": "réactive, tactique, littéraire." The desire to escape his
own subjectivity, history, and language is quite evidently an oppositional desire, still caught within the binary logic he seeks to avoid.
Japan is continually described with reference to the Occident, solely in
terms of what the Occident is *not*: the Japanese city is decentered,
Barthes claims, whereas Paris is oriented around a central *place*; chop-
sticks capriciously select, turn, and shift delicate pieces of food,
whereas knives and forks cut, pierce, and dominate; Japanese Bun-
raku puppet theater fragments the components of the drama and
reveals the puppeteers manipulating the puppets, whereas occidental
theater is an art of simulating the "naturalness" of the human figure, of
situating the origin of drama and emotion in the interior of the actor.
Thus, in *L'empire*, as in the construction of judo in *Mythologies*,

Barthes invokes Japanese cultural texts as antidotes to western institutions of meaning. In a sense, *L'empire* is structured as if it were a companion volume to *Mythologies*; for, as in *Mythologies*, the semiologist chooses cultural objects and practices to decode in terms of levels of denotation and connotation. In *L'empire*, however, the thwarted efforts of the semiologist are thematized. The semiologist discovers that the Japanese forms precisely do not mean, do not signify, in western terms. Barthes's invention of Japan is a reactive formation; its cultural texts are important to the degree that they do not conform to western systems of signification. In the discussion of the relationship between the paradigm of semiology and the theory of a polysemous Text, Barthes articulates the dilemma of reactive formation as one in which a *paradoxa*, erected as an antidote to a *doxa*, itself solidifies into a another *doxa*. In *L'empire* the utopian formulation of Japan, which represents an antithesis to western semiology, repeats this logic of reactive formation.

Alors la Chine?: "Où aller? J'en suis là."

Alors la Chine? (1975) is a much shorter, if no less "utopian," narrative about an invented Orient. Though not one of Barthes's more famous pieces, it is worthy of attention for not only does it develop further his search for a new form of writing, but also, along with Kristeva's *Des chinoises*, it emblematizes the powerful hold that China had on the imagination of certain French intellectuals during the mid-1970s. Like the Japan of *L'empire*, China is also constructed as a refutation of European hermeneutic and political traditions; the China evoked in this piece, however, elides the French writer's interpretive acts in a very different manner than does his Japan. In *L'empire*, even though the cultural texts are framed as ornate antitheses of French rites and practices, the Japanese texts are granted separate and independent symbolic logics (postulated, at times, as antilogics) of their own. In *Alors*, China is a text that completely lacks a symbolic function, is nothing but bland surfaces, contains no meanings to elucidate, no bodies to eroticize. It is constructed as offering only a single political Text, a set of coded clichés combined in various ways. The China described by Barthes is radically boring.

To a much greater degree than *L'empire, Alors* thematizes the project of writing about an absolute site of difference as the central topos of a writing strategy. This thematization is a consequence of the bipartite structure of the published text. Divided into two sections, which represent two writing situations, the text contains a first part written in a descriptive present made and a second part in a retrospective imperfect tense. The beginning section simulates the voice of an occidental traveler who experiences China; the final section (in italics) consists of reflective remarks and assessments about having written about China, an afterword composed after the "original" publication of the beginning section in *Le Monde*.

In the first section of *Alors*, China is hallucinated as a culture whose impossible homogeneity refuses to signify in western terms. Throughout the piece the traveler-narrator implies an antithesis between the cultural systems of France and China: French culture is a society structured on difference, differences being the source of occidental desire, meaning, and eroticism. Chinese society, he argues, is neutral, smooth, and prosaic, profoundly lacking conflict or difference. The undivided homogeneity is asserted in numerous remarks about the conformity, the undifferentiated appearances of the people, as well as the lack of color, and the bland, faded quality of everyday life: "La Chine n'est pas *coloriée*. La campagne . . . est plate . . . au loin, deux buffles gris, un tracteur, des champs réguliers mais asymétriques, un groupe de travailleurs en bleu, c'est tout" ("China is not *colorful*. The countryside . . . is flat . . . in the distance a few gray oxen, a tractor, orderly but asymmetrical fields, a group of workers dressed in blue, and that is all").[17] Yet it is precisely the peacefulness and tedium which are evoked as subversive and radically Other, insofar as they thwart the western subject's hermeneutic desire for closure, meaning, and correspondence.

> Nous voulons qu'il y ait des choses impénétrables pour que nous puissions les pénétrer: par atavisme idéologique, nous sommes des êtres du déchiffrement, des sujets hermeneutiques; nous croyons que notre

---

[17]Roland Barthes, *Alors la Chine?* (Paris: Christian Bourgois, 1975), p. 9. I am grateful to Steven Ungar for having referred me to this text. The translation is by Lee Hildreth from "Well, and China?" *Discourse* 8 (Fall–Winter 1986–87): 116–21; the quoted passage appears on p. 117.

tache intellectuelle est toujours de découvrir un sens. La Chine semble résister à livrer ce sens, non parce qu'elle le cache mais, plus subversive-ment, parce que (en cela bien peu confucéenne) elle defait la constitution des concepts, des thèmes, des noms; elle ne partage pas les cibles du savoir comme nous; le champ semantique est désorganisé . . . les objets idéologiques que notre société construit sont silencieusement déclaré *im-pertinents*. C'est la fin de l'hermeneutique.   (p. 8)

[We want there to be impenetrable phenomena, so that we can penetrate them: by an ideological atavism, we are deciphering beings, hermeneu-tic subjects. We believe our intellectual task is always to discover a meaning. China seems to resist delivering this meaning, not because it hides it, but more subversively, because (in this respect very un-Confu-cian) it defeats the constitution of concepts, themes, names. It does not divide up the targets of knowledge as we do; the semantic field is disorganized . . . the ideological objects of our society are silently de-clared *im-pertinent*. It is the end of hermeneutics.]   (p. 116–17)

In defining China as "subversive," as not yielding to the western subject's desire for meaning, Barthes specifies that his notion of China is not one in which China hides meaning from the western observer (a configuration within which China would again be invoked as a "reac-tive formation," "tactical, literary"). Rather, he asserts, from the point of view of the separate and different China, western hermeneutic desires are simply irrelevant. Barthes, the traveler-narrator, figures China as that long-imagined nonreactive atopia, confronted by which occidental systems of meaning totter and fail.

Although the narrator takes elaborate pains to declare China an independent phenomenon, the rhetorical and syntactical logic of the narrative description performs exactly the opposite function. First, a characterization of the western paradigm precedes each definition of China, rhetorically rendering each perception of China's difference dependent on an aspect of western ideology. Second, in contrast to the active subjectivity of *nous* in the syntactical constructions that describe western desires—"nous voulons," "nous sommes," "nous croyons"— "la Chine" occurs persistently as the subject of negations, of depen-dent clauses and qualifiers. Logically and syntactically, China is sub-versive if considered exclusively in terms of occidental cultural sys-tems; the narrator does not offer an explanation of how China is subversive within its own autonomous cultural system.

In a manner not unlike the invention of the mythical Japan, the subversive China is invoked according to a logic of opposition; it is described in terms of how it thwarts the will to decipher, and is described for the purpose of more thoroughly elaborating the western observer's hermeneutic desire. Even the description "bien peu confucéenne" does not denote an evolution or history within a specifically Chinese system of reference. For in this phrase "confucéenne" is appropriated to signify a hermeneutic "constitution des concepts, des thèmes, des noms." With this deft move Barthes snatches Confucian doctrine from China by equating it with western hermeneutics—stripping Chinese Confucianism of its lengthy history, condensing its myriad and diverse tenets into a single dimension—and assimilates it to an occidental characterization of itself.

There is another level on which *Alors* refuses to consider the independent status of China and relegates China to a position of serving the interests of the Occident; this is the tendency of the French leftist intellectual to make the Chinese communist example into a political fetish. The remark "bien peu confucéenne" refers to one of the goals of the Chinese Revolution of 1949, as well as to the cultural reform programs up through the Cultural Revolution: that the Confucian ethos of maintaining social order through correct hierarchical relationships should be purged from Chinese culture. In this one parenthetical phrase Barthes constructs a China that has successfully achieved Mao's Cultural Revolution by placing professors, officers, and administrators in the fields and factories. But the history, the struggle, the labors of restructuring are rendered invisible, and the implications of this enormous Chinese project are collapsed and reduced into one significance: that the otherness of the Chinese political experience should serve as a reified utopian moment for the contemporary French Left in the wake of May 1968, the Parisian attempt at "cultural revolution."

In a further elaboration of the irreducible political experience of China, Barthes asserts that whereas western ideology "depoliticizes" social practice, the political text is absolutely explicit in China: "En somme, à peu de choses près, la Chine ne donne à lire que son Texte politique. Ce texte est partout: aucun domaine ne lui est soutrait" (pp. 10–11) ("In short, China offers very little to be read aside from its political Text. That Text is everywhere: no area is exempt from it"; p. 118). What does it mean to be a pure "political text"? The background to this enigmatic gesture is provided in a much earlier discussion in

Mythologies, a discussion in which Barthes formulates an opposition between myth, or "depoliticized speech," and "political speech." Myth is *depoliticized* speech, he argues, because it represses the acts and processes of production, erasing ideological meanings, in order to represent the product and its values as both "natural" and "eternal." Yet, as early as *Mythologies* Barthes already gestures toward an essentialized kind of speech that is not susceptible to myth:

> Si le mythe est une parole dé-politisée, il y a au moins une parole qui s'oppose au mythe, c'est la parole qui *reste* politique. Il faut ici revenir à la distinction entre langage-objet et méta-langage. Si je suis un bûcheron et que j'en vienne à nommer l'arbre que j'abats, quelle que soit la forme de ma phrase, je parle l'arbre, je ne parle pas *sur* lui. Ceci veut dire que mon langage est opératoire, lié à son objet d'une façon transitive: entre l'arbre et moi, il n'y a rien d'autre que mon travail, c'est-à-dire un acte: c'est là un langage politique; il me présente la nature dans la mesure seulement où je vais la transformer, c'est un langage par lequel j'*agis* l'objet: l'arbre n'est pas pour moi une image, il est simplement le sens de mon acte. . . .
>
> Il y a donc un langage qui n'est pas mythique, c'est le langage de l'homme producteur. . . . Voilà pourquoi le langage proprement révolutionnaire ne peut être un langage mythique. . . . La bourgeoisie se masque comme bourgeoisie et par là même produit le mythe; la révolution s'affiche comme révolution et par là-même abolit le mythe.
>
> [If myth is depoliticized speech, there is at least one type of speech which is the opposite of myth: that which *remains* political. Here we must go back to the distinction between language-object and metalanguage. If I am a woodcutter and I am led to name the tree which I am felling, whatever the form of my sentence, I "speak the tree," I do not speak *about* it. This means that my language is operational, transitively linked to its object; between the tree and myself, there is nothing but my labor, that is to say, action. This is a political language: it represents nature for me only inasmuch as I am going to transform it, it is a language thanks to which I "*act the object*"; the tree is not an image for me, it is simply the meaning of my action. . . .
>
> There is therefore one language which is not mythical, it is the language of man as a producer. . . . This is why revolutionary language proper cannot be mythical. . . . The bourgeoisie hides the fact that it is the bourgeoisie and thereby produces myth; revolution announces itself openly as revolution and thereby abolishes myth.][18]

[18]Barthes, *Mythologies*, pp. 233–34; *Mythologies*, trans. Lavers, pp. 145–46.

As opposed to depoliticized speech, the labor of a specific worker acting upon an object is an enunciation of revolutionary "political speech." In asserting that this act in which the woodcutter *speaks* the tree can be invulnerable to myth—and is not subject to the repression of production or the erasure of history, which are functions of the metalanguage of myth—Barthes suggests that "political speech" does not conform to the outlined system of semiotic signification; indeed, this passage suggests that political speech is so powerful that it can "abolish myth." Earlier Barthes had argued that the arbitrariness of the sign—that is, the arbitrary, divisible, and relative relationship between any signifier and signified—makes most language objects vulnerable to invasion by the signification of myth. Here he suggests, however, that "political speech" is invulnerable because it is a special language object. There is an implied association of the semiotic sign constituted by political speech, which is indivisible and not arbitrary, and the notion of unalienated labor before the worker's labor is alienated and extracted as the surplus value of the product.[19] The act of the woodcutter upon the tree is pure political speech because, like the notion of unalienated labor, it is not yet separated from its object. Barthes's declaration that "revolution announces itself openly as revolution and thereby abolishes myth" suggests that a state of revolution might consist of the continual enunciation of political speech, in which speech could not be alienated from labor, and labor could not be alienated from the worker.

In the context of this earlier distinction between depoliticized (mythical) speech and political speech in *Mythologies*, it is possible to understand that *Alors la Chine?* celebrates China as a utopian site where this pure political speech is pronounced and iterated—everywhere. In China, Barthes contends, the political text is at one with social relations: with no mediation or gap between them, the sign *is* the referent.

[19]The notions of alienated and unalienated labor are elaborated in Marx's early writing, "The Economic and Philosophical Manuscripts of 1844." Marx argues that the worker's labor is alienated in the object of the product when the product of the worker's labor is appropriated by the owner of the means of production to earn profits from the surplus value of that product. "Through *estranged*, *alienated* labour, then, the worker produces the relationship to this labour of a man alien to labour and standing outside it. The relationship of the worker to labour engenders the relation to it of the capitalist, or whatever one chooses to call the master of labour. *Private property* is thus the product, the result, the necessary consequence, of *alienated labour*, of the external relation of the worker to nature and to himself." *Marx-Engels Reader*, p. 65.

Ai-je parlé de fadeur? Un autre mot me vient, plus juste: la Chine est *paisible*. La paix (à quoi l'onomastique chinoise fait si souvent référence) n'est-elle pas cette région, pour nous utopique, où la guerre des sens est abolie? Là-bas, le sens est annulé, exempté, dans tous les lieux où nous, Occidentaux, le traquons; mais il reste debout, armé, articulé, offensif, là où nous répugnons à le mettre: dans la politique.   (p. 10)

[Did I speak of blandness? Another word comes to me, one that is more accurate: China is *peaceful*. Is not peace (to which Chinese onomastics makes such frequent reference) the region, utopian for us, where the war of meaning is abolished? In China, meaning is annulled, exempted from being in all those places where we Westerners track it down, but it remains standing, armed, articulated, and on the offensive where we are loath to put it: in politics.]   (p. 118)

Thus, China provides a utopian site for Barthes, outside both the western "war of meaning" and the "war" of industrial capitalist production. It is an impossibly inaccessible Other for both aspects of Barthes's desire—for the semiotician who imagines an irreducible "semioclasm," as well as for the leftist intellectual who envisions an ideal model of cultural revolution where there is "un mouvement par lequel on empêche continûment la révolution de s'épaissir, de s'engorger, de se figer" (p. 11) ("a movement by means of which the revolution is continuously kept from losing its momentum, from choking on itself, from congealing"; p. 119). China—as semiotic and political utopia—is the sign under which Barthes's "poetics of escape" is written.

With the addition of a brief afterword to the text, Barthes complicates the first section by commenting on it. By writing about the first section from a different temporal location, he splits the text as a whole and renders it divided, troubled. The first section dramatizes the western subject's desire; the second section (in the past tense) frames the present tense of the first as a spontaneous utterance, proclaims it a discursive site, interprets it. In this sense the formal structure of the published text itself is ambivalent; it cannot be reduced to one mode or the other but is always divided, never static, always doubled.

In this second section the reflexive Barthes interprets the project of the narrator of the first section: "Sur la Chine, immense objet et, pour beaucoup, objet brûlant, j'ai essayé de produire—c'était là ma vérité—un discours qui ne fut ni assertif, ni négateur, ni neutre: un commentaire dont le ton serait: *no comment*" (p. 14) ("About China, an immense object, and for many, an urgent one, I tried to produce—and this was my truth—a discourse that was neither assertive nor negative, nor neutral: a commentary whose tone would be *no comment*"; p. 120). The afterword states the first narrator's wish for a mode of writing that would neither praise nor condemn, and thus could not be absorbed into either a *doxa* or a *paradoxa*. But there is an evident contradiction between what the second narrator declares and what the rhetorical logic of the first narration reveals. Despite the descriptions of China as bland, boring, and homogeneous, the evocation of China is nonetheless invested, committed, desiring; the entire piece is structured as an encomium praising the very subversive "fadeur" of China. For example, the statement "la Chine n'est pas *coloriée*" does not impartially comment that China is "uninteresting." On the contrary, it precisely posits China *in opposition to* the pervasive and overdetermined occidental systems of signification; "la Chine n'est pas *coloriée*" is a manner of saying that China is not "colonized" (*colorier* recalls the piece on exoticism, "Continent perdu," in which *colorier* is the means through which cultural domination takes place), and therefore offers to the western subject one pure, irreducible site from which western ideology can be criticized. The encomium constitutes China as a place of impossibility, the desire for which initiates and sustains the writer's writing. The project of writing about this inconceivably homogeneous Other is like the "discours amoureux," fragments uttered for a beloved whose absolute silence refuses the lover's words. It is the writing about the desired figure that founds the voice of the writer, and the closed inpenetrability of this Other that maintains the writing project, inasmuch as the Other can never be wholly written about. Again, as in traditional orientalism, the western writer's desire for the oriental Other structures the Other as forever separated, unpossessed, and estranged.

In the afterword to *Alors la Chine?* Barthes characterizes his aims and methods in the preceding narrative's description of China:

En hallucinant doucement la Chine comme un objet situé hors de la couleur vive, de la saveur forte et du sens brutal (tout ceci n'étant pas sans rapport avec la sempiternelle parade du Phallus), je voulais lier dans un seul mouvement l'infini féminin (maternel?) de l'objet lui-même, cette manière inouïe que la Chine a eue à mes yeux de déborder le sens, paisiblement et puissamment.   (p. 14)

[By gently hallucinating China as an object located outside any bright color or any strong flavor, any brutal meaning (all this not without a bearing on the relentless parade of the Phallus), I wanted to bring together in a single movement the infinite feminine (maternal?) of the object itself, that extraordinary way China, in my eyes, had of overflowing the boundaries of meaning, peacefully and powerfully.]   (p. 120)

If the first section of *Alors* emphasized China's otherness as a pure political text outside the logic and process of western signification, the remarks in the afterword figure China's otherness in psychoanalytic terms, and within a psychoanalytic paradigm. Barthes's association of China's "débordement" of western meaning with a feminine or maternal disruption of a phallic order locates China with reference to the Lacanian notions of the maternal Imaginary and the realm of the paternal Symbolic. Here we observe an interesting parallel between Barthes's and Kristeva's formulations. Kristeva places Chinese women in a pre-oedipal phase anterior to the castration and oedipalization that she associates with the processes of signification and subjectification in the sociosymbolic West. Like Kristeva, Barthes also makes use of Lacanian distinctions in order to posit a presymbolic space outside the Symbolic system based on the possession of, lack of, or desire for the masculine signifier of the phallus.[20] Both critics emphasize the nonintelligibility of western language within the context of their fictions of China in order to liken China to a preverbal psychoanalytic space, a site outside language and before the intervention of the Father. As the foregoing passage illustrates, this site is associated with the maternal, constituted by both Barthes and Kristeva as a powerful force for interrupting the overdetermined structures of relationship in the paternal Symbolic. Insofar as Barthes and Kristeva rely on the concepts of the Imaginary and the Symbolic in constructing the otherness of China, they situate China in a space akin to the Imaginary,

[20]In a sociological study of the emergence of psychoanalytic culture in France during the 1970s, *Psychoanalytic Politics: Freud's French Revolution* (Boston: Basic Books, 1978), Sherry Turkle analyzes the social circumstances that allowed the work of the psychoanalyst Jacques Lacan to exert such an influence on the thinking and politics of leftist intellectuals and literary theorists. The social revolts of May–June 1968 are central to Turkle's explanation of the particular form of psychoanalytic culture in France.

which Lacan poses as prior to, and recapitulated from, the sociolinguistic Symbolic.

In a sense, Barthes's projection of China in the first half of *Alors* as Other to western hermeneutics and politics coincides with the early desires in *Mythologies* and the middle-period desires of "La mythologie aujourd'hui" to locate a sociolinguistic position that is not subject to the overdetermination of western language, ideology, and practice. When Barthes associates this space with the "feminine" in *Alors*, and designates it as maternal and antiphallic, the frame of reference changes from a sociolinguistic one to one that is primarily psychoanalytic. Barthes's privileging of the psychoanalytic framework is what finally dehistoricizes and depoliticizes China, and ultimately reduces China's vast and heterogeneous history to an essentialized category within western psychoanalytic explanation. Indeed, one notes a methodological shift that privileges psychoanalysis, as opposed to the earlier sociolinguistic methods of semiotics, in the middle and later texts. The reduction of China to the maternal Imaginary in *Alors* is one telling example of the methodological shift in the larger corpus as a whole.

Some of the implications of Barthes's association of China with these psychoanalytic categories become clearer if we locate these categories in the middle works—*Fragments d'un discours amoureux*, *Barthes par Barthes*—and especially in the later work *La chambre claire* (1980). In these texts, as in *Alors*, Barthes constitutes maternal otherness as an irreducible difference against which social, linguistic, and ideological systems of meaning are distinguished. Barthes's texts consistently appeal to the presocial or extrasocial energies and desires of the maternal and the Imaginary in order to disrupt the Symbolic's order of meaning and law. In both *Fragments* and *Barthes par Barthes*, Barthes invents an Imaginary presocial order as part of devising writing strategies that oppose the paternal Symbolic order.[21] Both writing projects—*Fragments* and *Barthes*—metaphorically suspend the period of the Imaginary by refusing narrative, argument, or hierarchizing logics. Both texts associate the Imaginary with the Mother, and with a realm

[21]Gregory Ulmer, "The Discourse of the Imaginary," *Diacritics* 10, no. 1 (March 1980): 61–75. Ulmer asserts that in *Barthes* and *A Lover's Discourse*, Barthes attempts to open a "third front" in criticism, devising a "projective-productive style of reading" in which the relationship of reader and text imitates the Imaginary relationship of child-subject and Imaginary Other.

outside the sociosymbolic network of inscription and signified subjectivity.

The "figures" in *Fragments* dramatize a variety of possible desiring postures of the subject in love; they are presented in a random, nonlinear, nonexclusive order, as if the text were a simulation of the various topoi of desire that hover before speech in the unconscious. *Fragments* suggests that "love" occurs in the junction between the Imaginary and the Symbolic, that is, in the transitions between the preverbal and presocial desires (of child for Mother, for specular images, for absent others) and the articulation of this desire in the symbolic system of speech and language. The text portrays the source of the "lover's discourse" in the Imaginary, before selection, before being inserted into a narrative. *Fragments*, however, presents the lover's possible utterances as ends in themselves. Unhierarchized and coequal, they are suspended without emplotment, without destination. *Barthes par Barthes* is a somewhat random collection of fragments as well, simulating a presymbolic "antistructure" or "polygraphy" of photographic images, meditations, and aphorisms that makes up the "life" of Roland Barthes. The structure of the book simulates an Imaginary consisting of assorted visual images and aphorisms; the text places the reader in the position of analyst, or of secondary revisionist, by its demands on the reader to pull together the fragments, to interpret, to infer and consolidate. Associative connections are substituted for narrative logic; a diffused, shifting, fragmented voice—at times referred to as "je," at times as "il" or "R. B."—is substituted for a unified and oedipalized subject. In thematizing the Imaginary as those images before language, narrative, and oedipalization, the writing strategies of *Fragments* and *Barthes* metaphorically defer the processes of castration and socialization associated with entry into the Symbolic. In these texts, oedipalization is effectively displaced as the destination or end point of writing and narrative.

La chambre claire, the eulogy to Barthes's mother, finished just before his own death, also evokes a maternal realm, appealing to an impossible and irreducible maternal body which radically interrupts the social system. In *La chambre* the photograph is explored as a form of presentation, as opposed to representation, that is not subject to language, analysis, ideology; the meditation on the photograph is a vehicle for isolating and articulating a phenomenon that can be classified as prelinguistic. The shift to essentialized psychoanalytic categories, which marks both the later works and the final characterization of China in *Alors*, is perhaps best exemplified by the concept of the photographic *punctum*. Barthes asserts that an inexplicable element in the photo may trigger an inexpressible and overwhelming constellation of presocial desires, memories, and mourning. The *punctum* is a detail in a photograph—for Barthes it is a man's fingernails in one photo, a woman's shoes in another—that "punctures" the viewing subject and triggers a subjective experience. The *punctum* initiates a powerful contradiction in the viewer of the photo; suddenly the viewer is seized by the sense that although the photograph may declare the absolute presence of the person, place, or event in the photo, it is simultaneously an undeniable statement of the photographed subject's absence, the fact of its no longer existing as it does in the photo: "*Le punctum, c'est: il va mourir*. Je lis en même temps: *cela sera* et *cela a été*; j'observe avec horreur un futur antérieur dont la mort est l'enjeu. . . . Devant la photo de ma mère enfant, je me dis: ella va mourir" ("The *punctum* is: *he is going to die*. I read at the same time: *This will be* and *this has been*; I observe with horror an anterior future of which death is the stake. . . . Before the photo of my mother as a child, I tell myself: she is going to die").[22] Although different details and photos initiate the wounding paradox of the *punctum* for different individual viewers, the "original source" of the *punctum*, Barthes implies throughout, is the viewer's memory of the maternal body. Viewing Charles Clifford's photograph of a Mediterranean house, the Alhambra, Barthes declares:

> Il est fantasmatique, relève d'une sorte de voyance qui semble me porter en avant, vers un temps utopique, ou me reporter en arrière, je ne sais où de moi-même: double mouvement que Baudelaire a chanté dans l'*Invitation au Voyage* et *La Vie Antérieure*. Devant ces paysages de prédilection, tout se passe comme si j'étais sûr d'y avoir été ou devoir y aller. Or Freud dit du corps maternel qu' "il n'est point d'autre lieu dont on puisse dire avec autant de certitude qu'on y a déjà été." Telle serait alors l'essence du paysage (choisi par le désir): *heimlich*, réveillant en moi la Mère (nullement inquiétant).   (p. 68)
>
> [It is fantasmatic, deriving from a kind of second sight which seems to bear me forward to a utopian time, or to carry me back to somewhere (I don't know where) in myself: a double movement heralded by Baude-

[22]Roland Barthes, *La chambre claire: Note sur la photographie* (Paris: Editions de l'Étoile, Gallimard, Seuil, 1980), p. 150; translation from *Camera Lucida*, trans. Richard Howard (New York: Farrar, Straus and Giroux, 1981), p. 96. All translations are from this edition.

laire in *Invitation au voyage* and *La Vie Antérieure*. Looking at these land-scapes of predilection, it is as if I were certain of having been there or of going there. Now Freud says of the maternal body that "there is no other place of which one can say with so much certainty that one has already been there." Such then would be the essence of the landscape (chosen by desire): *heimlich*, awakening in me the Mother (and never the disturb-ing Mother).]   (p. 40)

In this description of the *punctum*, Barthes constitutes the maternal body as a fantasmatic yet essential site of origin. The viewer of the photograph is struck by a particular detail or aspect, something which is not perhaps even visually explicit, but which carries the viewer back to a notion of the mother's body. This experience is "uncanny"—that is, paradoxical, split—because this memory of the mother's body is at once immediately tangible in the subject's experience of the photo-graph and yet impossibly lost and immaterial. In this sense Barthes privileges the remembrance of the Mother as the prototypical *punctum*, and essentializes the Mother as origin. Throughout the text Barthes suggests that the *punctum* is crucial to the viewing subject's grasp of itself as subject, as existing. The phenomenological argument about the maternal body as the source of the *punctum* collapses back into a psychoanalytic argument about the Mother as the subject's first love and first source of love, before oedipalization and the intervention of the Father. As in other of Barthes's texts, the maternal is designated as a privileged and essentialized realm outside of, and more powerful than, sociosymbolic relations.[23]

Therefore, when the afterword to *Alors la Chine?* refers to "l'infini féminin (maternel?)" of China, which has no "rapport avec la sem-piternelle parade du Phallus," Barthes is situating the binarism of China and the West in an already familiar system of psychoanalytic terms: China occupies a maternal, Imaginary, unnarrativized space antithetical to the sociosymbolic paternal order exemplified by the West. The remarkable irony of this figuration of China as Other is that even though the early essays in *Mythologies* criticize the binary logic that invented oriental cultures as the antithesis of western societies, in *Alors* a version of this very logic continues to structure the evocation of

[23]Lynn Higgins points out that foreign cultures are consistently experienced as mater-nal in Barthes's travelogues. See "Barthes's Imaginary Voyages," *Studies in Twentieth-Century Literature* 5, no. 2 (Spring 1981): 157–74.

China in terms of a psychoanalytic binarism: China as maternal Imaginary and West as paternal Symbolic.

China is, in the binary logic of *Alors*, a fetish, in both the psychoanalytic sense of being a fixation, a repetition of the same illusion or disavowal, and the sense of being reified, as Marx writes of the fetishism of commodities in capitalist society. Freud discusses fetishism as the result of a splitting of the ego; it manifests itself in a fixation that allows a person to hold simultaneously two contrary beliefs. Freud cites the example of the male subject who disavows the sight of female genitals because the lack of the penis initiates his fear of castration; thus, he denies his own perception that female genitals lack a penis. Yet the disavowed perception is not without its own influence; although the subject cannot assert that he actually saw a penis, he substitutes (fetishizes) another part of the body, or another object, and assigns it the role of the penis. "The creation of the fetish was due to an intention to destroy evidence for the possibility of castration, so that fear of castration could be avoided."[24] Marx also uses the term *fetishism* to refer to the commodity form in capitalist society, particularly the process through which the value of the commodity on the market is a reification and mystification of the material and labor that went into producing the commodity.[25] Thus, when I refer to China as a fetish in Barthes's texts, I am referring both to the sustaining of two opposed systems of contrary beliefs and to the reification of China as a commodity/image for all that is subversive to western signification. For Barthes, on the one hand, western sociosymbolic relations are all-pervasive and determining; yet on the other hand, each of his texts since *Mythologies* insists there must be a site that is not determined by these relations—an "uncastrated" speech, an undifferentiated society, without hierarchy, outside western law. Furthermore, in each of these texts the sign for this utopian space is both reified and mystified; in rendering China a transcendent Other, he allows little correspondence between the China of *Alors* and the historical circumstances of struggle and change in the People's Republic of China.

[24]Sigmund Freud, *An Outline of Psycho-Analysis* (New York: Norton, p. 60). See also J. Laplanche and J.-B. Pontalis, "Splitting of the Ego," in *The Language of Psycho-Analysis* (London: Hogarth, 1973).

[25]Fetishism in Marx is introduced in the "Economic and Philosophic Manuscripts of 1844," in *Marx-Engels Reader*, as well as in *Capital*; see pt. 1, chap. 1, "Commodities" (New York: International, 1967). For a detailed discussion of the fetishism of commodities in Marx, see White, *Metahistory*, pp. 287–97.

China as Political Utopia: *Tel quel*, Mai '68, and
French Maoism

In attempting to place Barthes's and Kristeva's formulations of
China in the context of each critic's theoretical project and agenda, I
have discussed Kristeva's notion that ancient Chinese matriarchy represented a pre-oedipal linguistic and social moment in the context of
structuralist, psychoanalytic, and feminist debates of the period, and
have placed Barthes's figuration of China as pure maternal speech in
terms of the critical aims of his larger corpus. A third context for these
figurations of China can be found in the political circumstances in
France during the 1960s and early 1970s, particularly the revolutionary
events of May 1968, as well as the subsequent attempts to grapple,
politically and theoretically, with the significance of those events. In
the aftermath of the widespread student revolts that were coordinated
with massive workers' strikes in May 1968, critics and activists debated
whether the crisis signaled a new age of European revolution or resulted in the consolidation of authoritarian rule. Numerous accounts
asserted that May 1968 created "revolutionary possibilities," and that
the events had suggested for the first time (as Marx had indicated in
the *Communist Manifesto*) that revolution could occur in an industrialized European nation.[26] At the same time, other analyses weighed
more heavily the ultimate repression of the revolts, the failures of the
Popular Front and the Communist party, and finally the recovery and
swift electoral victory of the Gaullists in June.[27] It is in the context of
the judgments of the May events as a failure of revolutionary possibilities that one faction of leftists, intellectuals, students, and workers
admired the People's Republic of China, constituted the Chinese Cultural Revolution as an example for the French Left, and celebrated
Maoism as true revolutionary theory. Within this context the journal
Tel quel provides another figuration of China—compatible with, yet
inflected differently from, Kristeva's and Barthes's figurations—as ab-

[26]See Daniel Singer, *Prelude to Revolution: France in May 1968* (New York: Hill and
Wang, 1970), and George Katsiaficas, *The Imagination of the New Left: A Global Analysis of
1968* (Boston: South End Press, 1987), which celebrate May 1968 in France in terms of its
importance to the history of Eurocommunism.

[27]Critics who underscored the failures of the potential of May 1968 include Jean-Paul
Sartre, André Barjonet, Jean-Marie Vincent, and Alain Touraine.

solute political utopia, the Maoist Other of western Marxist theory and practice.

The Communist party of France (PCF, Parti communiste français) has a very different status and history from that of communist parties elsewhere, particularly in the United States. The strength and credibility of the PCF following the Second World War had much to do with the persuasiveness of the Marxist analysis of fascism and Nazism, as well as the PCF's role in the Resistance, and in leading union activity. In the period from 1945 to 1970, however, both the theory and the practice of traditional French Marxism and French communism were challenged. Critiques of traditional Marxism, disillusionment with Soviet communism, and fragmentation of the French communist parties during the 1950s made Chinese Maoism in the 1960s an attractive alternative for a section of the French Left. The example of the Cultural Revolution, which placed professors, officers, and administrators in the fields and factories on the principle of reconnecting the government and the masses, provided a theoretical coherence for the fragmented parties.

On a theoretical level, well-known radical critiques of traditional Marxism were carried out by Jean-Paul Sartre, Henri Lefebvre, Cornelius Castoriadis, and others. Sartre's existential critique of Marxism concerned itself with what he considered to be the lack of a Marxist theory of subjectivity; Lefebvre's revisionist critique questioned the traditional Marxist view of advanced industrial society; the *gauchiste* Castoriadis criticized authoritarianism and hierarchy in the communist bureaucracy, ultimately claiming that revolutionary Marxism had ossified into a bureaucratic ideology.[28] These critiques contributed to the disillusionment of some students, workers, and intellectuals with the theory, policies, and machinery of the traditional PCF. Some older communists concerned about French involvement in Algeria and Indochina (of which the PCF was not greatly critical), and those disillusioned with Stalin and Soviet communism, considered Maoism an alternative to the orthodox stance of the PCF. Because the PCF dominated the CGT (Confédération générale du travail), the largest of the three major labor unions, the *gauchistes* viewed the PCF as a bureau-

[28]Arthur Hirsh, *The French New Left: An Intellectual History from Sartre to Gorz* (Boston: South End Press, 1981).

cratic machine interested in integrating the working classes into the status quo. Other factions that were disenchanted with, or had been expelled from, the PCF looked toward "antihierarchical" Maoism for theoretical and organizational ideals.[29] The social upheaval of May 1968 was an essential turning point in the challenges to traditional communism, for the themes of May were the very ones raised by the leftist critiques of Marxism: antihierarchicalism, self-management, the revolt against alienation in a bureaucratic society. At the same time, the events of May also seemed to reveal some of the limitations of both traditional Marxism and its new leftist critiques and in this sense represent an origin of the turn toward Maoism by *Tel quel*.

In 1968 the range of revolutionary activities against the Gaullist government which called for the dramatic expansion of freedoms for students and workers was neither singular nor peculiar to France. This was a time of popular protest in many nations; in Washington, D.C., Chicago, and San Francisco students and other citizens demonstrated against the involvement of the United States in the Vietnam war. In Rome, London, Tokyo, and Prague as well, dissident groups were spontaneously challenging ruling establishments.[30] In France, student demonstrations in the universities began at Nanterre and spread across the nation. Students occupied universities and issued a far-reaching critique of the university system which included specific protests against the authoritarian structure of the university (admissions policies, the repression of political meetings, examinations, the faculty rank system) and denunciations of the curriculum. But, unlike in the United States, for example, the French students were joined by

[29]At this particular historical juncture Maoism captured the imagination of a number of French radical groups: the Parti communiste Marxiste-Léniniste de France (PCMLF), the Union des étudiants communists (UEC) and its later Union des jeunesses communistes—Marxiste-Léniniste" (UJC–ML), the Gauche prolétarienne (GP), and Vive la Révolution (VLR), from which grew the feminist movement, Mouvement de libération des femmes (MLF), and the gay movement, Front homosexuel d'action révolutionnaire (FHAR).

For a short history of French Maoism, see Beldon Fields, "French Maoism," in *The Sixties without Apology*, ed. Sohnya Sayres et al. (Minneapolis: University of Minnesota Press, 1984).

[30]Two accounts of the global phenomenon of 1968 represent different tendencies in the interpretation of the events of that year. David Caute's *Year of the Barricades* (New York: Harper and Row, 1988) is somewhat more revisionist in its approach, whereas George Katsiaficas's *Imagination of the New Left* represents a more decidedly socialist interpretation.

workers who occupied factories and subsequently organized a two-week general strike affecting all industry, services, and trades. By May 13 workers had occupied factories throughout France; soon after, factory workers were joined by the public sector of industry—the railways, postal services, and airlines—as well as workers in services and trades such as hotels, banks, restaurants, and gas stations. The general strike of May 1968 resulted in a political crisis which so dramatically shook the structure of Gaullist power that the government retaliated with desperate and brutal repression. On June 1 the government stepped up the police and military suppression of demonstrations and occupations, while the unions negotiated with the government to stop the strikes, industry by industry; by June 6 workers in public transportation, mining, and some factories were forced to resume work. Ultimately, President Charles de Gaulle opportunistically invoked the threat of "totalitarian communism," just as the FGDS (Fédération de la gauche démocratique et socialiste) was in the midst of an organizing effort to launch the leftist coalition of the Popular Front. In the general elections at the end of June, the PCF and the FGDS lost over 10 percent of their votes, while the Gaullists (UDR, Union pour la défense de la République) gained almost 20 percent and were returned to power with an unmatched victory. The Left did not recover power until 1981 with the election of the Socialist PSU (Parti socialiste unifié) candidate, François Mitterrand.

For leftist intellectuals and students, the suppression and ultimate failure of the promising May events exacerbated their disillusionment with the French Communist party. The PCF and its paper *L'humanité* had not supported the student revolts; the party's traditional emphasis on the proletarian class as the only revolutionary class had led the PCF to condemn the uprising as petit-bourgeois anarchism, thus greatly alienating students and intellectuals. The party had argued that they chose to behave in an orderly electoral manner because the situation had not been revolutionary. Disappointed by the outcome of the May efforts, some Marxists criticized the PCF's shunning of the popular movement in favor of electoral politics, and credited the PCF with making possible the Gaullist repression and electoral victory. It must be said that the French communists in 1968 received blame from both sides: they had sufficient organizational strength and numbers to be scapegoated as a threatening specter by General de Gaulle, and at the same time severe criticisms fell on them from the Left. Sartre, Jean-Marie Vincent, and André Barjonet charged that the PCF had misunderstood both the aims and the means of the revolution, that it was doctrinal rigidity that had refused to accord importance to the student insurrections, and finally, that the emphasis on electoral politics implied less a reversal of the Gaullist regime than a friendly transmission of power from one party apparatus to another.[31] Furthermore, as a result of the CGT's efforts to harness the workers' strikes and to separate them from the student movement, as well as the FGDS's electoral ambitions, certain leftist critics questioned whether western Marxism had not itself become part of the existing political system. Critics such as Philippe Sollers, Marcelin Pleynet, Jean Ricardou, Jean-Louis Baudry, and Julia Kristeva, for whom the journal *Tel quel* was a center, sought to form a more radical Marxist critique of culture and society which would take its theoretical inspiration from a source outside western Marxism.

In this sense the journal *Tel quel* exemplifies an intellectual topos peculiar to Paris in the early 1970s, in which those leftist intellectuals disillusioned by 1968 came to consider the FGDS and PCF as agents for reinforcing the existing political system, and thus sought another kind of political model in Maoism and the Cultural Revolution. In 1971 *Tel quel* constituted the People's Republic and the Cultural Revolution as absolutely nonoccidental phenomena, which, owing to their very situation outside western European political experience, represented a model for revolution and ongoing cultural criticism that could not be recontained by western ideological systems. It was not a long-lived phenomenon—French Maoism at *Tel quel* subsided by 1975—but it is noteworthy to the extent that it illustrates yet another field touched by the pervasive logic of the Orient as Other. At this particular moment the fascination with China was a means of figuring not only the feminist-psychoanalytic desires of Kristeva, and the semiotic-psychoanalytic desires of Barthes, but also the political desires of the intellectuals at *Tel quel* (including Kristeva and Barthes) as well.

[31]André Barjonet was an economist, and former head of the social research department of the CGT, who resigned in protest against the CGT's role in the strikes on May 25. In "C.G.T., 1968," *Les temps modernes*, no. 265 (July 1968): 94–103. Barjonet objected to the authoritarianism of the communist leadership; he asserted that the leaders of both the CGT and the PCF dictated a narrow, undialectical sense of the relationship between "consciousness" and "social practice," and fought ceaselessly against the spontaneity of the masses, positions, he argued, that were fundamentally antimarxist.

The journal *Tel quel*, founded in 1960, published essays in avant-garde literary criticism and semiotic theory. Its inclination toward a leftist politics developed, by 1966, into a deep interest, among certain members of its editorial committee, in the Chinese Cultural Revolution. In the summer of 1968 *Tel quel* described the May events as "la Révolution ici maintenant" (the Revolution here now) and heralded May as a Parisian version of the Cultural Revolution. A Groupe d'études théoriques was set up, which met weekly to construct "une théorie tirée de la pratique textuelle" (a theory drawn from textual practice), declaring that "cette construction devra faire partie, selon son mode de production complexe de la théorie marxiste-léniniste, seule théorie révolutionnaire de notre temps, et porter sur l'intégration critique des pratiques les plus élaborés (philosophie, linguistique, sémiologie, psychanalyse, 'littérature,' histoire des sciences)" (this construction will have to form a part, in accordance with its complex mode of production, of Marxist-Leninist theory, the only revolutionary theory of our time, and work toward the critical integration of the most developed practices of philosophy, linguistics, semiology, psychoanalysis, "literature," and the history of science).[32] Thus, the ambitious program of the *telquelistes* called for the elaboration of theories of "textual politics," that is, a politics inhering in writing practices and in the subject's relationship to language and signification. During this time *Tel quel* investigated those textual practices—in poetics, in cultural texts, in psychoanalysis—that radically subverted the subject's stable self-identification in language. The most powerful work developed by theorists at *Tel quel* was the argument for the materiality of language and literature, the consequences of which were that the economic was no longer considered the only realm of political change, and that linguistic and formal experiments in art and literature were considered to have the power to transform the very structures of bourgeois ideology that determined subjectivity. As early as the winter of 1970, Sollers had translated some of Mao's poems in the journal, but it was not until 1971 that China was hailed as the revolutionary Other, a site of revolutionary practice which those at *Tel quel* believed closely embodied the very "textual politics" they desired. By 1971 a manifesto indicating the journal's enthusiastic embrace of Maoism had been published; the political tenets of the Mouvement de juin 71 were

[32]*Tel quel*, no. 34 (Summer 1968): 4.

consolidated, with the publication of a "Déclaration" and list of "Positions" appearing in *Tel quel*, no. 47 (Autumn 1971).

The declaration began with a protest against the censoring of Maria-Antonietta Macciocchi's *De la Chine* at a commercial display by *L'humanité*, the Communist press. *Tel quel* editors viewed the suppression of this book about the Chinese Revolution and Chinese society to be one of the most revealing and dangerous choices of the PCF (referred to with lower-case letters as "pcf"). They argued that the choice to suppress *De la Chine* indicated a repressive and dogmatic policy, which colluded with and made possible the revisionist "line." Furthermore, they declared that revisionism—policies such as belief in the electoral process followed by the PCF and FGDS—was the primary instrument in support of bourgeois hegemony. In this sense the declaration of *Tel quel*'s Maoism was specifically a reaction to the PCF's prohibitions; China was embraced as a privileged topos of revolution precisely because information about China was suppressed by *L'humanité* and the PCF: "La censure inévitable du révisionnisme sur la Chine est le prix à payer *par lui* pour que cette hégémonie soit *totale*. . . . On comprend donc comment, dans ces conditions, la révolution culturelle prolétarienne chinoise, plus grand événement historique de notre époque, dérange le calcul révisionniste et qu'il fera tout pour la falsifier. Eh bien, nous, nous ferons tout pour l'éclairer, l'analyser et la soutenir" (p. 134) (Revisionism's inevitable censuring of China is the price *it* pays so that this hegemony remains *total*. . . . We understand how, then, that under these conditions the Chinese Cultural Proletarian Revolution, the greatest historical event of our epoch, so disturbs the revisionist reasoning that they will do everything to falsify it. And so, for our part, we will do everything to illuminate it, to analyze it, and to support it). In 1971 the Maoist *telquelistes* described themselves less by means of new tenets or associations with the writings of Mao Zedong and more by distinguishing themselves from PCF positions and in terms of what was suppressed from the PCF line. In this sense the *Tel quel* Maoists did not identify Maoism as an agenda or a program of initiatives but rather identified with China as the suppressed Other of French communism.

The "Positions du Mouvement de juin 71," which followed the "Déclaration," included a list of distinctions between the Maoism of *Tel quel* and the older communism. In these positions the PCF line was characterized as a "ligne petit bourgeois," serving the bourgeoisie and revisionism, whereas Maoism was declared the "ligne révolutionnaire" (p. 136) directly serving the proletariat.

> Le mouvement de juin 71 luttera à l'intérieur et à l'extérieur de *Tel Quel* pour développer . . . ses thèses. . . . *Tel Quel* doit être: un instrument de travail et d'analyse révolutionnaire, un instrument actif de la transformation actuelle de l'idéologie . . . [une revue qui réfléchit] la production du nouveau dans le procès d'avant-garde littéraire, philosophique, scientifique, politique.   (p. 136)

> [The June '71 movement will struggle on the inside and outside of *Tel quel* to develop its theses. . . . *Tel quel* must be: an instrument for work and revolutionary analysis, an active instrument in the current transformation of ideology . . . (a review that reflects) the new production in the literary, philosophical, scientific, and political avant-gardes.]

The position statement began by characterizing *Tel quel* in a number of ways that implicitly criticized, or differentiated itself from, the PCF: the notions that its struggle would occur "à l'intérieur" and "à l'extérieur" of the theory-setting body of the journal, and that its primary field of action would be ideology. The location of struggle both inside and outside the journal implied a reaction against the closed body of the PCF leadership, and described a model of decision making that would be self-critical and would not exclude divergent opinions. In targeting the transformation of ideology as the primary field of activity, *Tel quel* joined its concerns with several other Marxist theories (those of Louis Althusser or others such as Macciocchi interested in Gramsci), which were concentrating less on action against the economic base per se (that is, changes in the economic mode of production) and more on the development of a critique of ideology, or theories of cultural intervention. In general, the emphasis on ideology reflected a desire to find a theory of cultural revolution in the largest sense, one that would call for a complete disruption of customs and ways of thinking, with the goal of eradicating from them vestiges of structures carried over from the past. For *Tel quel* this desire was a result of interpreting May 1968 as a failure, as the revolution's having been defeated by the overpowering body of administrative, pedagogical, and cultural superstructures. The position statement continued:

"Le lecteur de *Tel Quel*" . . . est en mesure de reconnaître, à l'intérieur et à l'extérieur de *Tel Quel*, deux lignes, deux voies, deux objectifs antagonistes. De l'issue de la lutte entre ces deux lignes dépend soit la victoire de l'avant-garde, soit sa défaite dans l'académisme, l'opportunisme, la répétition. Camarades! nous ne sommes pas en 1920 ou 1930, ni même en 1960, mais en 1971. Notre avant-garde n'est pas le formalisme, le futurisme, le surréalisme, le "nouveau *nouveau roman*," etc. mais la percée d'une production révolutionnaire *aujourd'hui*. Aujourd'hui, c'est-à-dire à l'époque qui a vu la révolution culturelle prolétarienne chinoise, Mai 1968 en France et, sur la scène internationale, le resurgissement, la propagation irréversible de la théorie et de la pratique révolutionnaire de notre temps: la pensée-maotsétoung.   (p. 136)

["The reader of *Tel quel*" will recognize that, inside and outside *Tel quel*, there are two lines, two views, two antagonistic objectives. Out of the issue of the struggle between these two lines results either the victory of the avant-garde, or its defeat in academicism, opportunism, and repetition. Comrades! We're not in 1920 or 1930, not even in 1960, but in 1971. Our avant-garde is not formalism, futurism, surrealism, or a "new *nouveau roman*," but rather a breakthrough of revolutionary production for *today*. A today, that is, which has seen the Chinese Cultural Revolution, May 1968 in France, and, on the international scene, a resurgence and irreversible spread of the revolutionary theory and practice of our time: Maoism.]

In this passage an even more emphatic opposition is drawn between a traditional line and Maoism as its critique. For *Tel quel* Maoism was not the theory of Mao Zedong as it functioned in the Chinese Cultural Revolution but rather an abstract notion of "le plus avant-garde et révolutionnaire"—an analogue of what was for Baudelaire, in his time, "le plus moderne"—the Other of established orthodoxy. The definition of "today" as a period that "has seen the Chinese Cultural Revolution, May 1968 in France" associates the Cultural Revolution with May 1968 as if they represented parallel, though perhaps unequal, events. In historical terms this parallel ignores many things, the least of which is mere scale: it is fair to say that more than a decade of immense upheaval in the social, economic, military, and bureaucratic areas of Chinese life, affecting hundreds of millions of people, can only with difficulty be glibly compared to one month of strikes in France. It is the very nonequivalence of these two events that underscores the logic of desire and substitution through which the imagined success of the Chinese Cultural Revolution is substituted for the judged failure of the events of May, which is essentially what the French Maoists were doing in turning to China after 1968.

It must be noted that in 1971, before their 1974 visit, the *telquelistes* knew very little about China. And because of this limited knowledge, both of these 1971 documents invoke repeatedly "la pensée maotsé-toung" without reference to either the political leader Mao, his writings, or the People's Republic of China. Rather, "Maoism," conjured as French communism's Other, was a manner of signifying a revolutionary practice whose very political and geographic distance from the West rendered it more powerful because it could not be subsumed by western social systems or western explanations. Even more particularly, French intellectuals at *Tel quel* in 1971 were searching precisely for a *nonoccidental* "Marxist" theory and practice of cultural revolution, because they claimed that May 1968 foregrounded the danger that western Marxisms could themselves be co-opted by the capitalist system.

The lack of knowledge about China also enabled *Tel quel*'s theorists to idealize the Cultural Revolution as the epitome of "permanent revolution," a revolution which they constituted as having successfully reintegrated into the factories and countrysides the solidifying elite strata of administrators, bureaucrats, and technicians. In addition, *Tel quel* elaborated on the then popular notion of the Chinese Cultural Revolution as a continuous critique of ideology, imagining that the Chinese Cultural Revolution also included a vigorous and continual critique of art and literature, resulting in an ever-changing and ultimate avant-garde. It is in this latter sense particularly that *Tel quel* romanticized China as a utopian aesthetic; because information about China was prohibited and censored, the theorists at *Tel quel* were able to situate their abstract notions of textual practice there without risk of contradiction or disillusionment.

Even in 1974, however, after *Tel quel*'s group trip to China, which included Philippe Sollers, Marcelin Pleynet, and François Wahl, as well as Barthes and Kristeva, the utopianization of China continued. The China evoked in the issue "En Chine" (no. 59, Autumn 1974), did not represent the economic and political struggles throughout the People's Republic of the early 1970s as it recovered from, and reassessed the gains and losses of, the Cultural Revolution. Rather, *Tel quel* praised and objectified China as a type of revolutionary practice in the realm of the "poetic"; *Tel quel* projected China as the location of a unique textual politics and practice, and proposed that this textual activity was central to Chinese society in a manner entirely different from the place of art in western society. In this issue Sollers wrote about China's "dimension 'poétique'": "Ces poèmes ne sont pas un décoration, comme trop d'Occidentaux ont tendances à la penser. Ils ont une triple portée: émotive-historique, graphique, politique. . . . [Le lyrisme chinois est] un dynamisme du geste, de la transformation" (pp. 15–16) (These poems are not a decoration, as many Westerners have the tendency to think. They carry a triple function: historical-emotive, graphic, political. . . . [Chinese lyricism is] a dynamism of physical action, of transformation). Even after *Tel quel*'s visit to the People's Republic, China is selectively idealized as "poesis"; more than that, Sollers suggests that the visit there revealed China to be the very embodiment of *Tel quel*'s critical and aesthetic project. This fictionalizing of China as a poetic avant-garde occurs in Kristeva's *Des chinoises* (p. 16) as well, where she describes the Chinese revolutionary example as being visible through "le 'dada' de la politique," thus conflating China (and ignoring China's predominant socialist realism) with the proto-surrealism of the French dada movement. These final representations of China as a poetic avant-garde illustrate the degree to which *Tel quel*'s embrace of Maoism was commensurate with the valorization of an Imaginary textual politics over any dimension of social politics in France. Even after *Tel quel* no longer advocated Maoism, those associated with the journal did not take up the social struggles of the French Left. French Maoism served initially as the vehicle for *Tel quel* to differentiate itself from traditional Marxism, but ultimately, the result was that *Tel quel* expanded its theories of textuality and retreated from activist social politics.[33]

Indeed, when we consider the political context of this interest in China represented by *Tel quel*, Kristeva, and Barthes, it is evident that the embrace of Maoism and the fetishizing of China represent more than a projection of the Orient as Other by a group of leftist intellectuals disillusioned after May 1968. It also reveals their judgment that

[33]For a satiric commentary on the conservatism of former French Maoists, see Guy Hocquenghem, *Lettre ouverte à ceux qui sont passés du col Mao au Rotary* (Paris: Albin Michels, 1986).

socialist revolution could never occur in France and therefore that nothing would be sacrificed if they withdrew their political focus from France and turned their gaze toward a political utopia elsewhere. In a sense it represented a desertion of the revolutionary possibilities and the continuing contradictions created by May 1968. The French romance with Maoism in the early 1970s served as an escape from the demanding struggles in France itself. In turning to China, these writers could ignore not only the continuing conflicts with a conservative regime, and the important work of forging dialogues among various old and new Left factions, but also a new situation of growing social inequality as immigrant populations from North Africa and Indochina settled in France, constituting a new class of workers in the French economy. The fetishizing of China was symptomatic of an all-or-nothing absolutism, which readily substituted an imaginary Cultural Revolution elsewhere because it was thought that the revolution could not be achieved at home.

Although the May events did not bring about a revolutionary transformation of French society, they did imply that large-scale and far-reaching popular movements are possible. The student and workers' strikes of 1968 addressed issues that extended beyond each group's individual demands; together for one month, the two popularly based movements had called the entire structure of society into question. The students' critique of the university became a broad critique of French society itself, a challenging of the consumer society, class privileges, and authoritarian structures, as well as a bold rejection of social regulation and determination. In addition to higher wages, the workers had called for self-management, demanding that they should be involved in decision making at the plant level, and that all information about operations should be spread throughout the work force; a view heard constantly among workers during the May uprising was that work is more than money and that human dignity is as valid a union demand as higher pay. After 1968 Gaullist state power was never the same; the 12 million no votes to a Gaullist referendum in April 1969 sent De Gaulle into retirement. The strikes brought many significant changes in the structure of the university and the factory. Most significant, the social movements of feminism, gay liberation, and self-determination emerged out of the events of 1968. Not only did the turn toward an imaginary Maoism refuse to recognize the advances that were actually achieved at the time but, more important, it neglected the mandate that there was still work to be done.   ⟶

The (Post)colonial Gaze

The social productions, historical frameworks of inscription, and cultural functions of these three postcolonial French representations of the "maternal," imaginary Orient differ greatly from Flaubert's nineteenth-century representations of "la femme orientale," Kuchuk-Hânem, discussed in Chapter 3. Nonetheless, these twentieth-century projections of China as a fiction of absolute cultural and sexual difference from the West are more similar to Flaubert's representation of the oriental woman than one might at first imagine; Kristeva's and Barthes's rhetorical postures particularly recall Flaubert's orientalism. Kristeva's description of her first encounter with the Chinese is reminiscent of Flaubert's *Correspondance*: she not only duplicates the structure of address which makes the oriental Other an object of exchange between occidental writer and receivers, but also she attributes to that otherness similar qualities of silence, inertia, and indifference:

> Une foule immense est assise sous le soleil: elle nous attend sans mot, sans mouvement. Des yeux calmes, même pas curieux, mais légèrement amusés ou anxieux, en tout cas perçants, et sûrs d'appartenir à une communauté avec laquelle nous n'aurons jamais rien à voir. Ils ne fixent pas en nous l'homme ou la femme, le jeune ou le vieux, le blond ou le brun, tel trait du visage ou du corps.[34]

> [An immense crowd is seated in the sun; it waits for us without a word, without moving. Calm eyes, not even curious, but slightly amused or anxious, in any case piercing, and certain of belonging to a community with which we will never have anything to do. They don't distinguish among us man or woman, young or old, blonde or brunette, this or that feature of face or body.]

The Chinese crowd is homogenized and distanced as Other to the group of French intellectuals traveling in China in 1974. They are still and silent, their collective gaze distant, impenetrable, yet piercing—

[34]Kristeva, *Des chinoises*, pp. 13–14.

excluded and excluding—and of one blended character, as if the crowd were like a single mirror reflecting the travelers' "étrangeté." "Ils ne fixent pas en nous l'homme ou la femme, le jeune ou le vieux" resonates with Flaubert's assertion that the oriental woman "ne fait aucune différence entre un homme et un autre homme." In both situations the oriental is represented by the French writers as speechlessly Other, indiscriminate rather than distinguishing among observers. The undifferentiating gaze of the French text is attributed to the gaze of the (undifferentiated) Chinese; that is, the Chinese are represented as doing the very thing that the textual representation does to them. In both, the French readers are the audience who receive and, as addressees, participate in these representations. This early passage from *Des chinoises* strikes the keynote of the entire text, in which the Chinese, and ultimately Chinese women as inheritors of a matriarchal tradition and maternal culture, are homogenized as the absolute cultural and sexual Others of the occidental tradition.

In Barthes's piece *Alors la Chine?* as well no one person is ever engaged or described. China exists only as a vast landscape of faceless, indistinguishable people—"ce peuple immense"—who are of one homogeneous character: "Dans le pénombre calme des salons d'accueil, nos interlocuteurs (des ouvriers, des professeurs, des paysans) sont patients, appliqués (tout le monde prend des notes: nul ennui, un sentiment paisible de travail commun)" (In the calm half-light of the reception room, our interlocutors [workers, professors, peasants] are patient, conscientious [everyone takes notes, not a trace of boredom, rather a peaceful feeling of teamwork]).[35] In Barthes's description, although the Chinese people speak and communicate ("nos interlocuteurs"), they are also evoked as indistinguishable and collective. The parenthetical gloss—"des ouvriers, des professeurs, des paysans"—suggests that there are no class divisions in the new China, that workers, professors, and peasants all do the same work in an identical manner. In less than three decades, this suggests, China has achieved an egalitarianism unparalleled—as well as impossible, the essay implies—in the western world. In other words, a tautological rhetoric is used in this evocation of China: the quality of homogeneity among the Chinese is asserted as the evidence that Chinese society is

[35]Barthes, *Alors la Chine?*, p. 7; the translation is my own.

without class divisions. As in the earlier orientalist portraits, the notion of the oriental people as unvaried and indistinguishable recurs. Like many of the preceding orientalist texts, including Flaubert's *Voyage en Orient*, both Kristeva's and Barthes's texts are also travelogues; to the degree that both narratives about the People's Republic of China reiterate certain generic and rhetorical features of travel literature (the trope of arrival, as well as the requisite description of the foreign people as incomprehensible), they fall very much within the body of French orientalism.

The theoretical projects of *Tel quel* and the semioticians Barthes and Kristeva were concerned with criticizing the power of the French state and its ideology, an ideology that had justified, among other things, imperialist policies in North Africa and Indochina. In this sense the constructions of China in *Tel quel*, *Des chinoises*, and *Alors la Chine?* conjured the oriental Other not as a colonized space but as a desired position outside western politics, ideology, and signification. Yet a final irony remains: these postcolonial refigurations of China continued to figure the Orient as the Other, no longer as colonized but as utopian, and this romantic regard for China permitted intellectuals to disregard the situation of actual postcolonial peoples residing and laboring in France itself. By the 1950s French colonialism in Africa and Asia had been rigorously challenged by nationalist groups in Algeria, Tunisia, Morocco, and Indochina, as well as by leftist groups within France critical of French policy. Intensification of the anti-French nationalist movements in Morocco and Tunisia forced France to agree to the independence of these countries in the early 1950s. Defeats in both Indochina in 1954 and in the Algerian war of the late 1950s marked the decline of French imperial power, and in 1958 De Gaulle was forced to seek an end to the war in Algeria on the terms of the FLN (Front de libération national), the Algerian nationalist organization. Algeria received its independence in 1962. Yet, despite the policies of French decolonization during the late 1960s, it is evident that the French involvement with Asia and the Third World continued into the 1970s, even though some of the more overt political apparatuses of colonialism had ended. In the postcolonial period the former colonial "gaze" toward Asia may have disappeared from official ideology, but it persists nonetheless, on the parts of both the political Right and Left. We need only consider the surprising credibility of Jean-Marie Le Pen and the Front national (FN) to appreciate that even though French colonialism has ended in name in North Africa, the Caribbean, and Indochina, the displaced populations from these regions have not encountered vastly changed relations between "colonizer" and "colonized" in the French metropolis. From this discussion of Kristeva, Barthes, and *Tel quel*, we understand that even on the Left the orientalist gaze may reemerge, even when the purpose of its project is to criticize state power and social domination. In this regard, for activists and intellectuals of the contemporary Left the example of French Maoism suggests that the continuing utopian tendency of projecting revolutionary, cultural, or ethnic purity onto other sites, such as the Third World, must be scrutinized and challenged. For those critical articulations that successfully break with orientalism, that resist the logic of otherness, we must finally look away from the European context of orientalism to other locations on the discursive terrain, such as spaces of decolonization, subalternity, and feminism.[36]

[36]For a brief discussion of the dangers of essentializing the position of the "Third World woman," see my review of Trinh T. Minh-ha's *Woman, Native, Other: Writing Postcoloniality and Feminism, Sub-Stance* 62–63 (1991); 213–16.

Conclusion:
Orientalism Interrupted

> The socialist conception of the revolutionary process is characterized by two fundamental features that Romain Rolland has summed up in his watchword: "pessimism of the intellect, optimism of the will."
>
> Antonio Gramsci, *L'ordine nuovo* (1920)

Frantz Fanon, the Martiniquan psychiatrist who served in an Algerian hospital during the French-Algerian war, gives us in *L'an cinq de la révolution algérienne* (1959) a study of how objects and practices that had been used previously by the colonizing power can be appropriated by the "native" group seeking independence. He describes how apparatuses that began as vehicles of French oppression, such as the radio, medical practices, or law enforcement, were reappropriated by the Algerians and turned to serve in the war against the French. When forms within the native culture, such as the women's custom of wearing veils or the patriarchal structure of the Algerian family, were manipulated or exploited by the colonizing forces, the Algerians were able to redefine their meaning and to practice them differently, in order to make themselves less vulnerable to French rule and to struggle more effectively against French colonialism.[1] Fanon explains, for example, that until 1945 the radio had represented the voice of the occupier—Frenchmen speaking to Frenchmen—a system of signs that

[1]For a feminist analysis of Fanon's discussion of the French attempt to raise the veils of Algerian women, see Winifred Woodhull's "Unveiling Algeria," *Genders* (1991; in press).

altogether excluded Algerians. As the Algerian struggle against the French occupation developed, however, Algerians began to listen to the French news reports in order to gain a sense of the progress of the revolution. In the French broadcasts' fabrications and distortions, Algerians were able to read the degree to which the occupiers were threatened. Radio became a means of measuring "the dying colonialism"; it became essential for the Algerians to be informed, both of the French losses and of their own. By 1956 Algerians of all economic levels were buying radio receivers; indeed, listening to the radio—even when the wavelengths that the Algerians depended on had been jammed and it was impossible to hear anything but static—became a signifier of Algerian commitment to the revolution itself.

In the preceding chapters I have located moments of intersection, conflict, multivalence, and incommensurability that illustrate the heterogeneity of the orientalist terrain. It has been my contention throughout that these moments represent the vulnerability of orientalist formations. Although these readings of destabilized moments of orientalism provide a starting point for articulating resistance, one finds among theorists of decolonization, subalternity, feminism, and minority discourse even more explicit and suggestive discussions of the possibilities for opposition to and transformation of cultural domination. In foregrounding the locations of dissent and the emergent spaces of the oppressed, Fanon's text offers an explicit mandate in a way that Foucault's notion of *heterotopia* does not; that is, his narrative makes evident the spaces of otherness on the social terrain from which transforming interventions may be articulated. Fanon's account grounds literary and theoretical analysis by focusing on explicit practices of dissent that produce significant changes to an existing colonialist hegemony, and by further emphasizing that the social and discursive locations of dissent are of utmost importance in the dismantling of colonialism. The account of the Algerian adaptation of the radio illustrates remarkably well the principle discussed throughout—that cultural shifts can be achieved through the appropriation and rearticulation of existing cultural objects or practices, for these objects and practices signify differently depending on social context and on whether they are articulated by dominant or emergent relations of representation. Furthermore, the insertion of an object into a new practice does not simply shift the meaning of the object, such as the radio's signifying initially the presence of the French colonialists and ultimately the presence of Algerian commitment to revolution. The rearticulated practice of Algerians listening to the radio also transformed the very construction of meaning under French colonialism, the ways in which meaning was attached to objects; that is, it destabilized the formerly secure connection between French objects and French rule. Fanon offers a practical and historical example of how the struggle for meaning in discourse forms an integral part of the struggle for hegemony. One can see how the dialogues between the Indian and Anglo-American scholars discussed in Chapter 4 exemplify a structurally, though not materially, analogous struggle for meaning; in their various claims to the right to interpret Forster's novel and, finally, to define the significance of India, the Indian scholars appropriate the objects and practices of the colonialist discourse and rearticulate a system of signs that had formerly excluded them.

Like Fanon, the Subaltern Studies Group, a group of contemporary Indian historians, is also concerned with positionality, or the question of from where interventions in "official" narratives are made, and in this sense they extend the present discussion of orientalism as a heterogeneous discursive terrain. The Subaltern Studies Group's concern with the problem of subalternity takes place in a more textual arena than Fanon's, however, in that their project is historiographic. Having specifically taken up Gramsci's notion of subalternity as the emergent classes whose practices are identified only when viewed with historical hindsight, they have targeted as their arena of contestation the way in which the history of Indian independence is told, from whose point of view, and with what materials. Within the context of the historiography of Indian nationalism and independence, they take *subalternity* to mean not simply the situations of the Indians vis-à-vis the British imperialists but, more specifically, the role of the masses of Indian peasants and urban poor, whose demonstrations of resistance have not been as celebrated as those of the Indian elite, and indeed whose means of articulating resistance to British rule were quite different from those of the Indian landlords and bourgeois nationalists. The project of the Subaltern Studies Group is to rewrite the history of Indian independence from the point of view of these voiceless insurgent masses, in defiance of historical accounts that place either Indian elites or British colonialists as the primary subjects of history. The

Group's histories of peasant rebellions and worker revolts narrate some of what is missing from official histories; they contest the totalizing authority of elite histories and assert, as Dipesh Chakrabarty does, that "ruling-class documents often used for historical reconstructions of working-class conditions can be read both for what they say and for their 'silences.' "[2] Thus, they reconstitute other versions of history from these "silences," as well as by rereading historical materials such as letters, state archives, public health reports, district handbooks, or Labour Department files in ways that are informed by attention to these silences. Their interventions work to unmask and displace the colonialist ideology of official historical narrative.

It is worth remembering, however, that subalternity is, in Gramsci's account, unclosed, episodic, and in process; the subaltern masses and their histories, by definition, cannot be fixed and narrated. Like the dominant component of the hegemonic process to which it is inextricably bound, subalternity is always emerging and in flux. To the degree that some of the narratives of these radical historians posit an insurgent subject of history as they chart the progress of the working class or peasant masses, they, like official historians, risk reducing and appropriating subalternity. For the process of narration inevitably effaces and displaces the untextualizable properties of subaltern historical material. For this reason certain historians of the Subaltern Group are suspicious of seamless narratives and essentialized subjects (such as the "Indianness of the native point of view" posited by Vasant Shahane), and prefer to render history in terms of struggles and contradictions, in order that their histories do not appropriate and neutralize the agents of subaltern struggles. Others consider that the positing of a subaltern subject may be a necessary and strategic fixing of subalternity for the political purposes of launching a critique of official history and its structures of exclusion. In his analysis of the semiotic codes of colonialist discourse, "The Prose of Counter-Insurgency," Ranajit Guha foregrounds this dilemma, explaining that even the history of insurgency, like colonialist historiography, "excludes the rebel as the conscious subject of his own history," for an "abstraction called Worker-and-Peasant, an ideal rather than the real historical

[2]Dipesh Chakrabarty, "Conditions for Knowledge of Working-Class Conditions," in Guha and Spivak, *Selected Subaltern Studies*, p. 179. Chakrabarty and other radical historians of the Subaltern Studies Group are represented in this volume.

personality of the insurgent" is made to replace the specific rebel forces, with their conflicts and contradictions.[3] Yet Guha ultimately argues for the political importance of positing such an ideal, and for the *strategic* necessity of inserting the ideal into a constructed chronology for the purpose of displacing official narrative and the ideological domination that it represents.

Gayatri Spivak further elaborates the *"strategic* use of a positive essentialism in a scrupulously visible political interest." Spivak explains that if the representation of subaltern subjectivity is "strategic," and such a subjectivity is posited while one simultaneously acknowledges that subalternity is by definition always unstable and heterogeneous to the narrative project of any historian, then this accomplishes an "affirmative deconstruction." If, by contrast, "the restoration of the subaltern's subject-position in history is seen by the historian as the establishment of an inalienable and final truth of things, then [this restoration will] inevitably objectify the subaltern and be caught in the game of knowledge as power."[4] The practice of strategic essentialism, then, as an "affirmative deconstruction" inserts a variety of insurgent subjects into historical discourse, and in the same move metaphorically brackets or annuls these insertions. By bracketing and suppressing subalternity-as-essence, the very same gesture by which the historian calls the subaltern subject into being in turn calls it into question. That gesture accomplishes an articulation of subaltern identity as a point of opposition to cultural domination yet avoids reducing or compromising the subaltern subject's state of persistent emergence. By inserting a number of different subjects and writing the histories of their struggles—peasant movements, workers' revolts—strategic essentialism also multiplies the terrain of the history of dissent, positing subjects without privileging the singularity or centrality of any one.

The Subaltern historian's problematic relationship to subalternity is not dissimilar to the relationship of critical readers of orientalism to the critical category of otherness, and indeed Spivak's discussion of strategic essentialism is instructive for my own discussion of reconstructing

[3]Ranajit Guha, "The Prose of Counter-Insurgency," in Guha and Spivak, *Selected Subaltern Studies*, p. 77.
[4]Gayatri Spivak, "Subaltern Studies: Deconstructing Historiography," in *In Other Worlds*, pp. 205, 207.

orientalism. Just as the Subaltern historian's insertion of a subaltern subject into historical narrative risks reducing and fetishizing subalternity, the critical problem of demystifying the discursive management and production of otherness is fraught with similar difficulties. For if one's task is in part to identify constituted otherness, one must take care to do this work of identification without reiterating, in the analysis of the formation, the apparatuses of management and exclusion, without overdetermining such otherness according to the very structures and disciplines that one wishes to displace. The practice of strategic essentialism suggests that it is possible for one to posit certain historically and textually specific essentialized notions of otherness—for example, the Orient, woman, the poor, the colonized—in order to challenge the discourses that produce such notions, while nonetheless placing the notion of the Other under erasure so as to ensure that such essentialisms will not be reproduced and proliferated by those very efforts to criticize their use.

It is not insignificant that one of the more important formulations of subalternity should come from Gayatri Spivak, a theorist whose body of work is not exclusively concerned with subaltern criticism but rather with theorizing the nexus of anticolonialism, deconstruction, marxism, and feminism. At this particular moment in the history of theory, I believe that feminist theory contains the most suggestive analyses of the problems of positionality, intersection, and multivalence.[5] I am referring here to feminist projects—in addition to Spivak's those of Trinh T. Minh-ha, Donna Haraway, or Evelyn Nakano Glenn—for which the focus is not exclusively the topics of women, gender, and sexuality, but in which issues such as poverty, classism, racism, and

[5]It is clear to any reader of feminist theory that what I refer to as feminism does not represent a homogeneous ideology, agenda, or approach, although it includes—but is not limited to—theories and practices that address the situation and construction of women in a number of arenas: social, cultural, literary, economic, and historical. Feminist concerns range from the struggle for reproductive rights, to psychoanalytic discussions about sexual difference, to rewriting history in terms of women as agents of history, to critiques of the implicit gendering of academic disciplines and fields of knowledge, to theories of gay and lesbian subjectivities, to studies of female domestic space in the novel. Yet feminist attention is also directed toward the feminization of poverty, the concentration of women of color in domestic labor and service jobs, the conditions of women in Asia, Africa, and Latin America. Thus, feminism is remarkable in the degree to which it has theorized and comprehended that gender is inextricably linked to inscriptions of class, race, and nationality, perhaps because it is evident that many women are poor, are workers, are of different races, are colonized.

colonialism are approached *as feminist issues* in the sense that the critiques of the oppression and exclusion of workers, men and women of color, and colonized populations are seen to be congruent with or implicated in the critique of sexism. This type of feminist theory is the least restrictive, and perhaps the most capable—among other paradigms of analysis, such as Marxism, anticolonialism, or psychoanalysis—of accounting for and theorizing heterogeneity to the degree that it considers a privileged category, gender, to be a powerful valence of human subjectivity, yet at the same time to be inseparable from other classifications such as class, race, or nationality.

Some of the feminist theorists who address the question of intersecting discursive formations do so through a discussion of gendered subjectivity, or the multiplicity of social relations across which a subject is constructed and signified. These theorists take as a fundamental premise that gender as a social classification is not produced in isolation; rather, its articulation is always also linked to the constructions of race, class, caste, nationality, and so forth. Teresa de Lauretis, for example, theorizes gendered subjectivity as both an active construction and a discursively mediated political interpretation of one's history.[6] For de Lauretis, all subjects are semiotic productions, both the result and the condition of the social production of meaning. The construction of subjectivity is in process, in that each position of the dialectic—the complex of practices she calls "experience" and the set of social relations—shifts and alters as the subject is signified. In *Technologies of Gender* (1987), de Lauretis elaborates her description of the gendered subject as "multiple," as simultaneously a racial, ethnic, and class-determined subject: "Feminist understanding: that the female subject is en-gendered, constructed and defined in gender across multiple representations of class, race, language, and social relations; and that, therefore, differences among women are differences *within* women, which is why feminism can exist despite those differences and, as we are just beginning to understand, cannot continue to exist without them."[7] Conceived as multiple, rather than divided or unified, the subject theorized by de Lauretis's feminism is not only a subject-in-process but, more important, a subject that occupies dis-

[6]Teresa de Lauretis describes her project in these terms in her article "The Essence of the Triangle or, Taking the Risk of Essentialism Seriously: Feminist Theory in Italy, the U.S., and Britain," in *differences* 1, no. 3 (Summer 1989).

[7]Teresa de Lauretis, *Technologies of Gender: Essays on Theory, Film, and Fiction* (Bloomington: Indiana University Press, 1987), p. 139.

tinctly different social positions at different moments, and at times several positions at once. Because it is multiply inscribed, the subject theorized by de Lauretis remains undetermined by any single discursive apparatus; by virtue of its multiplicity, this subject cannot be totalized as it *exceeds* dominant discursive formations, is always both *inside* and *outside* the apparatuses that inscribe any particular category, such as its gender, race, or class.

This suggests political implications beyond the narrower concern of de-essentializing female identity, namely that subjects conceived as multiply constructed are capable of a range of commitments. They may act, for example, at one time for feminist issues, while at others for racial or ethnic groups, for labor unions, or in anticolonialist or antiwar activities. The notion of a subject who represents the juncture of a multiplicity of social contradictions allegorizes the possibility of a site across which different counterhegemonic movements may be affiliated, through which diverse groups and sectors may cooperate to form a "new historical bloc." In this regard, theorists of coalition politics and minority discourse in Europe and the United States have elaborated Gramsci's notion in order to define a common agenda that could bring together heterogeneous minorities—racial and ethnic groups, women, postcolonial populations—who suffer political and material marginality in relation to dominant institutions.[8] Furthermore, the concepts of hybrid subjectivity and minority coalitions thematize not only a heterogeneity of counterhegemonic interests, but also, more strategically, the heterogeneity of different "fronts" in which the struggles of cultural politics, feminism, or anticolonialism may take place—the neighborhood, the workplace, the university, the picket line—and the necessity of not privileging a single site or struggle to the exclusion or suppression of others.

[8]See Stuart Hall, "Gramsci's Relevance for the Study of Race and Ethnicity," *Journal of Communication Inquiry* 10 (1986): 5–27; Abdul JanMohamed and David Lloyd, "Introduction: Toward a Theory of Minority Discourse: What Is to Be Done?" in *The Nature and Context of Minority Discourse,* ed. JanMohamed and Lloyd (Oxford: Oxford University Press, 1990); and Radhakrishnan, "Toward an Effective Intellectual."

For discussions of new historical blocs from the perspectives of specific minority communities, see, for example, George Lipsitz, "Cruising around the Historical Bloc: Postmodernism and Popular Music in East Los Angeles," in *Time Passages: Collective Memory and American Popular Culture* (Minnesota: University of Minnesota Press, 1990); Cornel West, "Marxist Theory and the Specificity of Afro-American Oppression," in *Marxism and the Interpretation of Culture,* ed. Lawrence Grossberg and Cary Nelson (Urbana: University of Illinois Press, 1988); and Lisa Lowe, "Heterogeneity, Hybridity, Multiplicity: Marking Asian American Differences," *Diaspora: A Journal of Transnational Studies* 1 (Spring 1991): 24—44.

Fanon, the Subaltern Studies Group, the feminist discussion of
multiplicity—each represents postcolonial theories of resistance that
contextualize the meanings of the discursive instabilities identified in
the preceding chapters by offering examples in which multivalence
and heterogeneity constitute the bases of significant transformations
of existing hegemonies. These postcolonial theorists write from sites
other than the European contexts of the theorists Foucault and Gramsci, with whom I opened my discussion of orientalism, and in this they
symptomatize the "heterotopical" property of discursive terrains.
Fanon's description of the multivalent meaning of the radio during the
French-Algerian war provides a historical and material example of
how the appropriation and rearticulation of objects and practices,
discussed in textual terms in the foregoing chapters, can alter the
structure and the distribution of power; the example of the radio
further foregrounds the importance of the political and geographic
locations of these oppositional practices. The multivalence of signs is
likewise emphasized by the Subaltern Studies Group. The practice of
"strategic" essentialism described by Guha and Spivak suggests that it
is possible to constitute specific signifiers of otherness, such as Indianness, for the purpose of disrupting the discourses that exclude Indians
as Other while simultaneously revealing the internal contradictions
and slippages of "Indianness" so as to ensure that the signifier *Indianness* will not be reappropriated by the very efforts to criticize its use. In
light of the discussion in Chapter 4 of the different constructions of
Indianness deployed by Anglo-American and Indian critics, Guha and
Spivak's deconstruction of "subalternity" may be considered as constituting a more contemporary third discussion of Indian "difference,"
one that provides critical commentary on the practices of critics such as
Shahane who intervene in the English discourse under the sign of
Indianness. In this sense one can map a series of heterogeneous sites
in which Indianness as difference is a structuring trope, beginning
with the British representation of Indianness as subordinated otherness, then the Indian critics who propose a countertradition named
Indianness, and then, in a more recent moment, critics such as Spivak
and Guha who take issue with an essentialized notion of Indianness.

The feminist discussion of multivalence and positionality implies
that because subjects are the sites of a variety of social relations, the
interdependence and conflict between different inscriptions provide

unique political opportunities to destabilize the power of any single particular inscription. Because the site of any cultural text is also crossed by multiple and unequal figurations, my interpretations have focused on those heterogeneous sites within French and British orientalism in which constructions of the Orient as Other are destabilized by intersecting or conflicting representations in the text itself, in intertextual dialogues, or from other discursive formations. In Lady Mary Wortley Montagu's *Turkish Embassy Letters*, both an eighteenth-century feminist discourse and a rhetoric about English class privilege provide discursive challenges to a prior tradition of seventeenth-century orientalist travel writing. The multivocality of the epistolary genre and the conflicting narratives about slaves and wives challenge the orientalizing framework of Montesquieu's *Lettres persanes*. Parody and multivalence in Flaubert's nineteenth-century work also contribute to the critique of orientalism as regressive sentimentality in *L'éducation sentimentale*.

Moments of heterogeneity occur in critical discourses, as well, and I have framed these moments of discursive instability in the dialogues between the Anglo-American and Indian critics, as well as in the postcolonial orientalist moment of Kristeva, Barthes, and *Tel quel*. In this last example the multivalent trope of the Orient as Other was reappropriated and refigured in the 1970s by the French Left, which constituted China as its revolutionary Other. Although semiotics, French Maoism, and psychoanalysis deployed the trope in order to criticize particular apparatuses of power, the use of the orientalist formation inevitably upheld many of the logics and relationships that the *Tel quel* theorists wished to topple. I have suggested that there is much to learn about our contemporary critical moment from this example of orientalist discourse. From it we understand that multivalence or heterogeneity in themselves do not by any means ensure a transformation of the status quo, that colonialist logics persist despite decolonization, and furthermore, that theoretical discourses are not invulnerable to these logics.[9]

[9]For postcolonial articulations that succeed in shifting the discursive terrain in ways that Barthes, Kristeva, and the writers of *Tel quel* do not, it is necessary to look at the interventions of "native" or diaspora postcolonial writers who have formulated polyvocal models of resistance to the discourses that presume to define them. In this regard I have suggested a number of postcolonial theorists who critically address British orientalist discourse, but to this one must add the North African critique of French oriental-

In this sense a consideration of heterogeneity and contradiction is likewise crucial to the framework within which the positions and responsibilities of critics are theorized. The notion of intellectual work must not be limited to the reproduction and restatement of a previous legacy of literary critical formulation. Rather, literary and cultural criticism must be made vital sites of productive, imaginative conflict between differing formulations and positions. New statements may not be enough, for although some may shift previously accepted paradigms, others will be neutralized and have little transforming effect. Therefore, it might be considered that the power of statements to alter specific cultural arrangements may not necessarily be due to an inherent quality or content, and may not even always be the exclusive result of the form of the statement. Rather, single articulations are apt to be less resistant to appropriation to the extent that they are not linked with other challenges to domination, and theories that are connected to a diversity of actions and practices are more powerful than those that are not connected. In other words, when intellectuals link theoretical concerns with activities inside and outside the university—when feminism and anticolonialism and antiracism are considered different but connected, and when otherness is not essentialized but is interpreted as a multivalent signifier making distinctly different relations of power possible at various historical moments— then this critical work can contribute to the building of pressures and resistances against the voice of the one and the silencings of others.

---

ism articulated in the novels of Assia Djebbar, Tahar Ben Jelloun, and Leïla Sebbar, among others, or the essays of Abdelkebir Khatibi.

Works Cited

Adamson, Walter. *Hegemony and Revolution: A Study of Antonio Gramsci's Political and Cultural Theory*. Berkeley: University of California Press, 1980.

Allen, Glen O. "Structure, Symbol, and Theme in E. M. Forster's *A Passage to India*." *PMLA* 70 (December 1955), 934–54.

Alloula, Malek. *The Colonial Harem*. Translated by Myrna Godzich and Wlad Godzich. Minneapolis: University of Minnesota Press, 1986.

Althusser, Louis. *Politics and History: Montesquieu, Rousseau, Hegel, and Marx*. Translated by Ben Brewster. London: New Left Books, 1972.

Anand, Mulk Raj. *Conversations in Bloomsbury*. New Delhi: Arnold-Heinemann, 1981.

Anderson, Benedict. *Imagined Communities: Reflections on the Origin and Spread of Nationalism*. London: Verso, 1983.

Barjonet, André. "C. G. T., 1968." *Les temps modernes*, no. 265 (July 1968): 94–103.

Barthes, Roland. *Mythologies*. Paris: Seuil, 1957. Published in English as *Mythologies*. Translated by Annette Lavers. New York: Farrar, Straus and Giroux, 1972.

——. *Éléments de sémiologie*. Paris: Gonthier, 1965.

——. *L'empire des signes*. Geneva: Skira, 1970. Published in English as *Empire of Signs*. Translated by Richard Howard. New York: Farrar, Straus and Giroux, 1982.

——. *Le plaisir du texte*. Paris: Seuil, 1973.

——. *Alors la Chine?* Paris: Christian Bourgois, 1975.

——. *Roland Barthes par Roland Barthes*. Paris: Seuil, 1975. Published in English as *Roland Barthes by Roland Barthes*. Translated by Richard Howard. New York: Farrar, Straus and Giroux, 1977.

——. *Fragments d'un discours amoureux*. Paris: Seuil, 1977.

——. *Image Music Text*. Edited and translated with an introduction by Stephen Heath. New York: Farrar, Straus and Giroux, 1977.

——. *La chambre claire: Note sur la photographie*. Paris: Éditions de l'Étoile, Gallimard,

Seuil, 1980. Published in English as *Camera Lucida*. Translated by Richard Howard. New York: Farrar, Straus and Giroux, 1981.

Bensmaïa, Réda. *The Barthes Effect*. Minneapolis: University of Minnesota Press, 1987.

Berchet, Jean-Claude, ed. *Le voyage en Orient: Anthologie des voyageurs français dans le Levant aux XIXᵉ siècle*. Paris: Robert Laffont, 1985.

Bhabha, Homi K. "The Other Question: The Stereotype and Colonial Discourse." *Screen* 24, no. 6 (November–December 1983): 18–36.

———, ed. *Nation and Narration*. London: Routledge, 1990.

Bloch, Marc. *Les caractères originaux de l'histoire rurale française*. 2 vols. Paris: Armand Colin, 1952, 1956.

Bourdieu, Pierre. "The Invention of the Artist's Life." Translated by Erec R. Koch. *Yale French Studies* 73 (1987): 75–103.

Brantlinger, Patrick. *Rule of Darkness: British Literature and Imperialism, 1830–1914*. Ithaca: Cornell University Press, 1988.

Braudel, Fernand. *Civilisation matérielle et capitalisme*. Paris: Armand Colin, 1967.

Brennan, Timothy. *Salman Rushdie and the Third World*. New York: St. Martin's, 1989.

Brombert, Victor. *Flaubert*. Paris: Seuil, 1971.

Brower, Reuben A. *The Fields of Light*. New York: Oxford University Press, 1951.

Brown, E. K. *Rhythm in the Novel*. Lincoln: University of Nebraska Press, 1950.

Bruneau, Jean. *Le "conte oriental" de Gustave Flaubert*. Paris: Denöel, 1973.

Burra, Peter. *The Novels of E. M. Forster*. London: Whitefriars Press, 1934.

Butor, Michel. *Improvisation sur Flaubert*. Paris: Éditions de la Différence, 1984.

Cabral, Amilcar. *Unity and Struggle: Speeches and Writings*. Translated by Michael Wolfers. New York: Monthly Review Press, 1979.

Carthill, Al. [Calcraft-Huntingdon]. *The Lost Dominion*. London: Blackwood, 1924.

Castle, Terry. *Masquerade and Civilisation*. Stanford: Stanford University Press, 1986.

Caute, David. *The Year of the Barricades*. New York: Harper and Row, 1988.

Chakrabarty, Dipesh. "Conditions for Knowledge of Working-Class Conditions." In *Selected Subaltern Studies*, edited by Ranajit Guha and Gayatri C. Spivak. New York: Oxford University Press, 1988.

Chaudhuri, Nirad. "Passage to and from India," *Encounter* 2, no. 6 (June 1954): 19–24.

Chodorow, Nancy. *The Reproduction of Mothering: Psychoanalysis and the Sociology of Gender*. Berkeley: University of California Press, 1978.

Christian, Barbara. *Black Women Novelists*. Westport, Conn.: Greenwood Press, 1980.

Clifford, James. "On *Orientalism*." In *The Predicament of Culture*. Cambridge, Mass.: Harvard University Press, 1988.

Clifford, James and George Marcus, eds. *Writing Culture: The Poetics and Politics of Ethnography*. Berkeley: University of California Press, 1986.

Cohn, Bernard S. "The Command of Language and the Language of Command." In *Subaltern Studies*, edited by Ranajit Guha. Vol. 4. Delhi: Oxford University Press, 1985.

———. *An Anthropologist among the Historians and Other Essays*. Delhi: Oxford University Press, 1987.

———. "Law and the Colonial State." In *History and Power in the Study of Law*, edited by Jane Collber and June Starr. Ithaca: Cornell University Press, 1989.

Colmer, John. *E. M. Forster: The Personal Voice*. London: Routledge and Kegan Paul, 1975.

Covel, John. *Early Voyages and Travels in the Levant.* London, 1670.

Coward, Rosalind, and John Ellis. *Language and Materialism.* London: Routledge and Kegan Paul, 1977.

Crews, Frederick. *E. M. Forster: The Perils of Humanism.* Princeton: Princeton University Press, 1962.

Culler, Jonathan. *Flaubert: The Uses of Uncertainty.* Ithaca: Cornell University Press, 1974.

Czyba, Lucette. *La femme dans les romans de Flaubert: Mythes et idéologie.* Lyons: Presses universitaires de Lyon, 1983.

Das, G. K. *E. M. Forster's India.* Totowa, N.J.: Rowman and Littlefield, 1977.

Das, G. K., and John Beer, eds. *E. M. Forster: A Human Exploration: Centenary Essays.* London: Macmillan, 1979.

Davis, Natalie Zemon. *Society and Culture in Early Modern France.* Stanford: Stanford University Press, 1975.

Defoe, Daniel. *Robinson Crusoe.* New York: Oxford University Press, 1972.

de Lauretis, Teresa. *Alice Doesn't: Feminism, Semiotics, Cinema.* Bloomington: Indiana University Press, 1984.

——. *Technologies of Gender: Essays on Theory, Film, and Fiction.* Bloomington: Indiana University Press, 1987.

——. "The Essence of the Triangle or, Taking the Risk of Essentialism Seriously: Feminist Theory in Italy, the U.S., and Britain." *Differences* 1, no. 3 (Summer 1989): 3–37.

de Man, Paul. *Allegories of Reading: Figural Language in Rousseau, Nietzsche, Rilke, Proust.* New Haven: Yale University Press, 1979.

Derrida, Jacques. "Différance." In *Speech and Phenomena,* translated by David B. Allison. Evanston, Ill.: Northwestern University Press, 1973.

——. *Of Grammatology.* Translated with a preface by Gayatri Spivak. Baltimore: Johns Hopkins University Press, 1976.

——. *Spurs: Nietzsche's Style/Eperons: Les Styles de Nietzsche.* Translated by Barbara Harlow. Chicago: University of Chicago Press, 1979.

duBois, Page. *Centaurs and Amazons: Women and the Pre-History of the Great Chain of Being.* Ann Arbor: University of Michigan Press, 1982.

——. *Sowing the Body: Psychoanalysis and Ancient Representations of Women.* Chicago: University of Chicago Press, 1988.

Dumont, Jean. *A New Voyage to the Levant.* London, 1696.

Edwardes, Michael. *British India, 1772–1947: A Survey of the Nature and Effects of Alien Rule.* New York: Taplinger, 1967.

——. *Bound to Exile: The Victorians in India.* London: Sidgwick and Jackson, 1969.

Endrikar, Y. *Gamblers in Happiness: An Indian Episode.* London: Heath Cranton, 1930.

Escobar, Arturo. "Discourse and Power in Development: Michel Foucault and the Relevance of His Work to the Third World." *Alternatives* 10 (Winter 1984–85): 377–400.

Fanon, Frantz. *L'an cinq de la révolution algérienne.* Paris: F. Maspero, 1959.

——. *Les damnés de la terre.* Paris: F. Maspero, 1961.

Fields, Beldon. "French Maoism." In *The Sixties without Apology,* edited by Sohnya Sayres et al. Minneapolis: University of Minnesota Press, 1984.

Flaubert, Gustave. *Salammbô* (1862). Paris: Garnier Flammarion, 1961.

——. *L'éducation sentimentale* (1869). Paris: Garnier Flammarion, 1969.

——. *Oeuvres complètes de Gustave Flaubert.* Vols. 10 and 13. Paris: Club de l'Honnête homme, 1973.

——. *Madame Bovary* (1857). Paris: Garnier Flammarion, 1979.

Forster, E. M. *A Passage to India*. New York: Harcourt, Brace and World, 1924.

——. *Two Cheers for Democracy*. London: Edward Arnold, 1951.

Foster, Hal, ed. *The Anti-Aesthetic: Essays on Postmodern Culture*. Port Townsend, Washington: Bay Press, 1983.

Foucault, Michel. *Archaeology of Knowledge*. Translated by A. M. Sheridan Smith. New York: Pantheon, 1972.

——. *The History of Sexuality*. Vol. 1. Translated by Robert Hurley. New York: Pantheon, 1978.

——. "Of Other Spaces." Translated by Jay Miskowiec. *Diacritics* 16, no. 1 (Spring 1986): 22–27.

Fraser, Andrew H. L. *Among Rajahs and Ryots*. London: Seeley, 1911.

Freud, Sigmund. *An Outline of Psycho-Analysis*. Translated by James Strachey. New York: Norton, 1949.

——. *New Introductory Lectures on Psychoanalysis*. Translated by James Strachey. New York: Norton, 1964.

Furbank, P. N. *E. M. Forster: A Life*. New York: Harcourt Brace Jovanovich, 1977.

Gallop, Jane. *The Daughter's Seduction*. Ithaca: Cornell University Press, 1982.

Gates, Henry Louis, Jr., ed. *"Race," Writing, and Difference*. Chicago: University of Chicago Press, 1986.

Gilbert, Sandra, and Susan Gubar. *Madwoman in the Attic: The Woman Writer and the Nineteenth-Century Imagination*. New Haven: Yale University Press, 1979.

——, eds. *Norton Anthology of Literature by Women*. New York: Norton, 1985.

Goubert, Pierre. *The Ancien Régime: French Society, 1600–1750*. Translated by Steve Cox. New York: Harper and Row, 1973.

Gowda, H. H. Anniah, ed. *A Garland for E. M. Forster*. Mysore: Literary Half-Yearly Press, 1969.

Gramsci, Antonio. *Selections from "The Prison Notebooks."* Edited and translated by Quintin Hoare and Geoffrey Nowell Smith. New York: International Publishers, 1971.

——. *Selections from Political Writings, 1910–1920*. Selected and edited by Quintin Hoare, translated by John Mathews. New York: International Publishers, 1977.

Greenberger, Allen. *The British Image of India: A Study in the Literature of Imperialism, 1880–1960*. New York: Oxford University Press, 1969.

Greenblatt, Stephen. "Invisible Bullets: Renaissance Authority and Its Subversion." *Glyph* 8 (1981): 40–61.

Grosrichard, Alain. *La structure du sérail: la fiction du despotisme asiatique dans l'occident classique*. Paris: Seuil, 1979.

Guha, Ranajit, and Gayatri Chakravorty Spivak. *Selected Subaltern Studies*. New York: Oxford University Press, 1988.

Hall, Stuart. "Signification, Representation, Ideology: Althusser and the Post-Structuralist Debates." *Critical Studies in Mass Communication* 2, no. 2 (June 1985): 91–114.

——. "Gramsci's Relevance for the Study of Race and Ethnicity." *Journal of Communication Inquiry* 10 (1986): 5–27.

Harari, Josué, ed. *Textual Strategies: Perspectives in Post-Structuralist Criticism*. Ithaca: Cornell University Press, 1979.

Haraway, Donna. "A Manifesto for Cyborgs: Science, Technology, and Socialist Feminism in the 1980s." *Socialist Review* 80 (March–April 1985): 65–107.

——. *Primate Visions: Gender, Race, and Nature in the World of Modern Science*. London: Routledge, 1989.

Heath, Stephen. *Le vertige du déplacement*. Paris: Fayard, 1974.

Hegel, G. W. F. *Phenomenology of Mind*. Translated by J. B. Baillie. London: Macmillan, 1910.

Heidegger, Martin. *Being and Time*. Translated by John Macquarrie and Edward Robinson. New York: Harper and Row, 1962.

Higgins, Lynn. "Barthes's Imaginary Voyage." *Studies in Twentieth-Century Literature* 5, no. 2 (Spring 1981): 157–74.

Hill, Aaron. *A Full and Just Account of the Present State of the Ottoman Empire*. London, 1709.

Hill, Christopher. *The Century of Revolution, 1603–1714*. New York: Norton, 1961.

Hirsh, Arthur. *The French New Left: An Intellectual History from Sartre to Gorz*. Boston: South End Press, 1981.

Hobsbawm, Eric. *The Age of Empire, 1875–1914*. New York: Random House, 1987.

Hocquenghem, Guy. *Lettre ouverte à ceux qui sont passés du col Mao au Rotary*. Paris: Albin Michels, 1986.

hooks, bell. *Ain't I a Woman: Black Women and Feminism*. Boston: South End Press, 1981.

Hutchins, Francis G. *The Illusion of Permanence: British Imperialism in India*. Princeton: Princeton University Press, 1967.

Jameson, Fredric. *The Prison-House of Language: A Critical Account of Structuralism and Russian Formalism*. Princeton: Princeton University Press, 1972.

——. "The Imaginary and Symbolic in Lacan: Marxism, Psychoanalytic Criticism, and the Problem of the Subject." *Yale French Studies* 55–56 (1977): 338–95.

——. *The Political Unconscious: Narrative as a Socially Symbolic Act*. Ithaca: Cornell University Press, 1981.

JanMohamed, Abdul R. *Manichean Aesthetics: The Politics of Literature in Colonial Africa*. Amherst: University of Massachusetts Press, 1983.

JanMohamed, Abdul R., and David Lloyd, eds. *The Nature and Context of Minority Discourse*. Oxford: Oxford University Press, 1990.

Jardine, Alice. *Gynesis: Configurations of Woman and Modernity*. Ithaca: Cornell University Press, 1985.

Johnson, Barbara. *The Critical Difference: Essays in the Contemporary Rhetoric of Reading*. Baltimore: Johns Hopkins University Press, 1980.

Jones, Ann Rosalind. "Writing the Body: Toward an Understanding of l'Écriture Féminine." *Feminist Studies* 7, no. 2 (Summer 1981): 247–63.

Katsiaficas, George. *The Imagination of the New Left: A Global Analysis of 1968*. Boston: South End Press, 1987.

Kim, Elaine. *Asian American Literature*. Philadelphia: Temple University Press, 1982.

King, Francis. *E. M. Forster and His World*. London: Thames and Hudson, 1978.

Klein, Melanie. *Developments in Psycho-Analysis*. New York: Da Capo, 1983.

Kopf, David. *British Orientalism and the Bengal Renaissance*. Berkeley: University of California Press, 1969.

Kristeva, Julia. *Des chinoises*. Paris: des Femmes, 1974.

——. *La révolution du langage poétique*. Paris: Seuil, 1974. Published in English as *The Revolution in Poetic Language*. Translated by Margaret Waller. New York: Columbia University Press, 1984.

———. "Women's Time." *Signs* 7, no. 1 (Autumn 1981): 5–35.

Lacan, Jacques. "The Function of Language in Psychoanalysis." In *The Language of the Self,* translated by Anthony Wilden. Baltimore: Johns Hopkins University Press, 1968.

———. *Écrits.* Translated by Alan Sheridan. New York: W. W. Norton, 1977.

———. *Feminine Sexuality: Jacques Lacan and the École Freudienne.* Edited and translated with a preface by Juliet Mitchell and Jacqueline Rose. New York: Norton and Pantheon. 1983.

LaCapra, Dominick. *"Madame Bovary" on Trial.* Ithaca: Cornell University Press, 1982.

———. *History and Criticism.* Ithaca: Cornell University Press, 1985.

Laclau, Ernesto, and Chantal Mouffe. *Hegemony and Socialist Strategy: Towards a Radical Democratic Politics.* London: Verso, 1985.

Laplanche, J., and J.-B. Pontalis. *The Language of Psycho-Analysis.* London: Hogarth, 1973.

Lavers, Annette. *Roland Barthes: Structuralism and After.* Cambridge, Mass.: Harvard University Press, 1982.

Lemaire, Anika. *Jacques Lacan.* London: Routledge and Kegan Paul, 1977.

Lévi-Strauss, Claude. *Structural Anthropology.* New York: Basic Books, 1963.

Lipsitz, George. *Time Passages: Collective Memory and American Popular Culture.* Minneapolis: University of Minnesota Press, 1990.

Lloyd, David. *Nationalism and Minor Literature: James Clarence Mangan and the Emergence of Irish Cultural Nationalism.* Berkeley: University of California Press, 1987.

———. "Genet's Genealogy: European Minorities and the Ends of Canon." In *The Nature and Context of Minority Discourse,* edited by Abdul JanMohamed and David Lloyd. Oxford: Oxford University Press, 1990.

Lowe, Lisa. Review of Trinh T. Minh-ha's *Woman, Native, Other: Reading Postcoloniality and Feminism. Sub-Stance.* 62–63 (1990): 213–16.

———. "Heterogeneity, Hybridity, Multiplicity: Marking Asian American Differences." *Diaspora: A Journal of Transnational Studies* 1 (Spring 1991): 24–44.

McConkey, James. *The Novels of E. M. Forster.* Ithaca: Cornell University Press, 1957.

McCully, Bruce. *English Education and the Origins of Indian Nationalism.* New York: Columbia University Press, 1942.

MacKinnon, Catharine. *Feminism Unmodified.* Cambridge, Mass.: Harvard University Press, 1987.

Maconochie, Evan. *Life in the Indian Civil Service.* London: Chapman and Hall, 1926.

Mahood, M. M. *The Colonial Encounter.* Totowa, N.J.: Rowman & Littlefield, 1977.

Mani, Lata. "Multiple Mediations: Feminist Scholarship in the Age of Multinational Reception." *Inscriptions* 5 (1989): 1–23.

Marcus, George, and Michael M. J. Fischer, eds. *Anthropology as Cultural Critique: An Experimental Moment in the Human Sciences.* Chicago: University of Chicago Press, 1986.

Marks, Elaine, and Isabelle de Courtivron, eds. *New French Feminisms.* Amherst: University of Massachusetts Press, 1980.

Marx, Karl. *Capital.* Vol. 1. New York: International Publishers, 1967.

———. "The Economic and Philosophical Manuscripts of 1844" and "The German Ideology." In *Marx-Engels Reader,* edited by Robert C. Tucker. New York: Norton, 1971.

Mason, Philip. *The Men Who Ruled India.* London: Jonathan Cape, 1985.

Miller, Christopher. *Blank Darkness: Africanist Discourse in French*. Chicago: University of Chicago Press, 1985.

Mitchell, Juliet. *Psychoanalysis and Feminism*. New York: Viking, 1974.

Moi, Toril. *Sexual/Textual Politics: Feminist Literary Theory*. London: Methuen, 1985.

Montagu, Lady Mary Wortley. *The Complete Letters of Lady Mary Wortley Montagu*. Vol. 1 (1708–1720). Edited by Robert Halsband. Oxford: Clarendon Press, 1965.

——. *Essays and Poems*. Edited by Robert Halsband and Isobel Grundy. Oxford: Clarendon Press, 1977.

Montesquieu, Charles Louis de Secondat, Baron de. *Lettres persanes*. Paris: Gallimard, 1973.

Moore-Gilbert, B. J. *Kipling and "Orientalism."* London: Croom Helm, 1986.

Moretti, Franco. *The Way of the World*. London: Verso, 1987.

Morgan, Susan. "Victorian Travel Writings." *Genre* 20, no. 2 (Summer 1987): 189–207.

Naik, M. K. "A Passage to Less than India." In *Focus on Forster's "A Passage to India,"* edited by Vasant A. Shahane. Bombay: Orient Longman, 1975.

Natwar-Singh, K. "'Only Connect . . .': E. M. Forster and India." In *Focus on Forster's "A Passage to India,"* edited by Vasant A. Shahane. Bombay: Orient Longman, 1975.

Natwar-Singh, K., ed. *E. M. Forster: A Tribute*. New York: Harcourt Brace, 1964.

Nelson, Cary, and Lawrence Grossberg, eds. *Marxism and the Interpretation of Culture*. Urbana: University of Illinois Press, 1988.

Omi, Michael, and Howard Winant. *Racial Formation in the United States*. London: Routledge, 1986.

O'Reilly, Robert. "The Structure and Meaning of the *Lettres persanes*." *Studies on Voltaire and the Eighteenth Century* 67 (1969): 91–131.

Orgel, Stephen. *The Illusion of Power*. Berkeley: University of California Press, 1975.

Pandey, Gyanendra. "Peasant Revolt and Indian Nationalism." In *Selected Subaltern Studies*, edited by Ranajit Guha and Gayatri C. Spivak. New York: Oxford University Press, 1988.

Parry, Benita. *Delusions and Discoveries: Studies on India in the British Imagination, 1880–1930*. Berkeley: University of California Press, 1972.

——. "The Contents and Discontents of Kipling's Imperialism." *New Formations*, no. 6 (Winter 1988): 49–63.

Pascal, Roy. *The Dual Voice: Free Indirect Speech and Its Functioning in the Nineteenth-Century European Novel*. Manchester: Manchester University Press, 1977.

Pechesky, Rosalind. "Antiabortion, Antifeminism, and the Rise of the New Right." *Feminist Studies* 7, no. 2 (Summer 1981): 206–46.

Pratt, Mary Louise. "Fieldwork in Common Places." In *Writing Culture: The Poetics and Politics of Ethnography*, edited by James Clifford and George Marcus. Berkeley: University of California Press, 1986.

Pucci, Suzanne L. "Orientalism and Representations of Exteriority in Montesquieu's *Lettres persanes*," *Eighteenth Century: Theory and Interpretation* 26 (1985): 263–79.

Radhakrishnan, Radha. "Toward an Effective Intellectual: Foucault or Gramsci." In *Intellectuals: Academics/Politics/Aesthetics*, edited by Bruce Robbins. Minneapolis: University of Minnesota Press, 1990.

Reig, Daniel. *Homo orientaliste: La langue arabe en France depuis le XIXe siècle*. Paris: Éditions Maisonneuve et Larose, 1988.

Rosecrance, Barbara. *Forster's Narrative Vision*. Ithaca: Cornell University Press, 1982.

Sahni, C. L. *Forster's "A Passage to India": The Religious Dimension*. Atlantic Highlands, N.J.: Humanities Press, 1981.

Said, Edward W. *Orientalism*. New York: Random House, 1979a.

——. *The Question of Palestine*. New York: Times Books, 1979b.

——. *After the Last Sky: Palestinian Lives*. New York: Pantheon Books, 1986.

——. "Identity, Negation, and Violence." *New Left Review*, no. 171 (December 1988): 46–60.

——. "Representing the Colonized: Anthropology and Its Interlocutors." *Critical Inquiry* 15, no. 2 (Winter 1989): 205–25.

Said, Edward, and Christopher Hitchens, eds. *Blaming the Victims: Spurious Scholarship and the Palestinian Question*. London: Verso, 1988.

Sanchez, Marta. *Contemporary Chicana Poetry: A Critical Approach to an Emerging Literature*. Berkeley: University of California Press, 1985.

Sandys, George. *Sandys Travailes*. London, 1658.

Sartre, Jean-Paul. *L'être et le néant: essai d'ontologie phénoménologique*. Paris: Gallimard, 1943.

Sassoon, Anne Showstack, ed. *Approaches to Gramsci*. London: Writers and Readers, 1982.

Schlenoff, Norman. *Ingres, ses sources littéraires*. Paris: Presses universitaires de France, 1956.

Schor, Naomi. *Breaking the Chain: Women, Realism, and the French Novel*. New York: Columbia University Press, 1985.

Schwab, Raymond. *The Oriental Renaissance: Europe's Rediscovery of India and the East: 1680–1880*. New York: Columbia University Press, 1984.

Shahane, Vasant A. *E. M. Forster: A Reassessment*. New Delhi: Kitab Mihal, 1963.

——, ed. *Perspectives on E. M. Forster's "A Passage to India": A Collection of Critical Essays*. New York: Barnes and Noble, 1968.

——, ed. *Focus on Forster's "A Passage to India": Indian Essays in Criticism*. Bombay: Orient Longman, 1975.

——. *"A Passage to India": A Study*. Bombay and London: Oxford University Press, 1977.

Shevelow, Kathryn. *Women and Print Culture*. London: Routledge, 1989.

Singer, Daniel. *Prelude to Revolution: France in May 1968*. New York: Hill and Wang, 1970.

Singh, Bhupal. *A Survey of Anglo-Indian Fiction*. Oxford: Oxford University Press, 1934.

Sivaramakrishna, M. "Marabar Caves Revisited." In *Focus on Forster's "A Passage to India,"* edited by Vasant A. Shahane. Bombay: Orient Longman, 1975.

Smith, Paul. *Discerning the Subject*. Minneapolis: University of Minnesota Press, 1988.

Spivak, Gayatri. "French Feminism in an International Frame." *Yale French Studies*, no. 62 (1981): 154–84.

——. *In Other Worlds*. London: Routledge, 1988a.

——. "Can the Subaltern Speak?" In *Marxism and the Interpretation of Culture*, edited by Cary Nelson and Lawrence Grossberg. Urbana: University of Illinois Press, 1988b.

Stevens, MaryAnne, ed. *The Orientalists: Delacroix to Matisse: The Allure of North Africa and the Near East*. London: Weidenfeld and Nicolson, 1984.

Stone, Wilfrid. *The Cave and the Mountain: A Study of E. M. Forster.* Stanford: Stanford University Press, 1966.

Swift, Jonathan. *Gulliver's Travels.* Oxford: Oxford University Press, 1986.

Tanner, Tony. *Adultery in the Novel.* Baltimore: Johns Hopkins University Press, 1979.

Tennenhouse, Leonard. *Power on Display: The Politics of Shakespeare's Genres.* New York: Methuen, 1986.

Terdiman, Richard. *Discourse/Counter-Discourse: The Theory and Practice of Symbolic Resistance in Nineteenth-Century France.* Ithaca: Cornell University Press, 1985.

Thomson, George. *The Fiction of E. M. Forster.* Detroit: Wayne State University Press, 1967.

Tocqueville, Alexis de. *L'ancien régime et la révolution.* Paris: Michel Levy, 1856.

Trilling, Lionel. *E. M. Forster.* Norfolk: New Directions, 1943.

Trinh T. Minh-ha. *Woman, Native, Other: Writing Postcoloniality and Feminism.* Bloomington: Indiana University Press, 1989.

Turkle, Sherry. *Psychoanalytic Politics: Freud's French Revolution.* Boston: Basic Books, 1978.

Ulmer, Gregory. "The Discourse of the Imaginary." *Diacritics* 10, no. 1 (March 1980): 61–75.

Ungar, Steven. *Roland Barthes: The Professor of Desire.* Lincoln: University of Nebraska Press, 1983.

Vartanian, Aram. "Eroticism and Politics in the *Lettres persanes.*" *Romanic Review* 60 (1969): 23–33.

Viswanathan, Gauri. *Masks of Conquest: Literary Study and British Rule in India.* New York: Columbia University Press, 1989.

West, Cornel. "Marxist Theory and the Specificity of Afro-American Oppression." In *Marxism and the Interpretation of Culture,* edited by Cary Nelson and Lawrence Grossberg. Urbana: University of Illinois Press, 1988.

White, Gertrude M. "A Passage to India: Analysis and Revaluation." *PMLA* 68, no. 4 (September 1953): 641–57.

White, Hayden. *Metahistory: The Historical Imagination in Nineteenth-Century Europe.* Baltimore: Johns Hopkins University Press, 1973.

——. *Tropics of Discourse.* Baltimore: Johns Hopkins University Press, 1978.

——. "The Problem of Style in Realistic Representation: Marx and Flaubert." In *The Concept of Style,* edited by Berel Lang. Philadelphia: University of Pennsylvania Press, 1979.

Wilden, Anthony. Introduction to Jacques Lacan, *The Language of the Self.* Baltimore: Johns Hopkins University Press, 1968.

Williams, Raymond. *Marxism and Literature.* Oxford: Oxford University Press, 1977.

Withers, Robert. *A Description of the Grand Signor's Seraglio or Turkish Emperor's Court.* London, 1650.

Wolf, Eric. *Europe and the People without History.* Berkeley: University of California Press, 1982.

Woodhull, Winifred. "Unveiling Algeria." *Genders* (1991; in press).

Index

Library of Congress Cataloging-in-Publication Data

Lowe, Lisa.
    Critical terrains : French and British orientalisms / Lisa Lowe.
      p.   cm.
    Includes bibliographical references and index.
    ISBN 0-8014-2579-4 (cloth : alk. paper)
      1. French literature—Oriental influences. 2. English literature—
Oriental influences.   3. French—Travel—Orient—History.
4. British—Travel—Orient—History. 5. Exoticism in literature.
6. Orient in literature. I. Title.
PQ143.O75L6 1992
840.9—dc20   91-55058